# Communications
# in Computer and Information Science       1805

## Rationale

The CCIS series is devoted to the publication of proceedings of computer science conferences. Its aim is to efficiently disseminate original research results in informatics in printed and electronic form. While the focus is on publication of peer-reviewed full papers presenting mature work, inclusion of reviewed short papers reporting on work in progress is welcome, too. Besides globally relevant meetings with internationally representative program committees guaranteeing a strict peer-reviewing and paper selection process, conferences run by societies or of high regional or national relevance are also considered for publication.

## Topics

The topical scope of CCIS spans the entire spectrum of informatics ranging from foundational topics in the theory of computing to information and communications science and technology and a broad variety of interdisciplinary application fields.

## Information for Volume Editors and Authors

Publication in CCIS is free of charge. No royalties are paid, however, we offer registered conference participants temporary free access to the online version of the conference proceedings on SpringerLink (http://link.springer.com) by means of an http referrer from the conference website and/or a number of complimentary printed copies, as specified in the official acceptance email of the event.

CCIS proceedings can be published in time for distribution at conferences or as post-proceedings, and delivered in the form of printed books and/or electronically as USBs and/or e-content licenses for accessing proceedings at SpringerLink. Furthermore, CCIS proceedings are included in the CCIS electronic book series hosted in the SpringerLink digital library at http://link.springer.com/bookseries/7899. Conferences publishing in CCIS are allowed to use Online Conference Service (OCS) for managing the whole proceedings lifecycle (from submission and reviewing to preparing for publication) free of charge.

## Publication process

The language of publication is exclusively English. Authors publishing in CCIS have to sign the Springer CCIS copyright transfer form, however, they are free to use their material published in CCIS for substantially changed, more elaborate subsequent publications elsewhere. For the preparation of the camera-ready papers/files, authors have to strictly adhere to the Springer CCIS Authors' Instructions and are strongly encouraged to use the CCIS LaTeX style files or templates.

## Abstracting/Indexing

CCIS is abstracted/indexed in DBLP, Google Scholar, EI-Compendex, Mathematical Reviews, SCImago, Scopus. CCIS volumes are also submitted for the inclusion in ISI Proceedings.

## How to start

To start the evaluation of your proposal for inclusion in the CCIS series, please send an e-mail to ccis@springer.com.

Toon Calders · Celine Vens · Jefrey Lijffijt ·
Bart Goethals
Editors

# Artificial Intelligence and Machine Learning

34th Joint Benelux Conference, BNAIC/Benelearn 2022
Mechelen, Belgium, November 7–9, 2022
Revised Selected Papers

Springer

*Editors*
Toon Calders (ID)
University of Antwerp
Antwerp, Belgium

Celine Vens (ID)
KU Leuven
Leuven, Belgium

Jefrey Lijffijt (ID)
Ghent University
Gent, Belgium

Bart Goethals
University of Antwerp
Antwerp, Belgium

ISSN 1865-0929        ISSN 1865-0937 (electronic)
Communications in Computer and Information Science
ISBN 978-3-031-39143-9        ISBN 978-3-031-39144-6 (eBook)
https://doi.org/10.1007/978-3-031-39144-6

This Springer imprint is published by the registered company Springer Nature Switzerland AG
The registered company address is: Gewerbestrasse 11, 6330 Cham, Switzerland

# Preface

We proudly present the post-proceedings of BNAIC/BeNeLearn 2022, the joint conference on Artificial Intelligence and Machine Learning in the BeNeLux. Originally organized separately as the BeNeLux Conference on AI (BNAIC) and the Belgian-Dutch Conference on Machine Learning (BeNeLearn), the conference has been co-organised since 2018. In 2022, BNAIC/BeNeLearn was organised under the responsibility of the University of Antwerp and held as a fully in-person event again in the beautiful city of Mechelen, Belgium. The event took place from Monday 7 November until Wednesday 9 November, with a full three-day programme, featuring oral and poster presentations of all contributed research papers, demo's, an industry session, and keynotes.

As in previous years, for the scientific track we welcomed four types of contributions, namely, a) regular papers, b) encore abstracts of recently published work, c) demonstrations, and d) thesis abstracts. We received 137 submissions overall, out of which 58 were regular papers, 35 encore abstracts, 12 demos, and 32 thesis abstracts. All submissions received two single-blind reviews by the program committee that consisted fully of senior researchers in the field. Of the regular papers, 11 (19%) were selected for inclusion in this volume of the Springer CCIS series. The authors were given the opportunity to revise their papers, after which they have been reviewed and possibly revised again.

All accepted scientific contributions were presented as 15-minute talks, in one of three parallel tracks. In addition to these scientific presentations, we had keynote presentations by Marcin Detyniecki (AXA France), Tinne Tuytelaers (Katholieke Universiteit Leuven), and Karl Tuyls (DeepMind). We also held a special FACt (FACulty focusing on the FACts of AI) session with presentations by Khalid Al Khatib (University of Groningen), Joost Vennekens (Katholieke Universiteit Leuven), and Gianluca Bontempi (Université Libre de Bruxelles). To conclude, we express our sincere appreciation to everyone who made this conference possible, including the BNVKI, the volunteers that helped with the local organisation, the programme committee members, the session chairs, and the sponsors: the Dutch Foundation for Neural Networks (SNN), the Foundation for Knowledge-Based Systems (SKBS), and the Benelux Association for AI (BNVKI). Finally, we also thank all the authors; you are the primary contributors to the conference and the community.

June 2023

Toon Calders
Jefrey Lijffijt
Celine Vens
Bart Goethals

# Organization

## General Chair

Bart Goethals       University of Antwerp, Belgium

## Program Committee Chairs

Toon Calders       University of Antwerp, Belgium
Jefrey Lijffijt       Ghent University, Belgium
Celine Vens       Katholieke Universiteit Leuven, Belgium

## Local Organization

Sam Pinxteren       University of Antwerp, Belgium
Daphne Lenders       University of Antwerp, Belgium
Arne Van Overloop       University of Antwerp, Belgium
Lien Michiels       Froomle, University of Antwerp, Belgium
Robin Verachtert       Froomle, University of Antwerp, Belgium
Len Feremans       University of Antwerp, Belgium
Ewoenam Kwaku Tokpo       University of Antwerp, Belgium
Jens Leysen       University of Antwerp, Belgium
Marco Favier       University of Antwerp, Belgium
Wannes De Breuck       University of Antwerp, Belgium
Joey De Pauw       University of Antwerp, Belgium

## Program Committee

Riad Aggoune       Luxembourg Institute of Science and Technology, Luxembourg
Wassila Aggoune-Mtalaa       Luxembourg Institute of Science and Technology, Luxembourg
Mitra Baratchi       University of Twente, The Netherlands
Tony Belpaeme       Ghent University, Belgium
Katrien Beuls       Université de Namur, Belgium
Floris Bex       Utrecht University, The Netherlands

Hendrik Blockeel             Katholieke Universiteit Leuven, Belgium
Bart Bogaerts                Vrije Universiteit Brussel, Belgium
Chiara Boldrini              CNR-IIT, Italy
Gianluca Bontempi            Université Libre de Bruxelles, Belgium
Tibor Bosse                  Radboud University, The Netherlands
Willem-Paul Brinkman         Delft University of Technology, The Netherlands
Jeska Buhmann                University of Antwerp, Belgium
Tom Claassen                 Radboud University, The Netherlands
Chris Cornelis               Ghent University, Belgium
Walter Daelemans             University of Antwerp, Belgium
Gregoire Danoy               University of Luxembourg, Luxembourg
Mehdi Dastani                Utrecht University, The Netherlands
Jesse Davis                  Katholieke Universiteit Leuven, Belgium
Tijl De Bie                  Ghent University, Belgium
Jasper de Boer               Katholieke Universiteit Leuven, Belgium
Mathijs De Weerdt            Delft University of Technology, The Netherlands
Thomas Demeester             Ghent University, Belgium
Kris Demuynck                Ghent University, Belgium
Chris Develder               Ghent University, Belgium
Robbe Dhondt                 Katholieke Universiteit Leuven, Belgium
Remco Dijkman                Eindhoven University of Technology,
                               The Netherlands
Sebastijan Dumančić          Katholieke Universiteit Leuven, Belgium
Ad Feelders                  Utrecht University, The Netherlands
Len Feremans                 University of Antwerp, Belgium
Elias Fernández Domingos     Université Libre de Bruxelles, Vrije Universiteit
                               Brussel, Belgium
Emma Frid                    KTH Sound and Music Computing, Sweden
Floris Geerts                University of Antwerp, Belgium
Pierre Geurts                University of Liège, Belgium
Alireza Gharahighehi         IMEC, Katholieke Universiteit Leuven, Belgium
Nicolas Gillis               Université de Mons, Belgium
Toon Goedemé                 Katholieke Universiteit Leuven, Belgium
Isel Grau                    Eindhoven University of Technology,
                               The Netherlands
Nick Harley                  Vrije Universiteit Brussel, Belgium
Arjen Hommersom              Open University of the Netherlands,
                               The Netherlands
Mark Hoogendoorn             Vrije Universiteit Amsterdam, The Netherlands
Lynn Houthuys                Thomas More University of Applied Sciences,
                               Belgium
Zhisheng Huang               Vrije Universiteit Amsterdam, The Netherlands

| | |
|---|---|
| Nils Jansen | Radboud University, The Netherlands |
| Merel Jung | Tilburg University, The Netherlands |
| Michel Klein | Vrije Universiteit Amsterdam, The Netherlands |
| Walter Kosters | Leiden University, The Netherlands |
| Jesse Krijthe | Leiden University, The Netherlands |
| Benno Kruit | Vrije Universiteit Amsterdam, The Netherlands |
| Johan Kwisthout | Radboud University, The Netherlands |
| Steven Latre | University of Antwerp, IMEC, Belgium |
| Kris Laukens | University of Antwerp, Belgium |
| John Lee | Université catholique de Louvain, Belgium |
| Luis A. Leiva | University of Luxembourg, Luxembourg |
| Jan Lemeire | Vrije Universiteit Brussel, Belgium |
| Tom Lenaerts | Université Libre de Bruxelles, Belgium |
| Marco Loog | Delft University of Technology, The Netherlands |
| Gilles Louppe | University of Liège, Belgium |
| Peter Lucas | University of Twente, The Netherlands |
| Réka Markovich | University of Luxembourg, Luxembourg |
| Maarten Marx | University of Amsterdam, The Netherlands |
| Wannes Meert | Katholieke Universiteit Leuven, Belgium |
| John-Jules Meyer | Utrecht University, The Netherlands |
| Pieter Meysman | University of Antwerp, Belgium |
| Felipe Nakano | Katholieke Universiteit Leuven, Belgium |
| Fateme Nateghi | Katholieke Universiteit Leuven, Belgium |
| Frans Oliehoek | Delft University of Technology, The Netherlands |
| Itir Onal Ertugrul | Utrecht University, The Netherlands |
| Sharon Ong | Tilburg University, The Netherlands |
| Daniel Peralta | Ghent University, Belgium |
| Guillermo A. Pérez | University of Antwerp, Flanders Make, Belgium |
| Romana Pernisch | Vrije Universiteit Amsterdam, The Netherlands |
| Aske Plaat | Leiden University, The Netherlands |
| Henry Prakken | University of Utrecht, University of Groningen, The Netherlands |
| Cédric Pruski | Luxembourg Institute of Science and Technology, Luxembourg |
| Roxana Radulescu | Vrije Universiteit Brussel, Belgium |
| Jan Ramon | INRIA, France |
| Valentin Robu | CWI Amsterdam, The Netherlands |
| Matthia Sabatelli | University of Groningen, The Netherlands |
| Yvan Saeys | Ghent University, Belgium |
| Fatiha Saïs | Paris-Saclay University, France |
| Walter Schaeken | Katholieke Universiteit Leuven, Belgium |
| Stefan Schlobach | Vrije Universiteit Amsterdam, The Netherlands |

# Contents

# Explainable Misinformation Detection from Text: A Critical Look

Suzana Bašić[(✉)], Marcio Fuckner, and Pascal Wiggers

Amsterdam University of Applied Sciences, Amsterdam, The Netherlands
{s.basic,m.fuckner,p.wiggers}@hva.nl

**Abstract.** With the proliferation of misinformation on the web, automatic methods for detecting misinformation are becoming an increasingly important subject of study. If automatic misinformation detection is applied in a real-world setting, it is necessary to validate the methods being used. Large language models (LLMs) have produced the best results among text-based methods. However, fine-tuning such a model requires a significant amount of training data, which has led to the automatic creation of large-scale misinformation detection datasets. In this paper, we explore the biases present in one such dataset for misinformation detection in English, NELA-GT-2019. We find that models are at least partly learning the stylistic and other features of different news sources rather than the features of unreliable news. Furthermore, we use SHAP to interpret the outputs of a fine-tuned LLM and validate the explanation method using our inherently interpretable baseline. We critically analyze the suitability of SHAP for text applications by comparing the outputs of SHAP to the most important features from our logistic regression models.

**Keywords:** misinformation detection · dataset bias · LLM · XAI · SHAP

## 1 Introduction

The increase of misinformation on the web is recognised as a socially relevant issue and acknowledged by several authors [2, 10, 23, 29, 31]. To mitigate the risks of exposing unreliable content, many initiatives took place to check the content's reliability, either manually or automatically. Manual checking could lead to reliable results using experts with access to external sources. However, this task comes at a price of low scalability, limiting checking to a small subset of news articles.

A plethora of techniques has been proposed to automate the verification of the integrity of the news. The main approaches encompass propagation-based and content-based methods, as well as combinations thereof. Propagation-based methods use network features, i.e. features that encode information about how news spreads on social networks. On the other hand, content-based methods use the linguistic features of the text of the article and possibly images in the case of

T. Calders et al. (Eds.): BNAIC/Benelearn 2022, CCIS 1805, pp. 1–15, 2023.
https://doi.org/10.1007/978-3-031-39144-6_1

multimodal methods. This encompasses a wide variety of methods, from traditional machine learning models using hand-engineered features or bag-of-words (BOW) representations to neural networks with non-contextual word embeddings and, most recently, transfer learning with large language models (LLMs). As with most natural language processing (NLP) tasks, LLMs reportedly achieve the best results among the content-based methods.

Fine-tuning such models requires a significant amount of training data, which can be found in various large-scale unreliable news datasets [7,8,11,12,14,19]. Since labelling a large dataset requires considerable time and expertise, large datasets are increasingly being created semi-automatically, which can cause problems with data quality. Therefore, the question is how well models trained on such data generalise in real-world settings. The results of our experiments on NELA-GT-2019 [7] show that models are at least partly learning the stylistic and other features of different news sources rather than the actual features of unreliable news. We observed a considerable reduction in model performance on unseen data when using training and test sets with no news site overlap as opposed to randomly selected sets. In addition, we observed that a simple baseline achieved comparable accuracy results to Transformer models when using non-biased data. We therefore suggest that a further investigation of potential improvements to the inherently interpretable baselines could lead to more sustainable and less resource-intensive procedures.

Apart from the ever increasing resource requirements of large language models, a major concern is their lack of explainability. That is especially relevant in real-world settings, where automatic methods are increasingly being applied to flag web content or limit its reach. In our view, such automated actions should be accompanied by some form of explanation so as to increase transparency and user trust. Since LLMs are not inherently interpretable, the dominant approach is to use a model-agnostic post-hoc explanation method, such as SHAP [9]. However, it is unclear to what degree SHAP-based explanations reflect the actual workings of language models. We found the NELA-GT dataset family to be the perfect testing ground for an exploratory investigation of that question because the datasets—and, consequently, the models trained on them—contain very specific biases, which were observed in previous work and confirmed by our own experiments. We therefore apply SHAP to interpret the outputs of a language model fine-tuned on NELA-GT-2019 and validate the explanation method using our inherently interpretable baseline. The main contribution of our work is a comparative analysis of feature importance between logistic regression and SHAP, which illuminates certain shortcomings of SHAP explanations for text applications.

## 2 Related Work

This section lists the most prominent datasets and methods used for automatic misinformation detection.

## 2.1   Misinformation Detection Datasets

Much attention has been dedicated in recent years to improving misinformation detection performance. The task of training effective models depends on high-quality datasets. This section lists the most prominent misinformation detection datasets in English.

**LIAR** [26] is a fake news detection dataset containing 12.8k human-annotated short statements collected from the fact-checking website PolitiFact. Statements are annotated using six fine-grained labels. Apart from the statements, the dataset contains metadata about the speaker and the statement's context. **Fakeddit** [11] is a multimodal dataset with over one million samples automatically collected from Reddit. The data samples include text, images, comments data, and metadata. The data is labelled using 2-way, 3-way, and 6-way labels, enabling both fine-grained and coarse-grained classification. **BuzzFace** [19] consists of over 1.6 million Facebook comments discussing 2,282 news articles. The articles were annotated by BuzzFeed using four labels. The dataset includes additional metadata.

The **NELA-GT** datasets [7,8,12] are large collections of news articles scraped from the web during 2018, 2019, and 2020. News outlets are labeled as *reliable, mixed* or *unreliable* based on the information from several fact-checking organisations. Individual articles are assigned the corresponding label automatically based on the site-level labels. This work focuses on the NELA-GT family of datasets as we are interested in misinformation in longer texts.

## 2.2   Misinformation Detection Methods

There is a rapidly growing literature on automatic misinformation detection. **Propagation-based methods** [10,23,29] use data from social networks, including data about the individual users who share and comment on news, as well as broader news sharing patterns in the network. **Content-based methods** use features based on the content of an article. Multimodal content-based methods use a combination of text and images contained in a piece of news [2,27,30]. Purely text-based methods are also frequently used [1,4,14]. However, it is not entirely clear what kind of linguistic features are most useful. For example, Bozarth and Budak [3] speculate that models based on engineered linguistic features are more robust, while Gravanis et al. [6] have found that they add little to the performance of word embeddings. Surprisingly, Zhou et al. [31] observe that BERT only slightly outperforms BOW on r/Fakeddit. **Mixed methods** use a combination of propagation-based and content-based features [2,17].

In the area of **explainable misinformation detection**, few inherently explainable systems have been developed, e.g. dEFEND [21]. Yang et al. [28] construct an explainable fake news detector that uses text and metadata. Reis et al. [15] conduct a large-scale exploration of linguistic and network features used for explainable misinformation detection. Since state-of-the-art NLP models are not inherently explainable, post-hoc explanation methods are typically used to explain the predictions of purely content-based models. These methods, like LIME [16] and SHAP [9], determine feature importance for individual prediction by observing the relationship between changes in the input to the model and the model's output.

Zhou et al. [31] highlight the importance of collecting high-quality datasets and suggests improvements to data collection, dataset construction and experiment design processes in order to avoid hidden pitfalls that lead to biased models. Since unreliable news detection is generally a classification task, datasets should have a pair of article features and annotated labels. Labels can be collected in different ways, and the level of effort may vary. For simplicity, we are taking into account only the outcome and not the process of assigning these labels. We can divide labels into two types: article-level and site-level labels. Article-level labels are fine-grained and found in smaller datasets because maintaining such datasets requires significant time and expertise. In contrast, site-level annotations are scalable since articles from the same news outlet receive the same label, favouring scalability but compromising performance.

Another concern regarding data collection pertains to biased resources. For example, FakeNewsNet [22] uses Google search to query the original news article. It comes with the price of potentially selecting the wrong article due to the ranking process. NELA datasets, on the other hand, collect news directly from outlets, avoiding such risk. Also, selection bias can be generated by fact-checking websites that link unreliable classes mostly with articles with click-bait titles containing celebrity names and similar. Bozarth and Budak [3] alert that models that used the random permutation approach to split train and test presented biased behaviour, bypassing the actual task of classifying reliable and unreliable news and just memorising the site identities or writing style of some news sources, even when the names of news sources are removed from the data.

## 3   Experimental Setup

This section describes the design choices we made to conduct the experiments in terms of data collection, model construction, and evaluation.

### 3.1   Data

We use a subset of the NELA-GT-2019 [7] dataset for misinformation detection in news articles. The entire 2019 dataset consists of 1.12M news articles published in 2019 and scraped from 260 different news sources. Each news source is labelled as "reliable", "mixed" or "unreliable" based on the reliability scores aggregated from seven fact-checking websites. Rather than containing article-level labels, the dataset contains site-level labels, meaning that all articles from the same news source receive the same label. This is a clear limitation because a predominantly unreliable news source can occasionally publish reliable news and vice versa.

For our experiments, we use two different subsets of NELA-GT-2019. Each subset consists of 10k training articles, 3k validation articles and 3k test articles. Preprocessing included removal of very short texts (<150 chars) and reducing the size of large texts to a maximum of 500 tokens. Preliminary experiments showed that a ten-fold increase in data size did not significantly influence model performance. We exclude the "mixed" category and balance the number of "reliable" and "unreliable" samples in each of the data splits. The two subsets are constructed in the same way as in Zhou et al. [31] Namely, in the first ("random") subset, articles are randomly split between the training, validation and test data splits. In the second ("disjoint") subset, we ensure that the news sources are strictly separated across the data splits, so that no articles from the same source appear both in the training and test data. This enables us to test the performance of our models on articles from previously unseen news sources.

## 3.2   Models

As a baseline model we use a logistic regression classifier on unigram, bigram and trigram features encoded using a TF-IDF vectorizer with a maximum vocabulary size of 30k. We purposefully do not exclude features that appear in a large number of documents because, as with news outlet names, preliminary experiments showed that they are useful for our feature importance analysis. We do, however, exclude features with low frequency in the entire dataset, retaining only the 30k most frequent features. The training and development sets were merged before training this model because, rather than using a separate development set, ten-fold cross-validation is used for hyperparameter search. Input documents are constructed by concatenating the title and article strings.

Furthermore, we fine-tune DistilBERT [18] for sequence classification. DistilBERT belongs to a family of large-scale pre-trained language models which have become popular in recent years thanks to their state-of-the art performance on many standard natural language processing tasks. It is a smaller, faster version of BERT [5], a language representation model which learns deep bidirectional (sub-)word embeddings using a Transformer encoder [25]. Compared to BERT, DistilBERT is reported to retain 97% of language understanding capabilities with a 40% smaller size and 60% more speed [18]. The optimal dropout values were obtained empirically and modified as follows: attention_dropout = 0.2, dropout = 0.2, seq_classif_dropout = 0.3. As input to the model, we use the title and text of an article separated by the special token [SEP].

## 3.3   Explanation Methods

SHAP (SHapley Additive exPlanations) [9] is a model-agnostic post-hoc explanation method for explaining individual model predictions. It is based on Shapley values [20,24], a method from cooperative game theory for assigning payouts to players based on their individual contributions to the total payout in the game. The SHAP framework encompasses model-specific variants of the explanation method for tree-based, linear, and deep models, as well as a kernel-based estimation method that connects Shapley values with LIME [16]. SHAP determines feature contributions by perturbing the values of input features and observing the effects on model output. We use SHAP to analyze the individual predictions of our fine-tuned Transformer models.

To assess the reliability of the method, we also apply SHAP to the baseline models. Since our subsets of the data are not too large, it was possible to calculate SHAP values for the simple baseline models on the entire dataset. That means that we were able to construct a global feature importance overview, aggregated from the individual feature importance of each prediction in the dataset. Thanks to this, we were able to analyze the global feature importance as constructed by SHAP, as well as compare it to the feature importance based on the logistic regression model coefficients.

## 4    Results

This section shows the results of our experiments, focused on the effect of the chosen dataset split strategy on model performance. A brief overview of results in terms of model explanations is given, but feature importance is analyzed in more detail in Sect. 5.

**Table 1.** Logistic regression results on the random data split

|            | Precision | Recall | F1-score | No. of documents |
|------------|-----------|--------|----------|------------------|
| 0          | 0.8482    | 0.8220 | 0.8349   | 3000             |
| 1          | 0.8273    | 0.8530 | 0.8399   | 3000             |
| Accuracy   | 0.8375    | 0.8375 | 0.8375   | 6000             |
| Macro avg. | 0.8378    | 0.8375 | 0.8374   | 6000             |

**Table 2.** Logistic regression results on the disjoint data split

|            | Precision | Recall | F1-score | No. of documents |
|------------|-----------|--------|----------|------------------|
| 0          | 0.7331    | 0.7700 | 0.7510   | 3000             |
| 1          | 0.7578    | 0.7196 | 0.7382   | 3000             |
| Accuracy   | 0.7448    | 0.7448 | 0.7448   | 6000             |
| Macro avg. | 0.7454    | 0.7448 | 0.7446   | 6000             |

### 4.1    Model Performance

The performance of the models is presented in Tables 1, 2, 3, and 4. The classes 0 and 1 represent reliable and unreliable news, respectively.

Our baseline model achieves an accuracy of 83.75% on the random data split and 74.48% on the disjoint split. DistilBERT performs significantly better on the random split, achieving 91.32%. However, on the disjoint split it performs comparably to the baseline, achieving an accuracy of 75.40%. Precision and recall are mostly balanced, except for the DistilBERT model on the disjoint data split.

Table 3. DistilBert results on the random data split

|            | Precision | Recall | F1-score | No. of documents |
|------------|-----------|--------|----------|------------------|
| 0          | 0.9116    | 0.9150 | 0.9133   | 3000             |
| 1          | 0.9146    | 0.9113 | 0.9130   | 3000             |
| Accuracy   | 0.9131    | 0.9131 | 0.9131   | 6000             |
| Macro avg. | 0.9131    | 0.9131 | 0.9131   | 6000             |

Table 4. DistilBert results on the disjoint data split

|            | Precision | Recall | F1-score | No. of documents |
|------------|-----------|--------|----------|------------------|
| 0          | 0.7119    | 0.8533 | 0.7762   | 3000             |
| 1          | 0.8169    | 0.6546 | 0.7268   | 3000             |
| Accuracy   | 0.7540    | 0.7540 | 0.7540   | 6000             |
| Macro avg. | 0.7644    | 0.7540 | 0.7515   | 6000             |

## 4.2 Model Explanations

This section presents the most important features of the logistic regression model as determined by both the model weights and SHAP. The analysis of the results in terms of feature importance is limited to logistic regression for two reasons. Firstly, we do not have access to an internal feature importance ranking of DistilBERT as we do for logistic regression. That means that we are unable to compare the results of SHAP to a straightforward "gold standard" of feature importance as in the case of logistic regression. Secondly, calculating SHAP values is computationally

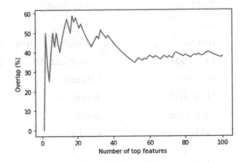

Fig. 1. The percentage of overlap between logistic regression and SHAP (y-axis) among n most important features identified by the two methods (x-axis) on the random data split

expensive. Therefore, it is impractical to run SHAP on the entire dataset to construct a global feature importance overview. We focus on the logistic regression model trained on the randomly split portion of the dataset, but similar effects can also be observed on the disjoint data split. The global ordering of features by SHAP values is built by averaging the absolute instance-level SHAP values for each feature.

Figure 1 illustrates the percentage of overlap between the top features learned by logistic regression and identified by SHAP. The overlap is higher than 50% only for certain values between 13 and 33, with the highest value of 58.82% for

**Table 5.** The top 50 most important features from the logistic regression model and SHAP on the random data split. The columns LR and SHAP contain features that are only identified as being in the top 50 by either logistic regression or SHAP, respectively. The middle two columns list the features that are found in both logistic regression and SHAP, ordered by the feature importance in the two models.

| LogReg | Intersection (LogReg order) | Intersection (SHAP order) | SHAP |
|---|---|---|---|
| ap | apos | apos | during |
| natural news | read more | said | us |
| com | tass | but | in |
| stated | read | mr | it |
| illegal | mr | this | had |
| article | but | video | on |
| mr trump | said | read | at |
| cnsnews | says | says | and |
| cnsnews com | video | read more | has |
| democrat | reported | media | year |
| 2019 at | according | according | was |
| ms | this | according to | first |
| natural | president trump | reported | trump |
| breitbart | according to | said the | america |
| centre | obama | president trump | war |
| this article | however | tass | its |
| buy new | media | obama | the |
| article was | said the | however | israel |
| vaccine | | | not |
| the democrats | | | say |
| this article was | | | even |
| music | | | epstein |
| msnbc | | | any |
| moscow | | | president |
| cnn | | | that |
| tass the | | | more than |
| trump donald john | | | or |
| rt | | | is |
| below | | | the us |
| schiff | | | that the |
| percent | | | an |
| donald john | | | than |

the 17 most important features. When the number of features is higher than 46, the percentage of overlap stabilises between 35 and 40%.

Table 5 shows the 50 most important features as identified by the logistic regression model and SHAP. The two outer columns, *LogReg* and *SHAP*, contain the features found among the 50 most important features only by the respective method. They are ordered by their importance rank, from the most important to the least important feature. The inner two columns, *Intersection (LogReg order)* and *Intersection (SHAP order)* contain the features found in the top 50 features by both methods. The only difference between those two columns is that the first one is ordered by the feature importance according to the logistic regression model, while the second one reflects the feature importance according to SHAP.

## 5  Discussion

In this section we discuss the results presented in Sect. 4 and dive deeper into the comparison of prediction explanations obtained from the logistic regression model and SHAP. Furthermore, we present the observations from a qualitative analysis of SHAP explanations of DistilBERT predictions.

### 5.1  Model Accuracy

On the portion of the dataset with no news site overlaps, the accuracy of our baseline decreases by 9.27% points, while the accuracy of DistilBERT decreases by 15.92 points. This indicates that a bias towards learning the features of news sources is present in both models. The DistilBERT models suffers a significantly larger decrease in accuracy, indicating that the more complex LLM is more biased than the baseline. These findings are in line with those of Zhou et al. [31], who looked at the generalisability of different models on the related NELA-GT-2018 dataset.

Apart from the need for data debiasing techniques already mentioned by Zhou et al. [31], these findings also point to potentially interesting considerations regarding model choice. While LLMs are very powerful models that achieve state-of-the-art results on most standard natural language processing tasks, they are not without flaws. They require significant data, time, and computing power to train and fine-tune, and their outputs are difficult to interpret. If a simple baseline achieves comparable results on reasonably non-biased data, it might be worth exploring potential improvements to the inherently interpretable baselines rather than using a more resource intensive model.

### 5.2  Logistic Regression Explanations

As can be seen from the results presented in Table 5, SHAP performs rather poorly in detecting the features that are relevant to the model. By inspecting the top features obtained from the logistic regression model and SHAP, we can observe two interesting effects.

Firstly, SHAP fails to identify nearly all news outlet names found among the 50 most important features learned by logistic regression. The outlet names not identified by SHAP, with their respective feature importance rank, are as follows: **ap** (7), **natural news** (9), **cnsnews** (23), **cnsnews com** (24), **breitbart** (30), **msnbc** (41), **cnn** (43), and **rt** (46). The only news outlet name that SHAP recognised is **tass**, but it was ranked much lower by SHAP than by logistic regression (the 30th vs 3rd most important feature). Furthermore, the bigram **tass the** additionally appears as the 44th most important feature in logistic regression, but not in SHAP. That means that SHAP fails to capture the source bias, which is present both in the data and the model, as confirmed by our data manipulation experiments. This might point to a general shortcoming of SHAP regarding bias detection in textual datasets.

The second effect that can be observed is that most of the top features that are identified only by SHAP do not carry much semantic content. In linguistics, only nouns, main verbs, adjectives, and adverbs are typically considered as content words. Word classes such as determiners, conjunctions, and prepositions, are considered to be function words, which primarily or exclusively carry grammatical rather than lexical meaning. While such features are typically excluded from BOW models based on word frequency or a predefined list of stop words, we intentionally include them in order to assess the faithfulness of SHAP explanations to the classification model. In fact, 20 out of the 32 features exclusive to SHAP are function words or combinations thereof. Those features and their respective ranking in the logistic regression feature importance are: **in** (179), **it** (116), **had** (67), **on** (114), **at** (86), **and** (462), **has** (139), **was** (557), **its** (358), **the** (6557), **not** (344), **even** (66), **any** (131), **that** (1125), **more than** (52), **or** (268), **is** (906), **that the** (247), **an** (353), and **than** (202). Most of the listed features are placed well below the rank of 50 by logistic regression. While the ranks of 200 or 300 might seem close to 50 in a space of 30,000 features in total, it is important to note that the distribution of feature contributions has a very long tail, as shown in Fig. 2. Figure 2a gives a broader overview of the top 1000 feature contributions, while Fig. 2b zooms in on the 100 most important features. It is clear that the features below the top 50 are far less important in the model.

## 5.3    DistilBERT Explanations

Since attempting to construct global SHAP explanations for DistilBERT would require subsampling the dataset due to computational complexity, we instead discuss the observations based on a qualitative inspection of the instance-level explanations of DistilBERT predictions. While we cannot make any conclusions about the global feature ranking, we have observed some patterns in the several dozen explanations we analysed. In this section, we focus on inconsistent explanations of feature contributions provided by SHAP, as well as on certain issues that are specific to LLM explanations. Those include punctuation, which is excluded in standard BOW implementations, and text highlights, which are only provided for Transformer-based models in the SHAP library.

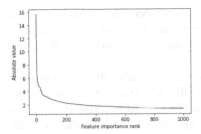

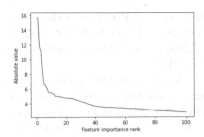

(a) Feature importance of the top 1000 features

(b) Feature importance of the top 100 features

**Fig. 2.** The long tail of feature contributions. a and b show the absolute feature contributions for the top 1000 and 100 most important features

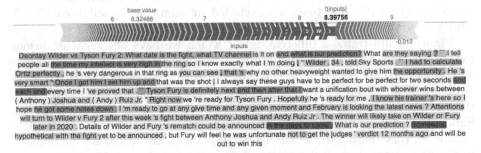

(a) SHAP explanation of an instance-level DistilBERT prediction, illustrating the prominence of function words in the explanation

(b) SHAP explanation of an instance-level DistilBERT prediction, illustrating an inconsistency in the explanation

**Fig. 3.** Two examples of SHAP explanations: Features are highlighted in different colours: red for those that contribute to unreliable news and blue for reliable news. (Color figure online)

As with the explanations of logistic regression predictions, function words seem to be rather prominent in the top 20 features for individual instances. This is illustrated in Fig. 3a. The highlighted words and phrases include **is it on**, **and**, **and each and**, **and then after that I**, **somewhat**, and similar. In this example, those sequences consist exclusively of function words. However, that is not always the case, especially with longer highlights. If an entire sentence is highlighted, one might intuitively expect that the content words have the highest SHAP values in the sentence, but that is not necessarily the case. That means that text highlights, which are used specifically to explain the output of LLMs, do not always clearly reflect the actual feature contributions determined by SHAP.

Apart from the function words, we can also see that individual punctuation marks are highlighted in this example. More specifically, 10 out of the top 20 features for this text are punctuation marks. As in the case of function words, this is not always as visible as in this example because punctuation marks are usually highlighted as a part of a longer phrase or sentence. We have also observed punctuation marks among the top features in other examples, but not as frequently as function words. Moreover, they seem to be much more frequent in examples from the test set on which the model makes an incorrect prediction. Therefore, the prominence of punctuation marks might indicate uncertainty of the predictive model on those examples. This effect was not observed with the BOW model because punctuation is excluded automatically by scikit-learn's [13] TfidfVectorizer.

Figure 3b illustrates a different issue, which we have observed in various examples. The article begins with the title: *Rivalry on ice: Zagitova zooms into lead at world figure skating championship*. In the title, the word **skating** is highlighted red, signifying that it contributes to the unreliable class. However, in the first sentence it is highlighted blue, as contributing to the reliable class. Similarly, the name Zagitova is highlighted in dark red in the title, signifying a significant contribution to the unreliable class. In contrast, it is not highlighted in the first sentence at all. Even though the vector representations of the same word differ across contexts and the features are not independent, we consider it unlikely that these two features would drastically impact the model prediction in these two very similar contexts (the title and first sentence). While we did not perform an extensive analysis of instance-level explanations for the logistic regression model, we did notice a similar issue. In several instances, the same word was listed as the top contributing feature for both the reliable and unreliable class across different examples, which is impossible. That indicates an issue with the reliability of SHAP explanations.

# 6    Conclusion and Future Work

In this paper, we investigated how data collection approaches can directly affect the performance of models in realistic scenarios. Results indicated that models that apparently outperformed the baseline had a significant drop in performance when the news outlet name was used as a basis to create disjoint sets for training and testing. Furthermore, we conducted an extensive analysis of SHAP explanations of our models, highlighting potential shortcomings of the approach. The main contributions of this paper and potential future research directions are as follows.

**Data Bias.** We found that models trained on NELA-GT datasets learn certain features of news sources rather than the features of unreliable news. This confirms earlier findings on bias in the NELA-GT datasets [e.g. 31]. We showed that the same effects are still observed on an iteration of the dataset containing a significantly larger variety of news sources (260 sources in NELA-GT-2019 compared to 194 in NELA-GT-2018). That problem stems from the data collection method, where all articles from the same news source are automatically assigned the same label based on the rating of the news source by fact-checking organisations. This process results in a relatively unclean dataset containing an unknown number of mislabeled articles as well as biases based on news outlet names and on the lexical and stylistic choices of particular authors and/or outlets.

**Model Performance.** We found that a simple baseline almost matched the performance of a state-of-the-art Transformer model on a debiased portion of the dataset. Based on this, we recommend further investigation into the effects of data bias on comparative model performance. While LLMS achieve state-of-the-art results on a vast array of NLP tasks, we consider it worthwile to explore under which conditions a smaller, faster, more sustainable, and more interpretable model might achieve similar performance.

**Validity of SHAP Explanations for Text.** We discovered great inconsistencies between the most important features of our interpretable model and SHAP explanations of the same model. Our analysis showed that SHAP does not identify the news source biases present in the data and models, while it does highlight a large number of irrelevant features. We consider this our most important contribution because post-hoc explanations of black-box models are often taken for granted and they cannot be validated directly. We conclude that SHAP might not be a suitable method for textual data. In future work, we aim at the development of text-specific explanation methods or extensions of existing post-hoc explanation methods for text.

# References

1. Ahmed, H., Traore, I., Saad, S.: Detection of online fake news using N-gram analysis and machine learning techniques. In: Traore, I., Woungang, I., Awad, A. (eds.) ISDDC 2017. LNCS, vol. 10618, pp. 127–138. Springer, Cham (2017). https://doi.org/10.1007/978-3-319-69155-8_9
2. Ajao, O., Bhowmik, D., Zargari, S.: Fake news identification on twitter with hybrid CNN and RNN models. In: Proceedings of the 9th International Conference on Social Media and Society, Copenhagen, Denmark, pp. 226–230. ACM (2018)
3. Bozarth, L., Budak, C.: Toward a better performance evaluation framework for fake news classification. In: Proceedings of the International AAAI Conference on Weblogs and Social Media, vol. 14, no. 1 (2020)

4. Conforti, C., Pilehvar, M.T., Collier, N.: Towards automatic fake news detection: cross-level stance detection in news articles. In: Proceedings of the First Workshop on Fact Extraction and VERification (FEVER), Brussels, Belgium, pp. 40–49. Association for Computational Linguistics (2018)

5. Devlin, J., Chang, M.W., Lee, K., Toutanova, K.: BERT: pre-training of deep bidirectional transformers for language understanding. In: Proceedings of the 2019 Conference of the North American Chapter of the Association for Computational Linguistics: Human Language Technologies, Volume 1 (Long and Short Papers), pp. 4171–4186 (2019)

6. Gravanis, G., Vakali, A., Diamantaras, K., Karadais, P.: Behind the cues: a benchmarking study for fake news detection. Expert Syst. Appl. **128**, 201–213 (2019)

7. Gruppi, M., Horne, B.D., Adalı, S.: NELA-GT-2019: A Large Multi-Labelled News Dataset for The Study of Misinformation in News Articles. arXiv:2003.08444 (2020). arXiv: 2003.08444

8. Gruppi, M., Horne, B.D., Adalı, S.: NELA-GT-2020: A Large Multi-Labelled News Dataset for The Study of Misinformation in News Articles. arXiv:2102.04567 (2021). arXiv: 2102.04567

9. Lundberg, S.M., Lee, S.I.: A unified approach to interpreting model predictions. In: Advances in Neural Information Processing Systems, vol. 30 (2017)

10. Monti, F., Frasca, F., Eynard, D., Mannion, D., Bronstein, M.M.: Fake News Detection on Social Media using Geometric Deep Learning. arXiv:1902.06673 (2019). arXiv: 1902.06673

11. Nakamura, K., Levy, S., Wang, W.Y.: r/Fakeddit: a new multimodal benchmark dataset for fine-grained fake news detection. In: Proceedings of the 12th Language Resources and Evaluation Conference, pp. 6149–6157 (2020)

12. Norregaard, J., Horne, B.D., Adali, S.: NELA-GT-2018: a large multi-labelled news dataset for the study of misinformation in news articles. In: Proceedings of the International AAAI Conference on Web and Social Media, vol. 13, pp. 630–638 (2019)

13. Pedregosa, F., et al.: Scikit-learn: machine learning in python. J. Mach. Learn. Res. **12**, 2825–2830 (2011)

14. Rashkin, H., Choi, E., Jang, J.Y., Volkova, S., Choi, Y.: Truth of varying shades: analyzing language in fake news and political fact-checking. In: Proceedings of the 2017 Conference on Empirical Methods in Natural Language Processing, Copenhagen, Denmark, pp. 2931–2937. Association for Computational Linguistics (2017)

15. Reis, J.C.S., Correia, A., Murai, F., Veloso, A., Benevenuto, F.: Explainable machine learning for fake news detection. In: Proceedings of the 10th ACM Conference on Web Science - WebSci 2019, Boston, Massachusetts, USA, pp. 17–26. ACM Press (2019)

16. Ribeiro, M., Singh, S., Guestrin, C.: "'Why should i trust you?": explaining the predictions of any classifier. In: Proceedings of the 22nd ACM SIGKDD International Conference on Knowledge Discovery and Data Mining, pp. 1135–1144 (2016)

17. Ruchansky, N., Seo, S., Liu, Y.: CSI: A hybrid deep model for fake news detection. In: Proceedings of the 2017 ACM on Conference on Information and Knowledge Management, Singapore, Singapore, pp. 797–806. ACM (2017)

18. Sanh, V., Debut, L., Chaumond, J., Wolf, T.: DistilBERT, a distilled version of BERT: smaller, faster, cheaper and lighter. arXiv:1910.01108 (2020). arXiv: 1910.01108

19. Santia, G.C., Williams, J.R.: BuzzFace: a news veracity dataset with facebook user commentary and egos. In: Twelfth International AAAI Conference on Web and Social Media (2018)

20. Shapley, L.S.: A value for n-person games. In: Contributions to the Theory of Games, vol. 2, pp. 307–317. Princeton University Press, Princeton (1953)
21. Shu, K., Cui, L., Wang, S., Lee, D., Liu, H.: dEFEND: explainable fake news detection. In: Proceedings of the 25th ACM SIGKDD International Conference on Knowledge Discovery & Data Mining, Anchorage, AK, USA, pp. 395–405. ACM (2019)
22. Shu, K., Mahudeswaran, D., Wang, S., Lee, D., Liu, H.: FakeNewsNet: a data repository with news content, social context, and spatiotemporal information for studying fake news on social media. Big Data 8(3), 171–188 (2020)
23. Shu, K., Wang, S., Liu, H.: Beyond news contents: the role of social context for fake news detection. In: Proceedings of the Twelfth ACM International Conference on Web Search and Data Mining, Melbourne, VIC, Australia, pp. 312–320. ACM (2019)
24. Strumbelj, E., Kononenko, I.: Explaining prediction models and individual predictions with feature contributions. Knowl. Inf. Syst. 41(3), 647–665 (2014)
25. Vaswani, A., et al.: Attention is all you need. In: Advances in Neural Information Processing Systems, vol. 30 (2017)
26. Wang, W.Y.: "Liar, liar pants on fire": a new benchmark dataset for fake news detection. In: Proceedings of the 55th Annual Meeting of the Association for Computational Linguistics (Volume 2: Short Papers), pp. 422–426 (2017)
27. Wang, Y., et al.: EANN: event adversarial neural networks for multi-modal fake news detection. In: Proceedings of the 24th ACM SIGKDD International Conference on Knowledge Discovery & Data Mining, pp. 849–857 (2018)
28. Yang, F., et al.: XFake: explainable fake news detector with visualizations. In: The World Wide Web Conference on - WWW 2019, pp. 3600–3604 (2019)
29. Yang, S., Shu, K., Wang, S., Gu, R., Wu, F., Liu, H.: Unsupervised fake news detection on social media: a generative approach. In: Proceedings of the AAAI Conference on Artificial Intelligence, vol. 33, pp. 5644–5651 (2019)
30. Yang, Y., Zheng, L., Zhang, J., Cui, Q., Li, Z., Yu, P.S.: TI-CNN: Convolutional Neural Networks for Fake News Detection. arXiv:1806.00749 (2018). arXiv: 1806.00749
31. Zhou, X., Elfardy, H., Christodoulopoulos, C., Butler, T., Bansal, M.: Hidden biases in unreliable news detection datasets. In: Proceedings of the 16th Conference of the European Chapter of the Association for Computational Linguistics: Main Volume, pp. 2482–2492 (2021)

# Explaining Two Strange Learning Curves

Zhiyi Chen[1,3](✉), Marco Loog[1,2], and Jesse H. Krijthe[1]

[1] Delft University of Technology, Delft, The Netherlands
zhiychen@student.ethz.ch
[2] Radboud University, Nijmegen, The Netherlands
[3] ETH Zürich, Zürich, Switzerland

**Abstract.** Learning curves illustrate how generalization performance of a learner evolves with more training data. While this is a useful tool to characterize learners, not all learning curve behavior is well understood. For instance, it is sometimes assumed that the more training data provided, the better the learner performs. However, counter-examples exist for both classical machine learning algorithms and deep neural networks, where errors do not monotonically decrease with training set size. Loog *et al.* [12] describe this monotonicity problem, and present several regression examples where simple empirical risk minimizers display unexpected learning curve behaviors. In this paper, we will study two of these proposed problems in detail and explain what caused the odd learning curves. For the first, we use a bias-variance decomposition to show that the monotonic increase in the learning curve is caused by an increase in the variance, which we explain by a mismatch between the model and the data generating process. For the second problem, we explain the recurring increases in the learning curve by showing only two solutions are attainable by the learner. The probability of obtaining a configuration of training objects that leads to the high risk solution typically decreases as the training set size increases. However, for particular training set sizes, additional configurations that produce the high risk solution become possible. We prove that these additional configurations increase the probability of the high risk solution and therefore explain the unusual learning curve. These examples contribute to a more complete understanding of learning curves and the possibilities and reasons behind their various behaviors.

## 1 Introduction

Learning curves are plots demonstrating how the number of training samples influences the generalization performance of learners. They are essential tools to understand and compare the learning behavior of different machine learning models. Among others, they have been used to predict the maximum achievable accuracy, estimate how much data is required for the desired accuracy, predict the generalization performance of learners [5,9] to save computational costs and avoid the usage of the excess training samples [6].

A large quantity of research investigated learning curves for different problems or tried to find a common model for learning curves of various problems

© The Author(s), under exclusive license to Springer Nature Switzerland AG 2023
T. Calders et al. (Eds.): BNAIC/Benelearn 2022, CCIS 1805, pp. 16–30, 2023.
https://doi.org/10.1007/978-3-031-39144-6_2

[18]. Different models have been proposed to describe learning curves, such as exponential or logarithmic models [5, 6, 8]. While generating the learning curves for assorted problems, many unexpected behaviors of learning curves have been observed. Some learning curves exhibit non-monotonic behaviors. This phenomenon is opposed to the common assumption that "The more training data, the better the performance of the learner", as proposed in [6, 7, 15].

One well-known example is the sample-wise double descent learning curve, which exists not only in simple models such as linear regression, but also appears in deep neural networks [2]. Two other striking examples are presented in Loog *et al.* [12]. In the first, the expected risk increases as more training data are provided (Fig. 1a). In the second problem, the learning curve shows a periodic pattern (Fig. 1b). The reasons for the non-monotonically decreasing learning curves in these examples are poorly understood. Our goal in this work is to explain why these behaviors occur and to contribute to a better understanding of learning curve behavior.

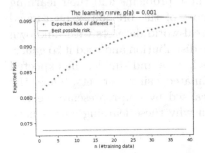

(a) Influence of the size of the training data on the risk of $\mathcal{A}_{erm}$ with L2 loss and linear functions without intercept.

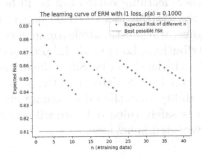

(b) Influence of the size of the training data on the risk of $\mathcal{A}_{erm}$ with L1 loss and linear functions without intercept.

**Fig. 1.** The two studied learning curves with unexpected behaviors

The remainder of this paper is structured in the following way. Section 2 will present other works in the field on learning curves and discuss how our work is related to them. Section 3 will introduce the problem settings of the investigated learning curves and our analysis methodology. Section 4 will display the results of the analysis. Finally, Sect. 5 will discuss how our study answers the research question, discuss its limitations and conclude.

## 2  Related Work

There is a large number of studies regarding learning curves in general. Many researchers have tried to find suitable functional models for learning curves [5, 6, 10, 18]. Duin [3] investigated the learning curves of a variety of algorithms to find a reasonably well-performing algorithm for small-sample-size problems. Likewise, much research has focussed on understanding the behavior of learning curves, leading to various assumptions about and insights into how learning curves can behave. Haussler *et al.* [7], as an example, developed a theory to find rigorous bounds for learning curves. Provost *et al.* [16] suggested that learning curves should exhibit a steep decrease in error at the early stage, a more gentle decrease in the middle stage, and a plateau afterward. Others have claimed that the accuracy should increase as more data is provided [6,7,15].

However, while investigating learning curves for various problems, many learning curves not conforming with these assumptions have been discovered. A well-known example is learning curves that exhibit a "double decent" or peaking pattern. This phenomenon was probably first recorded in [17] and relates to the currently equally popular double-descent complexity curves [1,4,13,15]. An fairly recent and complete overview of badly behaving learning curves can be found in [11].

In [12], the authors show that even with a simple distribution and a basic learner, learning curves can be ill-behaved. These problems and their learning curves are the focus of this paper. Unlike most of the previously mentioned studies, which estimate learning curves using real-world datasets with unknown distributions, Loog *et al.* [12] proposed a simple distribution and used it to generate artificial datasets. Since the distribution is known and simple, the expected risk can be calculated exactly, instead of estimated using test sets. Thus, the possibility that the odd learning curves are caused by non-representative test sets is safely ruled out. We will try to explain why these learning curves have unexpected behaviors.

## 3   Problem Setting and Methodology

We will first formally describe the two problems and introduce terminology in Sect. 3.1. Then, we will present the two disparate solution strategies we applied to explain the behavior of the learning curves in Sect. 3.2.

### 3.1   Problem Setting: The Distribution and the Learners

The two problems are originally proposed in [12]. In both problem settings, the following aspects are the same:

**The ground truth distribution** $\mathcal{D}$ is $(x, y) \in \mathbb{R} \times \mathbb{R} = \mathcal{Z}$, this distribution only has a non-zero probability at two points $a = (1, 1)$ and $b = (\frac{1}{10}, 1)$. Let $P((x, y) = a) = p_a$ and $P((x, y) = b) = 1 - p_a = p_b$.

**The hypothesis class** $\mathcal{H}$ is all linear functions without intercepts; i.e., $\mathcal{H} = \{h(x) = \beta x \mid \beta \in \mathbb{R}\}$.

**Both are regression problems and use ERM as the learner.** A learner $\mathcal{A}$ maps the set of all possible datasets to elements in the hypothesis class, i.e. $\mathcal{A}: \mathcal{Z} \cup \mathcal{Z}^2 \cup \mathcal{Z}^3 \cup ... \cup \mathcal{Z}^n \to \mathcal{H}$. Let $\mathcal{L}: \mathcal{H} \to \mathbb{R}$ denote the loss function,

$\mathcal{R} : \mathcal{H} \to \mathbb{R}$ denote the risk function, and $S^n = \{(x_1, y_1), (x_2, y_2), ..., (x_n, y_n)\}$ denote a set of samples with size $n$. The risk $\mathcal{R}(h)$ for a hypothesis $h \in \mathcal{H}$ is $\mathcal{R}(h) = \mathbb{E}_{(x,y)}\mathcal{L}(h(x), y)$ and the empirical risk $\hat{\mathcal{R}}(h)$, given a training dataset $S^n$, is $\hat{\mathcal{R}}(h) = \frac{1}{n}\sum_{i=1}^{n}\mathcal{L}(h(x), y)$. An empirical risk minimizer $\mathcal{A}_{erm}$ is a learner which outputs the hypothesis with minimum empirical risk, given a set of training data.

The main differences between the two problem settings we discuss lie in the value of $p_a$ and the loss function used.

**Problem I:** $p_a = 0.001$. The loss function is L2 loss: $\mathcal{L}(h) = (h(x) - y)^2$. The empirical risk minimizer $\mathcal{A}_{erm}$ has a closed-form solution $(X^T X)^{-1} X^T Y$, where $X = [x_1, x_2, \ldots, x_n]^T$ and $Y = [y_1, y_2, \ldots, y_n]^T$.

**Problem II:** $p_a = 0.1$. The loss function is L1 loss: $\mathcal{L}(h) = |h(x) - y|$. The empirical risk minimizer $\mathcal{A}_{erm}$ does not have a closed-form solution in general. However, we will show (Sect. 4.2) that it has a closed-form solution when $X, Y \in \mathbb{R}$.

### 3.2   Disparate Methods for Analyzing the Problems

Due to the divergent nature of the two problems, we will approach them using distinct methods. For **Problem I**, we use a bias-variance decomposition to break down the expected risk into *bias* and *variance* terms, and analyze the resulting terms. This method has previously been used in [14] to explain the double descent phenomenon occurring in the learning curves of linear regression (ERM with L2 loss). After observing the curves of these two terms, we focus on the *variance* term and further inspect the cause of its increase.

When interpreting the learning curve of **Problem II**, we will first derive the closed-form solution of $\mathcal{A}_{erm}$, to show only two solutions are possible: the risk optimal solution and a sub-optimal solution. We show that the expected risk depends on the probability of $\mathcal{A}_{erm}$ producing the sub-optimal hypothesis. We then show that this probability can be decomposed into the sum of the probability of different configurations of training objects. The periodic behavior is then explained by the interplay between the decreasing probability of existing configurations and periodic increases in probability due to new configurations becoming possible.

## 4   Analysis

### 4.1   Problem I

We apply a bias-variance decomposition to the expected risk for **Problem I** and identify the cause of the increase in the learning curve by observing how the resulting terms change with respect to the number of training samples. We show that ridge regression can mitigate the problem and then analyze why the problem occurs.

**Bias-Variance Decomposition.** In the setting of **Problem I**, given the L2 loss and linear hypotheses without intercept, the true risk for a fixed sample size $n$ is $\mathbb{E}_{S^n}\mathcal{R}(\mathcal{A}_{erm}(S^n)) = \mathbb{E}_{S^n}\mathbb{E}_{(x,y)}(\hat{\beta}x - y)^2$, $\hat{\beta} = \mathcal{A}_{erm}(S^n)$. This expression can be decomposed in the following way:

$$
\begin{aligned}
\mathbb{E}_{S^n}\mathcal{R}(\mathcal{A}_{erm}(S^n)) &= \mathbb{E}_{S^n}\mathbb{E}_{(x,y)}(\hat{\beta}x - y)^2 \\
&= \mathbb{E}_{(x,y)}\mathbb{E}_{S^n}(\hat{\beta}x - \mathbb{E}_{S^n}\hat{\beta}x + \mathbb{E}_{S^n}\hat{\beta}x - y)^2 \\
&= \mathbb{E}_{(x,y)}\mathbb{E}_{S^n}\left\{(\hat{\beta}x - \mathbb{E}_{S^n}\hat{\beta}x)^2 + (\mathbb{E}_{S^n}\hat{\beta}x - y)^2 \right. \\
&\qquad \left. +2(\hat{\beta}x - \mathbb{E}_{S^n}\hat{\beta}x)(\mathbb{E}_{S^n}\hat{\beta}x - y)\right\} \\
&= \mathbb{E}_{(x,y)}\left\{Var_{S^n}(\hat{\beta})x^2 + (\mathbb{E}_{S^n}\hat{\beta}x - y)^2 + \mathbb{E}_{S^n}G\right\} \\
\mathbb{E}_{S^n}G &= \mathbb{E}_{S^n}\left\{2(\hat{\beta}x - \mathbb{E}_{S^n}\hat{\beta}x)(\mathbb{E}_{S^n}\hat{\beta}x - y)\right\} \\
&= 2\mathbb{E}_{S^n}\left\{x^2\hat{\beta}\mathbb{E}_{S^n}\hat{\beta} - \hat{\beta}xy - x^2\mathbb{E}_{S^n}\hat{\beta}\mathbb{E}_{S^n}\hat{\beta} + \mathbb{E}_{S^n}\hat{\beta}xy\right\} \\
&= 2\left\{x^2\mathbb{E}_{S^n}\hat{\beta}\mathbb{E}_{S^n}\hat{\beta} - \mathbb{E}_{S^n}\hat{\beta}xy - x^2\mathbb{E}_{S^n}\hat{\beta}\mathbb{E}_{S^n}\hat{\beta} + \mathbb{E}_{S^n}\hat{\beta}xy\right\} \\
&= 0 \\
\mathbb{E}_{S^n}\mathcal{R}(\mathcal{A}_{erm}(S^n)) &= \mathbb{E}_{(x,y)}\left\{Var_{S^n}(\hat{\beta})x^2 + (\mathbb{E}_{S^n}\hat{\beta}x - y)^2\right\} \\
&= \mathbb{E}_{(x,y)}x^2 Var_{S^n}(\hat{\beta}) + \mathbb{E}_{(x,y)}(\mathbb{E}_{S^n}\hat{\beta}x - y)^2
\end{aligned}
$$

We will call the term $\mathbb{E}_x x^2 \cdot Var_{S^n}(\hat{\beta})$ *variance* and the term $\mathbb{E}_{(x,y)}(\mathbb{E}_{S^n}\hat{\beta}x - y)^2$ *squared bias*. Figure 2 shows how squared bias and variance are changing with respect to the training size $n$. This shows that the increase of the variance term surpasses the decrease of the squared bias term, leading to an increasing expected risk.

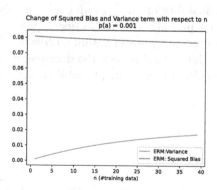

**Fig. 2.** Squared bias and Variance terms with respect to the growth of $n$ in Problem I

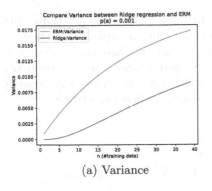
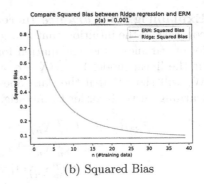

(a) Variance                                (b) Squared Bias

**Fig. 3.** Comparison of the variance and squared bias terms for ERM and ridge regression

**Mitigating the Variance Increase.** We consider ridge regression $\mathcal{A}_{ridge}$, to see whether regularization can mitigate the increase in variance and lead to a decreasing learning curve. $\mathcal{A}_{ridge}(S^n) = \arg\min_{\beta \in \mathbb{R}} \lambda||\beta||^2 + \sum_{i=1}^{n}(\beta x_i - y_i)^2$, where $\lambda \in [0, +\infty)$ is a hyper-parameter controlling the strength of the regularization effect. The larger the $\lambda$, the stronger the regularization effect is. The closed-form solution of $\mathcal{A}_{ridge}$ is $(X^TX + \lambda\mathbf{I})^{-1}X^TY$. As shown in Fig. 3a, with $\lambda = 0.1$, the variance is lower compared to $\mathcal{A}_{erm}$ and grows at a slower rate, while the squared bias starts at a higher value and decreases faster, as shown in Fig. 3b. Looking at different values for lambda, $\lambda = \{0.05, 0.1, 0.25, 0.5\}$, we find that learning curves of $\mathcal{A}_{ridge}$ decrease monotonically for $n = 1, 2, ...., 40$, (Fig. 4a), except when lambda is small. When zoomed in (Fig. 4b), the figure also shows that with a relatively small $\lambda$, $\mathcal{A}_{ridge}$ can achieve a lower expected risk compared to $\mathcal{A}_{erm}$, when $n$ is large enough.

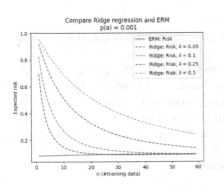
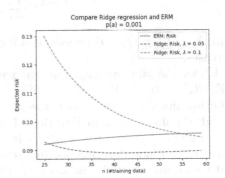

(a) Overview of performance with different lambda

(b) When zooming in, we can observe that lower expected risk is achieved when n is large enough with lambda 0.1 and 0.05.

**Fig. 4.** Compare the performance of different lambda values

**Explaining the *Variance* Increase.** The increase in the variance term runs contrary to the intuition that a larger number of training samples should lead to lower variance. One explanation for the effect is that the distribution does not fit the linear model $Y = \beta X + \epsilon$, where $\mathbb{E}\epsilon = 0$, and $X$ and $\epsilon$ are independent. We will show that if the data does fit this model, we can expect a decreasing learning curve. In order to investigate the variance, we first calculate $\mathbb{E}_{S^n}\hat{\beta}$:

$$
\begin{aligned}
\mathbb{E}_{S^n}\hat{\beta} &= \mathbb{E}_{S^n}(X_n^T X_n)^{-1}X_n^T Y \\
&= \mathbb{E}_{S^n}(X_n^T X_n)^{-1}X_n^T(X_n\beta + \epsilon_n) \\
&= \mathbb{E}_{X_n}(X_n^T X_n)^{-1}(X_n^T X_n)\beta + \mathbb{E}_{X_n}(X_n^T X_n)^{-1}X_n^T \mathbb{E}_{\epsilon_n}\epsilon_n
\end{aligned}
$$

Since $\mathbb{E}_{S^n}\epsilon_n = 0$, we have $\mathbb{E}_{S^n}\hat{\beta} = \beta$. Next consider $Var_{S^n}(\hat{\beta})$:

$$
\begin{aligned}
Var_{S^n}(\hat{\beta}) &= \mathbb{E}_{S^n}(\hat{\beta} - \beta)^2 \\
&= \mathbb{E}_{X_n}\mathbb{E}_{\epsilon_n}((X_n^T X_n)^{-1}X_n^T(X_n\beta + \epsilon_n) - \beta)^2 \\
&= \mathbb{E}_{X_n}\mathbb{E}_{\epsilon_n}((X_n^T X_n)^{-1}X_n^T X_n\beta + (X_n^T X_n)^{-1}X_n^T \epsilon_n - \beta)^2 \\
&= \mathbb{E}_{X_n}\mathbb{E}_{\epsilon_n}((X_n^T X_n)^{-1}X_n^T \epsilon_n)^2 \\
&= \mathbb{E}_{X_n}Var_{\epsilon_n}((X_n^T X_n)^{-1}X_n^T \epsilon_n) \\
&= \mathbb{E}_{X_n}\left[(X_n^T X_n)^{-1}X_n^T Cov_{\epsilon_n}\epsilon_n X_n(X_n^T X_n)^{-1}\right]
\end{aligned}
$$

Since all training samples are i.i.d., we have $Cov_{\epsilon_n}\epsilon_n = Var(\epsilon) \cdot \mathbb{I}_n$. Hence

$$
\begin{aligned}
Var_{S^n}(\hat{\beta}) &= \mathbb{E}_{X_n}\left[Var(\epsilon)(X_n^T X_n)^{-1}(X_n^T X_n)(X_n^T X_n)^{-1}\right] \\
&= Var(\epsilon)\mathbb{E}_{X_n}(X_n^T X_n)^{-1} \\
&= Var(\epsilon)\mathbb{E}_{X_n}\left(\sum_{i=1}^{n}x_i^2\right)^{-1}
\end{aligned}
$$

Since $\mathbb{E}_{X_n}(\sum_{i=1}^{n}x_i^2)^{-1}$ decreases as $n$ increases, the variance also decreases as $n$ increases.

Under the same assumptions, the squared bias term $\mathbb{E}_{(x,y)}(\mathbb{E}_{S^n}\hat{\beta}x - y)^2 = \mathbb{E}_{\epsilon}\mathbb{E}_x(\beta x - (\beta x + \epsilon))^2 = \mathbb{E}_{\epsilon}\epsilon^2$, which is a constant. Therefore, when the distribution fits the linear model, the learning curve will always decrease. Even though the distribution in **Problem I** can be modelled as $Y = \beta X + \epsilon$, where $\beta = \arg\min_{\beta \in \mathbb{R}}\mathbb{E}_{(x,y)}(\beta x - y)^2$, $\epsilon$ is dependent on $X$ and $\mathbb{E}\epsilon \neq 0$. We can therefore conclude that one possible reason for the increasing learning curve is that these two essential conditions are missing.

## 4.2   Problem II

To explain the unexpected periodic behavior of the learning curve for **Problem II**, we first derive the closed-form solution for both $\mathcal{A}_{erm}$ and the optimal $\beta$.

Then, we show that the expected risk depends on the probability of $\mathcal{A}_{erm}$ outputting a specific hypothesis. We then investigate why the curve of this probability has periodic behavior.

**Closed-form Solution of $\mathcal{A}_{erm}$ and the Optimal $\beta$.** In the setting of **Problem II**, the loss is L1 loss. Therefore, $\mathcal{A}_{erm}$ can be be expressed as $\mathcal{A}_{erm} = \arg\min_{\beta \in \mathbb{R}} \sum_{i=1}^{n} |\beta x_i - y_i|$. We first derive the closed form solution for $\mathcal{A}_{erm}$. Let $n$ denote the size of the training dataset, $n_a$ denote the number of points $a = (x_a, y_a)$ in the training dataset, and $n_b$ denote the number of points $b = (x_b, y_b)$. The empirical risk for all hypotheses $\beta$ is therefore

$$\frac{1}{n}\sum_{i=1}^{n} |\beta x_i - y_i| = \frac{1}{n}(n_a|\beta x_a - y_a| + n_b|\beta x_b - y_b|).$$

Consider the sign of the gradient with respect to $\beta$, we discard the positive $\frac{1}{n}$,

**(1)** For $\beta \in [0, \frac{y_a}{x_a})$

$$\frac{d}{d\beta}(n_a|\beta x_a - y_a| + n_b|\beta x_b - y_b|) = \frac{d}{d\beta}(n_a(y_a - x_a\beta) + n_b(y_b - x_b\beta))$$
$$= -n_a x_a - n_b x_b$$
$$< 0$$

**(2)** For $\beta \in [\frac{y_a}{x_a}, \frac{y_b}{x_b}]$

$$\frac{d}{d\beta}(n_a|\beta x_a - y_a| + n_b|\beta x_b - y_b|) = \frac{d}{d\beta}(n_a(x_a\beta - y_a) + n_b(y_b - x_b\beta))$$
$$= n_a x_a - n_b x_b$$

**(3)** For $\beta \in (\frac{y_b}{x_b}, +\infty)$

$$\frac{d}{d\beta}(n_a|\beta x_a - y_a| + n_b|\beta x_b - y_b|) = \frac{d}{d\beta}(n_a(x_a\beta - y_a) + n_b(x_b\beta - y_b))$$
$$= n_a x_a + n_b x_b$$
$$> 0$$

If $n_a x_a - n_b x_b > 0$, then the derivative is only negative when $\beta \in [0, \frac{y_a}{x_a})$, which means the function stops decreasing when $\beta \geq \frac{y_a}{x_a}$. Therefore, the minimum of this function is reached at the point $\beta = \frac{y_a}{x_a}$. In the other case, when $n_a x_a - n_b x_b < 0$, the derivative is negative when $\beta \in [0, \frac{y_b}{x_b})$, which means the function stops decreasing when $\beta \geq \frac{y_b}{x_b}$. Therefore, the minimum of this function is reached at the point $\beta = \frac{y_b}{x_b}$. Finally, when $n_a x_a - n_b x_b = 0$, both $\frac{y_a}{x_a}$ and $\frac{y_b}{x_b}$ are minima, among other solutions. In that case we pick $\beta = \frac{y_a}{x_a}$ as the minimizer. Note that this choice will not affect the qualitative behavior: it will merely shift the curve by one sample. The closed form solution of $\mathcal{A}_{erm}$ is thus the following.

$$\hat{\beta} = \begin{cases} \dfrac{y_b}{x_b} & \text{if } n_a x_a - n_b x_b < 0 \\ \dfrac{y_a}{x_a} & \text{else} \end{cases}$$

The same procedure is applied to find $\arg\min_{h \in \mathcal{H}} \mathcal{R}(h) = \mathbb{E}_{(x,y)}|\beta x - y| = p_a|\beta x_a - y_a| + p_b|\beta x_b - y_b|$ to give

$$\beta = \begin{cases} \dfrac{y_b}{x_b} & \text{if } p_a x_a - p_b x_b < 0 \\ \dfrac{y_a}{x_a} & \text{else.} \end{cases}$$

Under the setting of **Problem II**, $p_a x_a - p_b x_b = \frac{1}{10} \cdot 1 - \frac{1}{10} \cdot \frac{9}{10} > 0$, $\beta = \frac{y_a}{x_a}$.

**Analysis of the Expected Risk.** We now analyze the expected risk for a given $n$. Let $P_{S^n}(\hat{\beta} = \rho)$ denote the probability of $\mathcal{A}_{erm}$ outputting $\rho$ when the size of the training dataset is $n$, $\hat{\beta}_1 = \frac{y_a}{x_a}$, $\hat{\beta}_2 = \frac{y_b}{x_b}$ the two possible solutions, and $P_1^n = P_{S^n}(\hat{\beta} = \hat{\beta}_1)$ and $P_2^n = P_{S^n}(\hat{\beta} = \hat{\beta}_2) = 1 - P_1^n$ the probability of attaining these solutions. The expected risk can be written as the risk of each solution multiplied by the probability of attaining that solution:

$$\mathbb{E}_{S^n} \mathcal{R}(\mathcal{A}_{erm}(S^n)) = P_1^n \cdot \mathbb{E}_{(x,y)}|\hat{\beta}_1 x - y| + P_2^n \cdot \mathbb{E}_{(x,y)}|\hat{\beta}_2 x - y|.$$

As $\hat{\beta}_1 = \arg\min_{\beta \in \mathbb{R}} \mathbb{E}_{(x,y)}|\beta x - y|$, the risk of $\hat{\beta}_1$ is smaller than the risk of $\hat{\beta}_2$. Hence, the smaller $P_2^n$ is, the larger $P_1^n$ and the smaller the expected risk for $n$. Therefore, to explain the periodic behavior (shown in Fig. 5), we must investigate how $P_2^n$ changes with respect to the number of training samples.

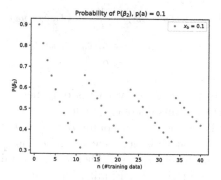

**Fig. 5.** The change of $P_2^n$ with respect to $n$

Note that if we change the value of $p_a$ such that $p_a x_a - p_b x_b < 0$, then $\beta = \frac{y_b}{x_b}$. In this case, $\hat{\beta}_2 = \arg\min_{\beta \in \mathbb{R}} \mathbb{E}_{(x,y)} |\beta x - y|$ and the smaller $P_2^n$ is, the larger the expected risk will be. An example is shown in Fig. 6 where we set $p_a = 0.05$ and all the other values remain the same.

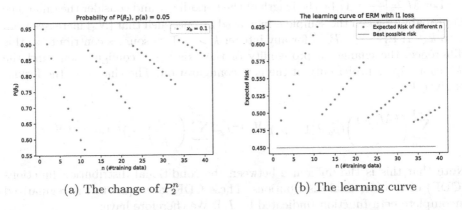

(a) The change of $P_2^n$        (b) The learning curve

**Fig. 6.** The curve of $P_2^n$ and the learning curve when $p_a = 0.05$ leading to $\beta = \hat{\beta}_2$

**Explaining the Periodic Pattern of $P_2^n$.** The question of why the learning curve behaves as in Fig. 1b can be reduced to the question why the curve of $P_2^n$ has the behavior shown in Fig. 5. To investigate $P_2^n$, we need to understand when $\mathcal{A}_{erm}$ will output $\hat{\beta}_2$. This happens when

$$\hat{\beta} = \frac{y_b}{x_b} = \hat{\beta}_2 \quad \text{if } n_a x_a - n_b x_b < 0.$$

Thus, for a given $n$, $P_2^n = P_{S^n}(n_a x_a - n_b x_b < 0)$. $n_b$ can be substituted by $n - n_a$.

$$n_a x_a - n_b x_b < 0$$
$$n_a x_a - (n - n_a) x_b < 0$$
$$n_a (x_a + x_b) < n x_b$$
$$n_a < \frac{x_b}{x_a + x_b} n$$
$$n_a < \frac{n}{\frac{x_a}{x_b} + 1}$$

$$P_{S^n}(n_a x_a - n_b x_b < 0) = P_{S^n}\left(n_a < \frac{n}{\frac{x_a}{x_b} + 1}\right) = \sum_{i \in N_A} P_{S^n}(n_a = i), \text{ where } N_A = $$

$\{i \in \mathbb{N}| \ i < \frac{n}{\frac{x_a}{x_b} + 1}\}$. Since $n, i \in \mathbb{N}$, $|N_A|$ increases by 1, when $n$ increases to

$\lceil \frac{x_a}{x_b} + 1 \rceil k + 1$, where $k \in \mathbb{N}$. In this problem setting $\lceil \frac{x_a}{x_b} + 1 \rceil = 11$ and as shown in the Figs. 1b and 5, the curves have an increase when $n \in \{x \in \mathbb{N} | x = 11k+1, k \in \mathbb{N}\}$. Therefore, we claim that the increase of $|N_A|$ is the cause of the sudden increase. In order to prove this, we consider $\sum_{i \in N_A} P_{S^n}(n_a = i)$ before and after $|N_A|$ increases by 1.

Let $M = \lceil \frac{x_a}{x_b} + 1 \rceil$ be the length of the periodicity and consider the difference in probability when the sample is increased by one, such that $|N_A|$ increases from $k$ to $k+1$: $P_2^{kM+1} - P_2^{kM}$ for any integer $k > 0$. Two sources contribute to this difference: the change in probability of the existing $k$ configurations and the addition of the probability of the new configuration. The change in the former is given by

$$\sum_{j=0}^{k-1} \binom{kM+1}{j} (p_a)^j (1-p_a)^{kM+1-j} - \sum_{j=0}^{k-1} \binom{kM}{j} (p_a)^j (1-p_a)^{kM-j}.$$

Note that this is the difference between the conditional distribution functions (CDF) of two binomial distributions. These CDFs are equal to the regularized incomplete beta function (indicated by $I_x$). We therefore have:

$$I_{(1-p_a)}((M-1)k+2, k) - I_{(1-p_a)}((M-1)k+1, k) =$$
$$- \binom{Mk+1}{k} \frac{k}{Mk+1} p_a^k (1-p_a)^{(M-1)k+1}, \quad (1)$$

using the identity $I_x(a+1, b) = I_x(a, b) - \binom{a+b}{a} \frac{b}{a+b} x^a (1-x)^b$. Note this difference is negative for any probability $p_a$.

Next consider the increase in $P_2^n$ caused by the additional configuration. This is given by

$$\binom{Mk+1}{k} (p_a)^k (1-p_a)^{(M-1)k+1}.$$

Comparing this to (1), we find that the decrease in probability is always $\frac{k}{Mk+1}$ times the increase caused by the additional configuration, hence the increase is always bigger than the decrease. So, whenever $|N_A|$ does not increase when $n$ increases, $P_2^n$ decreases. However, when $|N_A|$ increases as well (which happens every $M$ training objects), $P_2^n$ is guaranteed to increase. This also directly implies that the non-monotonic behavior for this learning curve keeps occurring for arbitrarily large $n$.

Moreover, we can conclude that the shape of the curve showing how $P_2^n$ changes with respect to $n$ will always demonstrate such periodic patterns regardless of the value of $p_a$. As shown in Fig. 7, with either larger or smaller values of $p_a$ the curve of $P_2^n$ still displays the same periodic pattern, which is sudden increase after a fixed period of decrease. Moreover, the duration of one period is dependent on $\lceil \frac{x_a}{x_b} + 1 \rceil$. As illustrated in Fig. 8, the duration of one period is always equal to $\lceil \frac{x_a}{x_b} + 1 \rceil$.

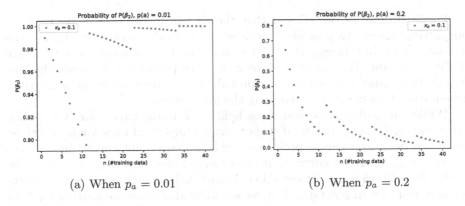

(a) When $p_a = 0.01$                    (b) When $p_a = 0.2$

**Fig. 7.** The behavior of $P_2^n$ with different values of $p_a$

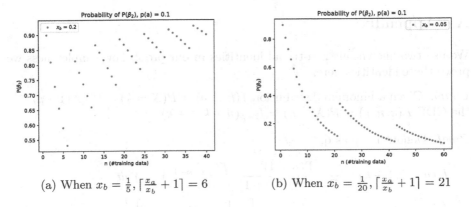

(a) When $x_b = \frac{1}{5}, \lceil \frac{x_a}{x_b} + 1 \rceil = 6$        (b) When $x_b = \frac{1}{20}, \lceil \frac{x_a}{x_b} + 1 \rceil = 21$

**Fig. 8.** The behavior of $P_2^n$ with different values of $\lceil \frac{x_a}{x_b} + 1 \rceil$

## 5   Discussion and Conclusion

Our goal was to explain why the learning curves generated under two problem settings proposed by Loog et al. [12] exhibit non-monotonic behavior. For **Problem I**, we adopted the bias-variance decomposition to split the expected risk into bias and variance terms. The visualization and analysis of these two terms have shown that the rapid increase in variance and the, in contrast, slower decrease in bias leads to the ascending learning curve. We demonstrated that ridge regression can suppress the rapid increase in variance. It is unexpected for variances to increase with more training samples. We suggested that this increase is caused by the fact that the distribution of this problem does not fit certain modeling assumptions (linearity, independence, and zero expected error). We supported this insight by showing that if these assumptions do hold, the variance decreases with more training samples. While this shows one way of adapting the problem to guarantee monotonicity, alternative assumptions about the problem are possible (for instance, letting go of linearity) that we have not explored here. In addition, these sufficient assumptions also do not offer a direct intuitive account of why the variance increases.

For **Problem II**, we showed that the change in the probability of $A_{erm}$ outputting one of two possible hypotheses leads to the periodic pattern of the learning curve. In this way, the problem is reduced to explaining why the curve of this probability has periodic behavior. For this probability, we prove that the factors that cause a decrease in the probability will periodically be negated by an additional configuration increasing the probability.

While our goal was to shed some light on learning curves for two specific problems, both using artificial distributions, an important question is how these insights generalize to similar problems, and how they can inform our understanding of strange learning curves that are observed empirically. Nevertheless, the study of specific cases, as presented in this work, helps to better understand learning behavior, also in general. In fact, we would be glad to see the study of artificial data sets to regain prominence within machine learning research in the large.

# A    Appendix

We use two known but non-trivial identities in our proof. For completeness we prove these identities here.

*Claim.* Given a binomial distribution $f(k, n, p) = P(X = k) = \binom{n}{k} p^k (1 - p)^{n-k}$, the CDF $F(k, n, p) = P(X \leq k) = I_{1-p}(n - k, 1 + k)$

*Proof.* Denote $1 - p$ as q,

$$
\begin{aligned}
I_q(n - k, 1 + k) &= \frac{\Gamma(n + 1)}{\Gamma(n - k)\Gamma(k + 1)} \int_0^q t^{n-k-1}(1 - t)^k dt \\
&= \frac{n!}{(n - k - 1)!k!} \left[ \frac{1}{n - k} t^{n-k}(1 - t)^k \right]\Big|_0^q \\
&\quad + \frac{n!}{(n - k - 1)!k!} \underbrace{\left[ \frac{k}{n - k} \int_0^q t^{n-k}(1 - t)^{k-1} dt \right]}_{\text{(Integration by parts)}} \\
&= \binom{n}{k} q^{n-k} p^k + \frac{n!}{(n - k)!(k - 1)!} \underbrace{\left[ \int_0^q t^{n-k}(1 - t)^{k-1} dt \right]}_{\text{Integration by parts}} \\
&= \binom{n}{k} q^{n-k} p^k + \binom{n}{k - 1} q^{n-(k-1)} p^{k-1} \\
&\quad + \frac{n!}{(n - k + 1)!(k - 2)!} \underbrace{\left[ \int_0^q t^{n-k+1}(1 - t)^{k-2} dt \right]}_{\text{Repeated application of integration by parts}} \\
&= \sum_{i=0}^{k} \binom{n}{i} q^{n-i} p^i \\
&= P(X \leq k)
\end{aligned}
$$

*Claim.* $I_x(a+1, b) = I_x(a, b) - \binom{a+b}{a}\frac{b}{a+b}x^a(1-x)^b$

*Proof.*

$$I_x(a+1, b) = \sum_{i=0}^{b-1}\binom{a+b}{i}x^{(a+b)-i}(1-x)^i$$

$$= \sum_{i=0}^{b-1}\left[\binom{a+b-1}{i} + \binom{a+b-1}{i-1}\right]x^{(a+b)-i}(1-x)^i$$

$$= x\sum_{i=0}^{b-1}\binom{a+b-1}{i}x^{(a+b-1)-i}(1-x)^i$$

$$+ \sum_{i=0}^{b-1}\binom{a+b-1}{i-1}x^{(a+b-1)-(i-1)}(1-x)^i$$

$$= xI_x(a, b) + \sum_{i=0}^{b}\binom{a+b-1}{i-1}x^{(a+b-1)-(i-1)}(1-x)^i$$

$$- \binom{a+b-1}{b-1}x^a(1-x)^b$$

$$= xI_x(a, b) + (1-x)I_x(a, b) - \frac{(a+b-1)!}{(b-1)!a!}x^a(1-x)^b$$

$$= I_x(a, b) - \frac{(a+b)!}{a!b!}\frac{b}{a+b}x^a(1-x)^b$$

$$= I_x(a, b) - \binom{a+b}{a}\frac{b}{a+b}x^a(1-x)^b$$

# References

1. Belkin, M., Hsu, D., Ma, S., Mandal, S.: Reconciling modern machine-learning practice and the classical bias–variance trade-off. Proc. Natl. Acad. Sci. **116**(32), 15849–15854 (2019). https://doi.org/10.1073/pnas.1903070116
2. d'Ascoli, S., Sagun, L., Biroli, G.: Triple descent and the two kinds of overfitting: where and why do they appear? J. Stat. Mech. Theory Exp. **2021**(12), 124002 (2021). https://doi.org/10.1088/1742-5468/ac3909
3. Duin, R.: Small sample size generalization. In: 9th Scandinavian Conference on Image Analysis, pp. 957–964 (1995)
4. Duin, R.: Classifiers in almost empty spaces. In: Proceedings 15th International Conference on Pattern Recognition, ICPR-2000, vol. 2, pp. 1–7 (2000). https://doi.org/10.1109/ICPR.2000.906006
5. Frey, L.J., Fisher, D.H.: Modeling decision tree performance with the power law. In: Proceedings of the Seventh International Workshop on Artificial Intelligence and Statistics. Proceedings of Machine Learning Research, vol. R2 (1999). https://proceedings.mlr.press/r2/frey99a.html

6. Gu, B., Hu, F., Liu, H.: Modelling classification performance for large data sets. In: Advances in Web-Age Information Management, pp. 317–328 (2001)
7. Haussler, D., Kearns, M., Seung, H.S., Tishby, N.: Rigorous learning curve bounds from statistical mechanics. Mach. Learn. **25**, 195–236 (1996). https://doi.org/10.1007/BF00114010
8. John, G.H., Langley, P.: Static versus dynamic sampling for data mining. In: Proceedings of the Second International Conference on Knowledge Discovery and Data Mining, KDD 1996, pp. 367–370. AAAI Press (1996)
9. Kolachina, P., Cancedda, N., Dymetman, M., Venkatapathy, S.: Prediction of learning curves in machine translation. In: Proceedings of the 50th Annual Meeting of the Association for Computational Linguistics (Volume 1: Long Papers), pp. 22–30 (2012). https://aclanthology.org/P12-1003
10. Last, M.: Predicting and optimizing classifier utility with the power law. In: Seventh IEEE International Conference on Data Mining Workshops (ICDMW 2007), pp. 219–224 (2007)
11. Loog, M., Viering, T.: A survey of learning curves with bad behavior: or how more data need not lead to better performance (2022). https://arxiv.org/abs/2211.14061
12. Loog, M., Viering, T., Mey, A.: Minimizers of the empirical risk and risk monotonicity. In: Proceedings of the 33rd International Conference on Neural Information Processing Systems, pp. 7478–7487 (2019)
13. Loog, M., Viering, T., Mey, A., Krijthe, J.H., Tax, D.M.: A brief prehistory of double descent. Proc. Natl. Acad. Sci. **117**(20), 10625–10626 (2020)
14. Nakkiran, P.: More data can hurt for linear regression: sample-wise double descent. arXiv (2019). https://arxiv.org/abs/1912.07242
15. Nakkiran, P., Kaplun, G., Bansal, Y., Yang, T., Barak, B., Sutskever, I.: Deep double descent: where bigger models and more data hurt. J. Stat. Mech. Theory Exp. **2021**(12), 124003 (2021). https://doi.org/10.1088/1742-5468/ac3a74
16. Provost, F., Jensen, D., Oates, T.: Efficient progressive sampling. In: Proceedings of the Fifth ACM SIGKDD International Conference on Knowledge Discovery and Data Mining, KDD 1999, pp. 23–32 (1999). https://doi.org/10.1145/312129.312188
17. Vallet, F., Cailton, J.G., Refregier, P.: Linear and nonlinear extension of the pseudo-inverse solution for learning boolean functions. Europhys. Lett. (EPL) **9**(4), 315–320 (1989). https://doi.org/10.1209/0295-5075/9/4/003
18. Viering, T.J., Loog, M.: The shape of learning curves: a review. CoRR abs/2103.10948 (2021). https://arxiv.org/abs/2103.10948

# Recipe for Fast Large-Scale SVM Training: Polishing, Parallelism, and More RAM!

Tobias Glasmachers[✉][ID]

Ruhr-University Bochum, Bochum, Germany
`tobias.glasmachers@ini.rub.de`

**Abstract.** Support vector machines (SVMs) are a standard method in the machine learning toolbox, in particular for tabular data. Non-linear kernel SVMs often deliver highly accurate predictors, however, at the cost of long training times. That problem is aggravated by the exponential growth of data volumes over time. It was tackled in the past mainly by two types of techniques: approximate solvers, and parallel GPU implementations. In this work, we combine both approaches to design an extremely fast dual SVM solver. We fully exploit the capabilities of modern compute servers: many-core architectures, multiple high-end GPUs, and large random access memory. On such a machine, we train a large-margin classifier on the ImageNet data set in 24 min.

**Keywords:** Support Vector Machine · Dual Budget Training · Graphics Processing Unit

## 1  Introduction

In this paper we pick up a classic learning algorithm, the support vector machine (SVM). Despite the impressive successes of deep learning in particular in the areas of image and language processing, there are still many applications in which the data does not obey a spatial or temporal structure. Sometimes, data comes as a large table of unstructured features. This is where classic methods like ensembles and large margin classifiers shine. Such problems show up regularly in many application domains like material science, medicine, bioinformatics, and many more [3,14,16].

One of the arguably most successful methods for processing tabular data is the support vector machine (SVM) [5]. From a modern perspective, it is limited by one out of two factors. In its linear form, training is fast, but models are limited to linear combinations of features, which often precludes accurate predictors. In its non-linear or kernelized form, high accuracy can be achieved at the price of long training times, which scale roughly quadratic with the number $n$ of data points. Since present-day data sets are orders of magnitude larger than what was common when SVMs were developed, this is a serious limiting factor for this otherwise highly valuable method.

The problem of long training times was a very active research topic for more than a decade, with considerable progress made. The most influential SVM implementation is for sure the seminal LIBSVM software [4]. It implements a variant

T. Calders et al. (Eds.): BNAIC/Benelearn 2022, CCIS 1805, pp. 31–46, 2023.
https://doi.org/10.1007/978-3-031-39144-6_3

of the sequential minimal optimization (SMO) method, a dual subspace ascent solver [17]. It is complemented by its spin-off LIBLINEAR [10], a conceptually similar solver, specialized in training linear SVMs. These solvers still represent the state-of-the-art for sequential SVM training of exact solutions on a single CPU core.

Broadly speaking, there are two types of acceleration techniques going beyond LIBSVM: approximation schemes and parallel algorithms. Most approximations are based on the insight that restricting the extremely rich reproducing kernel Hilbert space induced by the kernel to a much smaller subspace often works well, in the sense that considerable computational gains can be achieved while sacrificing only very little predictive performance [19, 23]. This is particularly true if the subspace is picked in a data-driven manner [6, 26]. As an orthogonal development, parallel algorithms aim to overcome the inherently sequential nature of subspace ascent, either by employing primal (mini-batch) training [15], or by resorting to heuristics [25].

In this work, we aim to combine both approaches by designing a GPU-ready dual coordinate ascent algorithm for approximate SVM training. To this end, we leverage a low-rank approximation technique combined with a dual linear SVM solver. We add vectorization, multi-core, and GPU processing to the picture. We achieve considerable speed-ups by paying attention to the memory organization of our solver. While several SVM solvers implement a kernel cache, our low-rank technique combined with the large amount of RAM available in modern server machines allows for a complete pre-computation of the relevant matrices. We also implement a simplistic yet robust and effective shrinking method, as well as proper support for cross-validation and parameter tuning using warm starts. We present an extremely fast solver suitable for large-scale SVM training on multi-core systems with and without GPUs. In a nutshell, our contributions are

- a GPU-ready approximate dual solver for large-scale SVM training in minutes (instead of hours or days),
- a significantly better compute/memory trade-off through complete precomputation of a low-rank matrix factor, and
- an robust and effective shrinking technique.

After recalling SVMs in the next section, we summarize existing speed-up techniques. Then we present our method and its fast implementation. We demonstrate its power through an empirical comparison with existing solvers, and finally draw our conclusions.

## 2   Support Vector Machines

*Primal and Dual Form.*   An SVM constructs a decision function of the form[1] $f(x) \mapsto \langle w, \phi(x) \rangle$. It is directly suitable for regression tasks, while its sign is considered for binary classification. Training is based on labeled data

---

[1] The angle brackets denote the inner product in the kernel-induced feature space. We drop the bias or offset term [22].

$(x_1, y_1), \ldots, (x_n, y_n) \in X \times Y$ and a kernel function $k : X \times X \to \mathbb{R}$ over the input space $X$. The weight vector $w^*$ is obtained by solving the (primal) optimization problem

$$\min_{w \in \mathcal{H}} \quad P(w) = \frac{\lambda}{2} \|w\|^2 + \frac{1}{n} \sum_{i=1}^{n} \ell(y_i, f(x_i)), \tag{1}$$

where $\lambda > 0$ is a regularization parameter, $\ell$ is a loss function (usually convex in $w$, turning problem (1) into a convex problem), and $\phi : X \to \mathcal{H}$ is an only implicitly defined feature map into the reproducing kernel Hilbert space $\mathcal{H}$, fulfilling $\langle \phi(x), \phi(x') \rangle = k(x, x')$. The representer theorem allows to restrict the solution to the form $w = \sum_{i=1}^{n} \alpha_i y_i \phi(x_i)$ with coefficient vector $\alpha \in \mathbb{R}^n$, yielding $f(x) = \sum_{i=1}^{n} \alpha_i y_i k(x, x_i)$. Training points $x_i$ with non-zero coefficients $\alpha_i \neq 0$ are called support vectors. For further details we refer the reader to the excellent review [1].

For the simplest case of binary classification (with $Y = \{\pm 1\}$), the equivalent dual problem [1] becomes

$$\max_{\alpha \in [0, C]^n} \quad D(\alpha) = \mathbb{1}^T \alpha - \frac{1}{2} \alpha^T Q \alpha. \tag{2}$$

This is a box-constrained quadratic program, with the notations $\mathbb{1} = (1, \ldots, 1)^T$, $C = \frac{1}{\lambda n}$, and $Q_{ij} = y_i y_j k(x_i, x_j)$. Corresponding problems for regression and ranking are of a similar form. Multi-class problems can either be cast into a larger problem of the same type [9], or they are handled in a one-versus-one manner [4].

*SVM Training.* Dual decomposition solvers [1, 4] are the fastest method for training a non-linear SVM to high precision. In each iteration, they solve a small sub-problem of constant size, which can amount to coordinate ascent in case of problem (2). The sub-problem restricted to a single dual variable $\alpha_i$ (a one-dimensional quadratic program) is solved by the truncated Newton step $\alpha_i \leftarrow \max\left\{0, \min\{C, \alpha_i + \frac{1 - Q_i \alpha}{Q_{ii}}\}\right\}$, where $Q_i$ is the $i$-th row of $Q$. In the simplest case (and in all solvers relevant to this work), the index $i$ is chosen in a round-robin fashion, possibly in a randomized order. In elaborate solvers like LIBSVM, considerable speed-ups can be achieved by a technique called shrinking, which amounts to temporarily removing variables $\alpha_i$ which remain at the bounds 0 or $C$ and hence do not change for a long time. This technique can reduce the number of active variables to a small subset, in particular in the late phase of the optimization.

Most alternative solvers operate on the primal problem (1). This has advantages and disadvantages. On the pro side, even simplistic methods like mini-batch stochastic gradient descent (SGD) [20] can add parallelism in the sense that multiple data points can enter an update step. This is exploited by the Eigen-Pro solver [15]. On the con side, convergence is slow (although finite-sum acceleration techniques are applicable in some cases [11]), while dual solvers enjoy linear convergence [13]. Therefore, primal solvers find rough approximate solutions quickly, while dual methods are the method of choice when the large margin principle is taken serious, which requires a rather precise solution.

In any case, the iteration complexity is governed by the computation of $f(x)$ (or equivalently, by the computation of a partial derivative of an update of the dual gradient), which is linear in the number of non-zero coefficients $\alpha_i$. Typically, for each non-zero coefficient, a kernel computation of cost $\mathcal{O}(p)$ is required, where $p$ is the dimension of the input space $X \subset \mathbb{R}^p$, or the average number of non-zeros for sparse data. The resulting complexity of $\mathcal{O}(np)$ is a limiting factor for large-scale data, since the number of support vectors grows linearly with $n$ [21]. In contrast, for linear SVM solvers, the iteration complexity is simply $\mathcal{O}(p)$, which is smaller by a factor of $n$ (often in the order of $10^5$ or more).

# 3    Speed-Up Techniques

*Budgeted and Low-Rank Solvers.* The iteration complexity of most primal as well as dual solvers is tightly coupled to the number of non-zero summands in the weight vector $w = \sum_{i=1}^{n} \alpha_i y_i \phi(x_i)$. Most approximate solvers significantly reduce the number of terms in one way or another. For a dataset with $n = 10^6$ points, a typical subspace is of dimension $B = 10^3$, where $B$ can be the budget or another parameter controlling the effective feature space dimension. Such a reduction can be interpreted as or even constructed through a low-rank approximation of the kernel matrix $Q$.

A low-rank method works well if and only if the optimal weight vector $w^*$ is well preserved by the projection to the low-dimensional subspace, in the metric induced by $Q$. The fact that low-rank approximations aim to preserve the eigenspaces corresponding to large eigenvalues of $Q$ explains why and when such approximations work well, namely when the spectrum of $Q$ decays sufficiently quickly. For kernel-induced Gram matrices, this is usually the case, see [2,15] and references therein.

Random Fourier Features [19] and related approaches approximate the most prominent directions of the kernel feature space $\mathcal{H}$. However, they can be inefficient since the approximation is performed *a priori*, i.e., without considering the data. Nyström sampling methods [26] address this issue by constructing a data-dependent subspace. In practice, this often amounts to simply reducing the available basis functions $\phi(x_i)$ to a small random subset of the training points $\{x_i\}$. Budget methods go even further by making the subspace adaptive during training [6,24]. This can be beneficial since in the end only a single direction needs to be represented in the feature space, namely the optimal weight vector $w^*$, which is however known (approximately) only in a late phase of the training process. Budget methods can be very efficient [18], but they are hard to parallelize due to their budget maintenance strategy, which usually amounts to merging support vectors [24].

Many different training schemes were designed along these lines. We can generally differentiate between two-stage methods in which the construction of the feature space and the training procedure are separated, and single-stage methods in which the two tasks are performed simultaneously. This distinction is generally useful, although it ignores a few variants like lazy learning schemes [12]. Generally speaking, two-stage methods like LLSVM [27] put considerable effort into constructing a suitable subspace and precomputing the projection of the feature vectors into that subspace. This has the advantage that the second stage reduces to training a *linear* SVM, which is relatively fast (although with an iteration complexity of $\mathcal{O}(B)$ instead of $\mathcal{O}(p)$, usually with $B > p$, but still independent of $n$). In contrast, single-stage approaches save the initial cost and pay the price of non-linear SVM training, in the hope that the initial saving amortizes. The latter strategy is generally applied by budget approaches.

*GPU-Ready Parallel Solvers.* The first GPU-ready SVM solver with a significant impact was ThunderSVM [25]. It is a parallel dual subspace ascent method. Algorithmically, it simply performs the same computations as LIBSVM, but it executes many subspace ascent steps in parallel. The steps are damped in order to avoid overshooting, but since there does not seem to be any rigorous justification (like a convergence proof) for the method, it should be considered a heuristic. Yet, in practice, it works very reliably, and it represents considerable progress over LIBSVM's sequential solver. To the best of our knowledge, it is the only GPU-ready SVM solver using a dual training scheme.

The EigenPro method [15] contrasts ThunderSVM im many aspects. The solver is based on modern deep learning frameworks (there are Tensorflow and PyTorch versions). Training is based on SGD on the primal problem. This naturally leverages opportunities for parallelism by means of mini-batch gradient descent, which comes with convergence guarantees, although at a slower rate than dual methods. Moreover, EigenPro is already an approximate solver. It is based on eigen decomposition of a sub-matrix of $Q$ (based on a random subset of the data, see Nyström sampling above). On this matrix it performs a whitening operation. This brings a decisive speedup, since it removes most of the ill-conditioning from the resulting optimization problem, which hence becomes much easier to solve with first order methods like SGD.

# 4   A Low-Rank Parallel Dual SVM Solver

For solving problem (2), we aim to combine three types of approaches: (1) we would like to build on the fast convergence of dual solvers, (2) we would like to achieve the fast iteration complexity of budget and low-rank methods, and (3) we aim for an algorithm with GPU-friendly computations. Any combination of two out of three goals was already demonstrated in the past, see [15,18,25]. In the design of such a method, the following considerations and trade-offs need to be taken into account:

- The matrix $Q$ is of size $n \times n$. For large data sets with millions of points, it does not fit into the RAM even of high-end server machines. Therefore, existing solvers either work with a (row/column-based) kernel cache, or they restrict training to chunks of data for a while, before moving on to the next chunk. However with a budget $B \ll n$ in place, a factor $G$ of a low-rank approximation of $GG^T \approx Q$ is only of size $n \times B$. For $B \approx 10^3$ and $n \approx 10^6$, such a matrix fits into the available memory of a laptop with 8 GB RAM. For server machines with large amounts of RAM, we can even afford two orders of magnitude more (e.g., $B \approx 10^4$ and $n \approx 10^7$). At the time of writing (March 2022), our largest server machine is equipped with 512 GB of RAM, while current high-end GPUs come with up to 80 GB of RAM. In other words, a complete pre-computation of a low-rank factor $G$ becomes feasible even for large[2] data sets.

- As a side effect, whitening the matrix $GG^T$ comes nearly for free based on the eigen decomposition of a $B \times B$ sub-matrix of $Q$, which is needed anyway for the computation[3] of the factor $G$. This is akin to the EigenPro method, but less relevant in our setting, since the dual coordinate ascent solver is not affected by the bad conditioning of the primal problem. On the other hand, it is relevant that for some data sets we find a highly skewed eigenvalue spectrum. As soon as the eigenvalues fall below a threshold close the machine precision times the largest eigenvalue, the subspaces are subject to strong numerical noise while contributing only minimally to the kernel computation. This allows us to drop such components, which further reduces the effective dimension (adaptively) and hence allows us to process even larger data sets.

- Pre-computing the kernel matrix precludes otherwise effective budget maintenance techniques like merging of support vectors, since merging alters $Q$ (and hence $G$) in a non-linear and kernel-dependent fashion. Therefore we settle on a fixed (yet data dependent) feature space representation based on a random sample. This turns out to be equivalent to the second-most attractive budget maintenance strategy: projection onto the remaining support vectors [24]. The difference is that all projections are pre-computed, hence avoiding an $\mathcal{O}(B^3)$ operation per SMO step.

- The precomputation of $G$ effectively turns our approach into a two-stage method. Performing a SMO step followed by a projection-based budget maintenance operation is exactly equivalent to performing a SMO step with an approximate kernel, which is given by $GG^T$ instead of $Q$. The second stage indeed reduces to solving a linear SVM problem where the original data points are replaced with the rows of $G$.

- The excellent study [10] and also our own experience clearly indicate that dual methods are generally superior to primal SGD-based solvers for obtaining SVM solutions of high quality. Therefore we apply a dual coordinate ascent solver, despite the fact that it offers fewer opportunities for parallelization. This decision is made in the expectation that the faster convergence in combination with additional opportunities for parallelization make up for it.

---

[2] These are surely not be the largest data sets in existence, but they are definitely large by the standards of the SVM literature.

[3] A Cholesky decomposition is an attractive alternative at first glance, but since kernel matrices can be ill-conditioned, it regularly runs into numerical problems by requiring *strict* positive definiteness.

As indicated above, a large number of approximate SVM training schemes was already proposed in the literature. Therefore it is not surprising that we arrived as a solution that is related to existing approaches. Our solver has conceptual similarity with the low-rank linearization SVM (LLSVM) [27], in the sense that it performs the same type of computations. LLSVM was proposed 10 years ago. Although the two-stage approach looks quite similar at first glance, there are major and highly relevant differences:

- LLSVM builds a model based on relatively few but carefully selected "landmark" points, by default 50. However, in our experience, the budget size should be in the order of hundreds or better thousands in order to achieve a sufficiently good approximation.
- LLSVM performs training by iterating over the data set only once, where linear SVM training proceeds in chunks of 50,000 points. In order to make good use of the precomputed kernel values, 30 epochs are performed within each chunk. Hence, each point is used exactly 30 times, irrespective of the achieved solution accuracy. In contrast, in our solver, a standard stopping criterion (similar to [10]) is employed to detect convergence.
- We remove the concept of chunks altogether and instead demand that the full matrix $G$ fits into memory. This leverages the capabilities of today's compute servers, simplifies the design, and maybe most importantly, it enables fast convergence to the optimal solution corresponding to the low-rank kernel represented by $G$ and the application of a corresponding stopping criterion.
- We implement all steps of the solver in a multi-core and GPU-ready fashion.

*Algorithm Overview.* The resulting algorithmic steps with their two-stage organization are depicted in Fig. 1. We call the resulting algorithm *low-rank parallel dual (LPD)* SVM. For a GPU implementation, it is important to design all processing steps in such a way that they work in a streaming fashion, at least for cases in which $G$ fits into CPU memory but not into GPU memory (this is similar to but not as restrictive as the chunking approach of LLSVM). The ability to split all computations into smaller chunks is also important when leveraging multi-GPU systems.

The multi-stage approach allows for considerable freedom. To this end, both stages (computation of $G$ and linear SVM training) can be performed by CPU and GPU, at the discretion of the user. This also holds for the prediction step (not shown), which is absent in training, but active in the prediction, test, and cross-validation modes of our software.

*Shrinking.* LIBSVM pays considerable attention to "details" like efficient caching and shrinking. Due to complete precomputation of $G$, we do not have a need for a kernel cache. However, shrinking plays an important role. The heuristic implemented in LIBSVM is known to be somewhat brittle, but it can be very effective when working well. We opt for a simplistic strategy: if a variable was not changed for $k$ steps in a row (we use $k = 5$) then we remove the variable from the problem, and we dedicate a fixed fraction $\eta$ of the total computation time (say, $\eta = 5\%$) to checking whether removed variables should be reconsidered. This heuristic turns out to be far more robust than LIBSVM's strategy which lacks a systematic way of re-activating variables. We will see in the next section that shrinking considerably accelerates the linear SVM training phase.

*Cross Validation, Parameter Tuning, and Multi-Class Training.* In reality, we rarely train a single SVM. Kernel SVMs have parameters like the kernel bandwidth and the regularization parameter $C$ (or $\lambda$) which absolutely need tuning in order to deliver top performance. While powerful parameter tuning procedures based on (Bayesian) optimization are widely available, for low-dimensional problems like this, a simple grid search does the job. It brings the additional benefit that multiple SVMs are trained with the same kernel, which allows to reuse the matrix $G$ and hence the complete first stage of the solver. The same applies to cross-validation: we simply fix the feature space representation once for the whole data set, pre-compute $G$, and only then sub-divide the data into folds.[4] Also, when searching a grid of growing values of $C$, we warm-start the solver from the optimal solution of the nearest value of $C$ already completed, while $G$ needs to be recomputed when the kernel changes. None of these techniques is novel, but they are rarely implemented, although they yield considerable speedups. In our solver their role goes well beyond pure convenience, since many linear training runs can share the first stage of the computation.

A further important point is the handling of classification problem with more than two classes. In this regard we follow the design of LIBSVM [4], which implements a one-versus-one approach. We do this for the following reason: one-versus one means that independent SVMs are trained to separate each pair of classes. What sounds like an immense burden at first, since the number of pairs grows quadratically with the number of classes, is more than alleviated by the fact that the sub-problems are relatively small. Moreover, creating independent subproblems is a welcome opportunity for parallelization. For an in-depth discussion

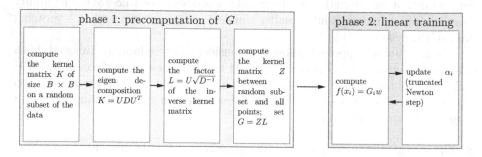

**Fig. 1.** Algorithm design as a two-stage method.

---

[4] While this proceeding may yield a slightly optimistic bias (since some basis vectors may stem from the validation set), it is perfectly suitable for parameter tuning (since all parameter settings profit in the same way), and offers a considerable computational advantage.

of the pros and cons of this approach we refer the interested reader to [8]. In our experiments we demonstrate high efficiency of this scheme on problems with up to 1000 classes, corresponding to roughly half a million pairs of classes.

*Multi-core and GPU Implementation.* Our implementation uses parallelism at three levels: vectorization within each single CPU core (implemented by the highly optimized Eigen C++ library[5]), multi-core parallelism (using OpenMP[6]), and GPU parallelism (using CUDA[7]). For the latter technology, we distinguish between a single streaming multiprocessor (SM) and a full GPU. We even implement multi-GPU support for problems where it makes sense, i.e., if there is sufficient opportunity for parallelism.

In the first stage of computing $G$, the computationally heavy steps are batch kernel computation, eigen decomposition, and matrix-matrix products. All of these are extremely efficient on the GPU, using our own CUDA kernels, the cuSOLVER library, and the cuBLAS library, respectively. On the CPU, we rely on Eigen, and we distribute chunks to multiple CPU cores using OpenMP. For all of these steps, the GPU turns out to be far superior to the CPU.

Sadly, ThunderSVM and EigenPro seem to lack proper support for sparse data, which is commonly encountered in the SVM context. For EigenPro (relying on deep learning software backends) this is understandable, since the focus is on images and similar data, which is usually dense. However, also ThunderSVM converts data to a dense format for kernel computations. The simple reason is that for most general-purpose kernels in common use (polynomial, Gaussian and hyperbolic tangent), batch kernel operations require a matrix-matrix multiplication at their core. It seems that only specific cases of such products are implemented in existing GPU libraries, including cuSPARSE. In our solver, we implemented all kernel operations based on efficient sparse matrix products. For CPU-based processing we rely on the Eigen C++ library, while for (far more efficient) GPU-based processing, we implemented sparse matrix products as custom CUDA kernels.

In the second stage of linear SVM training, the trade-offs turn out to be quite different. In contrast to ThunderSVM, all kernels are precomputed in the first stage. This is a logical and efficient step, but it removes most opportunities for parallelism. While ThunderSVM needs to process $n \cdot p$ floating point values per data points (where $p$ is the dimension of the input space $X \subset \mathbb{R}^p$), we only need to handle $B$ values. Although removing opportunities for parallelism, this is still a great acceleration, since the old wisdom that the fastest computation is the one that does not run at all still holds.

As a result, a single SMO (coordinate ascent) step runs extremely fast on a single CPU in a fully vectorized fashion. The corresponding GPU implementation is somewhat slowed down by the need for a parallel reduction operation. Also, the relatively low amount of parallelism precludes the use of more than one

---

[5] https://eigen.tuxfamily.org/.

[6] https://www.openmp.org/.

[7] https://developer.nvidia.com/.

streaming multiprocessor (SM) on the GPU, since a single SM can maintain the current weight vector in its fast scratchpad memory, while the communication cost of multiple SMs would slow down the extremely fast SMO loop. For current CUDA architectures this means that a total of "only" 1024 threads cooperate by computing $B$ summands per data point or dual variable. To make the orders of magnitude clear: in our solver, for a realistic value like $B = 10^3$, each CPU core performs several *million* coordinate ascent steps per second. At that pace, multi-core communication would incur an unacceptable overhead, and the same holds when communicating between multiple SMs within a GPU.

This leaves us with the (luxury) problem of fully leveraging server GPUs, which come with more than 100 SMs each. With a single training run of a binary classification problem this is simply not possible, and CPU-based training should be preferred. However, when performing even only a tiny $5 \times 5$ grid search using 10-fold cross validation on a 10-class dataset like MNIST, we need to train a total of $5 \times 5 \times 10 \times \binom{10}{2} = 11,250$ binary SVMs: one for each parameter vector, one for each hold-out set, and one for each pair of classes. This is far more parallelism than we need to fully exploit even multiple GPUs at the same time, while the first stage needs to run only five times (once for each kernel parameter).

Making predictions is relatively fast compared with training. One decisive difference is that predictions can be computed in parallel, so that for this task, the GPU is vastly superior to the CPU. Our implementation therefore defaults to the following behavior: computation of $G$ and prediction are performed by the GPU and SMO training runs on the CPU. This is confirmed in the next section as a solid default.

*Recipe.* In summary, our approach has conceptually close predecessors in the existing literature, which we polish up far beyond aesthetics by adding shrinking, a meaningful stopping criterion, warm starts, and proper support for cross-validation and parameter tuning. We put considerable effort into exploiting parallelism in all stages of the solver on CPU and GPU. Finally, we arrive at quite different trade-offs than older solvers through a combination of large available memory and memory saving techniques, in particular the low-rank approach, and by discarding small eigen values. This is how we arrive at the recipe *"polishing, parallelism, and more RAM"* for fast large-scale SVM training.

## 5   Experimental Evaluation

The main evidence for the value of our methodology is of empirical nature. We present experimental results to answer the following research questions:

- How fast and how accurate is our approach, compared with existing solvers?
- How scalable is our approach, in particular for multi-class problems?
- How do the various computational components perform on multi-core CPUs and on high-end GPUs?
- How does shrinking impact performance?

**Table 1.** Data sets used in this study, including tuned hyperparameters.

| data set | file size | # classes | size $n$ | budget $B$ | regular. $C$ | kernel $\gamma$ |
|---|---|---|---|---|---|---|
| Adult (a9a) | 2.3 MB | 2 | 32,561 | 1,000 | $2^5$ | $2^{-7}$ |
| Epsilon | 12 GB | 2 | 400,000 | 10,000 | $2^5$ | $2^{-4}$ |
| SUSY | 2.4 GB | 2 | 5,000,000 | 1,000 | $2^5$ | $2^{-7}$ |
| MNIST-8M | 12 GB | 10 | 8,100,000 | 10,000 | $2^5$ | $2^{-22}$ |
| ImageNet | 59 GB | 1000 | 1,281,167 | 1,000 | $2^4$ | $2^{-24}$ |

*Experimental Setup.* We trained SVMs on one mid-sized and four large data sets, see Table 1. The first four data sets are available from the LIBSVM website.[8] The ImageNet data set [7] can be obtained for free for non-commercial research.[9] We turned it into an SVM training problem by propagating the images through a pre-trained VGG-16 network (shipped with keras) and extracting the activations of the last convolution layer, which is of dimension 25,088. The resulting feature vectors are sparse due to the ReLU activation function.

We used the Gaussian kernel $k(x, x') = \exp(-\gamma \|x - x'\|^2)$ in all experiments. The hyperparameters $C$ and $\gamma$ were tuned with grid-search and cross-validation.

All timings were measured on a compute server with 512 GB of RAM, two Intel Xeon 4216 CPUs (up to 64 concurrent threads), and four NVIDIA A100 GPUs (40 GB RAM each).

In the spirit of open and reproducible research, our software is available under a permissive open-source BSD-3-clause license.[10]

*Comparison with Existing Solvers.* We aimed to compare with the following solvers: ThunderSVM,[11] EigenPro,[12] and LLSVM.[13] However, we failed to make (the PyTorch version of) EigenPro deliver meaningful results beyond the built-in MNIST example. On the chosen data sets, it seems to be quite sensitive data scaling, resulting in numerical instability. Despite our disappointment, we had to exclude EigenPro from the comparison. We therefore present performance data for ThunderSVM, LLSVM, and our own method LPD-SVM in Table 2. The same data is displayed graphically in Fig. 2.

First of all, while being quite fast (provided that only a single CPU core is used), LLSVM fails to deliver sufficiently accurate solutions. On the Epsilon problem, it consistently yields guessing accuracy (50% error). This is for its non-adaptive stopping rule, which does not check for convergence. It is of course easy to be fast if the job is not complete. This seems to be the case for LLSVM.

---

[8] https://www.csie.ntu.edu.tw/~cjlin/libsvmtools/datasets/.
[9] https://www.image-net.org/.
[10] https://github.com/TGlas/LPD-SVM.
[11] https://github.com/Xtra-Computing/thundersvm.
[12] https://github.com/EigenPro.
[13] https://github.com/djurikom/BudgetedSVM.

**Table 2.** Performance results of the different solvers: training and prediction time (seconds), and classification error (in percent). LLSVM is not applicable to data sets with more than two classes. ThunderSVM training on ImageNet stopped after 42 h with an out-of-memory error. At that point, training was about 83% complete. For LLSVM, we observed huge random deviations of predictive performance (about ±13.6% for Adult and about 4.6% for SUSY). In the table, we report mean values. Also the best values are cannot compete with the other solvers.

| solver | indicator | Adult | Epsilon | SUSY | MNIST-8M | ImageNet |
|--------|-----------|-------|---------|------|----------|----------|
| LLSVM | training | 1.51 | 48.38 | 71.93 | — | — |
| | prediction | 0.25 | 23.84 | 29.98 | — | — |
| | error | 27.3 | 50.0 | 27.52 | — | — |
| ThunderSVM | training | 2.25 | 5,315 | 14,604 | 7,517 | > 42 hours |
| | prediction | 1.42 | 470.51 | 5,128 | 11.07 | — |
| | error | 14.92 | 8.70 | 19.99 | 0.95 | — |
| LPD-SVM | training | 2.11 | 89.86 | 197.64 | 868 | 1,402.86 |
| | prediction | 1.62 | 12.94 | 1.22 | 2.08 | 36.22 |
| | error | 14.77 | 9.85 | 20.08 | 1.20 | 37.52 |

In terms of accuracy, LPD-SVM comes quite close to the (nearly exact) solutions obtained by ThunderSVM. On the Epsilon problem, we pay for the budget approximation with an increase of the error of a bit more than one percent, while in the other cases, error rates are quite close. This slight loss of predictive performance is expected and in line with the general experience with low-rank approximations in the SVM literature.

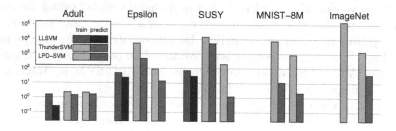

**Fig. 2.** Plot of the timing data from Table 2 on a logarithmic scale.

At the same time, LPD-SVM systematically outperforms ThunderSVM in terms of speed, both at training and at prediction time. This is particularly true for the large data sets where the low-rank approach makes a decisive difference by lowering the iteration complexity considerably. We see experimentally that the net difference is roughly one to two orders of magnitude. For the simple scenario of training a single SVM classifier, the GPU cannot be fully utilized during training. Hence, the speed-up over ThunderSVM is fully attributed to the low-rank approach.

*Multi-Class SVM Training.* Here, we are mostly interested in investigating the scaling of our solver to problems with many classes. Indeed, it takes LPD-SVM only about 24 min to train nearly half a million large-margin classifiers. This corresponds to less than 3 milliseconds per binary problem. It seems safe to conclude that—at least computationally—the one-versus-one approach is very well suited for training large-scale SVMs. It has its drawbacks in terms of accuracy, see [8], and indeed, we did not achieve a competitive error rate on the ImageNet problem (the VGG-16 network performs better). This is unsurprising, since convolutional neural networks are surely the better suited model class for the problem.

*CPU vs. GPU Performance.* When looking at the specifications of modern server CPUs and GPUs then one would expect the GPU to clearly dominate. However, despite our effort of implementing an efficient SMO solver natively on the GPU with custom CUDA kernels, CPUs are still a better match for the inherently sequential dual algorithm than GPUs. In our empirical data, the CPU wins the race on both data sets where $G$ fits into GPU memory, and in the other three cases GPU-based training is not an option at all. The GPU cannot play its strengths for the simple reason that the SMO loop is memory-bound, not compute-bound (it is dominated by computing inner products of vectors of dimension $B$, which is a far too low dimension for the GPU). While the GPU has a larger net memory throughput, the CPU has a faster clock speed, more efficient caches, and a very effective pre-fetching mechanism.

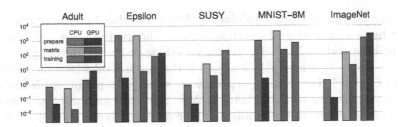

**Fig. 3.** Timing breakdown into the three stages "preparation" (red; first three steps in Fig. 1), "computation of the matrix $G$" (green; step four in Fig. 1), and "linear SVM training" (magenta), on CPU (bright) and GPU (dark). All durations are in seconds, depicted on a logarithmic scale. For two data sets, training times on the GPU are missing since the matrix $G$ does not fit into GPU memory. (Color figure online)

That being said, the overall role of the GPU must not be under-estimated. It vastly reduces the cost for preparing the matrix $G$, which can otherwise be the dominant cost on the CPU, and it also speeds up predictions. This way, the two types of processors (CPU and GPU) contribute jointly to fast training. If any of the two is dropped then the overall training times increase significantly.

Figure 3 gives a more detailed picture by breaking down the timings of the different stages for GPU and CPU. It becomes clear that the GPU is far more suitable for the preparation of $G$ and for making predictions, while the CPU outperforms the GPU for SMO training. This holds true even for the Imagenet problem where all $4 \times 108 = 432$ GPU processors are running SMO loops in parallel, as compared with 64 CPU cores.

It can also be observed that the trade-offs presented by the two-stage approach differ quite significantly between data sets, and depending on whether computations are carried out on CPU or GPU. When using the GPU then the first stage is generally faster than the second stage, which means that the investment made in the first stage amortizes. However, when solving the Epsilon problem completely on the CPU, this is not so clear, since the computation of $G$ takes the lion's share of the time.

*Shrinking.* We evaluate our shrinking algorithm by simply turning it on or off and measuring the optimization time. In order to achieve clean results, we restrict time measurements to the second phase (SMO training). Based on prior experience, we expect shrinking to yield a speed-up in general, but on the other hand, wrong shrinking decision can cost performance. It turns out that shrinking is a complete game-changer: without shrinking, the training time for the Adult data increases by factor 220, while for Epsilon it increases by factor of 350. Due to excessive training times, we did not perform the test for all data sets. This impressive speed-up is in part due to the fact that after removing many variable for fine tuning in the late phase of the optimization, at memory demand for the relevant sub-matrix of $G$ reduces and the processor cache becomes for effective.

*Parameter Tuning and Cross-Validation.* We tested the ability of our solver to support hyperparameter grid search and cross-validation as follows. For $\log_2(C)$, we defined the grid $\{0, 1, \ldots, 9\}$, and we varied $\log_2(\gamma)$ in the range $\{g^* - 2, g^* - 1, g^*, g^* + 1, g^* + 2\}$, where $g^* = \log_2(\gamma^*)$ is the optimal value, see the rightmost column of Table 1. For each hyperparameter setting, we performed 5-fold cross validation. Hence, we trained a total of $N = 250 \cdot \binom{c}{2}$ binary SVMs, where $c$ is the number of classes of the problem. The results are found in Table 3. It lists the total time, the time per binary problem (the first value divided by $N$), and the speed-up, which is estimated from the training time from Table 2 divided by the time per binary problem.

The speed-up is around a factor of two in most cases, and more than seven for the Epsilon data. This is in part because the first stage needs to run only five times (once for each value of $\gamma$), while previous computations can be reused for the remaining $N - 5$ training runs. This reuse of the precomputation of $G$ is only responsible for one part of the speed-up, while another part comes from warm-starts with solutions corresponding to smaller values of $C$, and from a better utilization of the compute resources (cores).

**Table 3.** Timings of the hyperparameter search and cross-validation experiments. All times are in seconds.

|                        | Adult  | Epsilon | SUSY    | MNIST-8M |
|------------------------|--------|---------|---------|----------|
| total time             | 247.43 | 2,837   | 28,163  | 84,600   |
| time per binary problem| 0.99   | 11.34   | 112.65  | 7.52     |
| speed-up               | ×2.1   | ×7.3    | ×1.75   | ×2.6     |

*Discussion.* Our experimental findings answer our research questions as follows. The proposed LPD-SVM is extremely fast, with a speed-up of roughly one to two orders of magnitude over ThunderSVM on large problems. This is despite the fact that the SMO loop runs on the CPU. LPD-SVM suffers only a minimal increase of error rates due to the budget approach. It scales very well to multi-class problems with many classes. We see performance gains from properly implemented cross-validation and grid search, and our shrinking algorithm turns out to be extremely effective. We believe that these results are a valuable addition to the state of the art, and that our solver provides an interesting alternative existing SVM software.

## 6 Conclusion

We have presented a GPU-ready SVM solver optimized for compute servers, called *Low-rank Parallel Dual* (LPD) SVM. It fits into the common framework of low-rank or budgeted schemes for approximate SVM training. It takes the typical capabilities of modern server machines into account: large random access memory, many-core CPUs, and high-end server GPUs. We demonstrate its potential on a number of large-scale data sets, achieving state-of-the-art results.

**Acknowledgements.** This work was supported by the Deutsche Forschungsgemeinschaft under grant number GL 839/7-1.

## References

1. Bottou, L., Lin, C.J.: Support vector machine solvers (2006)
2. Braun, M.L.: Accurate error bounds for the eigenvalues of the kernel matrix. J. Mach. Learn. Res. **7**, 2303–2328 (2006)
3. Byvatov, E., Schneider, G.: Support vector machine applications in bioinformatics. Appl. Bioinform. **2**(2), 67–77 (2003)
4. Chang, C.C., Lin, C.J.: LIBSVM: a library for support vector machines. ACM Trans. Intell. Syst. Technol. **2**(3), 1–27 (2011)
5. Cortes, C., Vapnik, V.: Support-vector networks. Mach. Learn. **20**(3), 273–297 (1995)
6. Dekel, O., Singer, Y.: Support Vector Machines on a Budget. MIT Press, Cambridge (2007)

7. Deng, J., Dong, W., Socher, R., Li, L.J., Li, K., Fei-Fei, L.: ImageNet: a large-scale hierarchical image database. In: IEEE Conference on Computer Vision and Pattern Recognition (CVPR), pp. 248–255 (2009)
8. Doğan, Ü., Glasmachers, T., Igel, C.: A unified view on multi-class support vector classification. J. Mach. Learn. Res. **17**(45), 1–32 (2016)
9. Doğan, Ü., Glasmachers, T., Igel, C.: A unified view on multi-class support vector classification. J. Mach. Learn. Res. (JMLR) **17**(45), 1–32 (2016)
10. Fan, R.E., Chang, K.W., Hsieh, C.J., Wang, X.R., Lin, C.J.: LIBLINEAR: a library for large linear classification. J. Mach. Learn. Res. **9**, 1871–1874 (2008)
11. Glasmachers, T.: Finite sum acceleration vs. adaptive learning rates for the training of kernel machines on a budget. In: NIPS Workshop on Optimization for Machine Learning (2016)
12. Kecman, V., Brooks, J.P.: Locally linear support vector machines and other local models. In: The 2010 International Joint Conference on Neural Networks (IJCNN), pp. 1–6. IEEE (2010)
13. Lin, C.J.: On the convergence of the decomposition method for support vector machines. IEEE Trans. Neural Networks **12**(6), 1288–1298 (2001)
14. Lu, W.C., Ji, X.B., Li, M.J., Liu, L., Yue, B.H., Zhang, L.M.: Using support vector machine for materials design. Adv. Manuf. **1**(2), 151–159 (2013)
15. Ma, S., Belkin, M.: Diving into the shallows: a computational perspective on large-scale shallow learning. In: Advances in Neural Information Processing Systems, vol. 30 (2017)
16. Ma, Y., Guo, G.: Support Vector Machines Applications, vol. 649. Springer, Cham (2014). https://doi.org/10.1007/978-3-319-02300-7
17. Osuna, E., Freund, R., Girosi, F.: An improved training algorithm of support vector machines. In: Neural Networks for Signal Processing VII, pp. 276–285 (1997)
18. Qaadan, S., Schüler, M., Glasmachers, T.: Dual SVM training on a budget. In: Proceedings of the 8th International Conference on Pattern Recognition Applications and Methods. SCITEPRESS - Science and Technology Publications (2019)
19. Rahimi, A., Recht, B.: Random features for large-scale kernel machines. In: Advances in Neural Information Processing Systems, pp. 1177–1184 (2008)
20. Shalev-Shwartz, S., Singer, Y., Srebro, N.: Pegasos: primal estimated sub-gradient solver for SVM. In: Proceedings of the 24th International Conference on Machine Learning, pp. 807–814 (2007)
21. Steinwart, I.: Sparseness of support vector machines. J. Mach. Learn. Res. **4**, 1071–1105 (2003)
22. Steinwart, I., Hush, D., Scovel, C.: Training SVMs without offset. J. Machine Learn. Res. **12**(Jan), 141–202 (2011)
23. Tsang, I.W., Kwok, J.T., Cheung, P.M., Cristianini, N.: Core vector machines: fast SVM training on very large data sets. J. Mach. Learn. Res. **6**(4) (2005)
24. Wang, Z., Crammer, K., Vucetic, S.: Breaking the curse of kernelization: budgeted stochastic gradient descent for large-scale SVM training. J. Mach. Learn. Res. **13**(1), 3103–3131 (2012)
25. Wen, Z., Shi, J., Li, Q., He, B., Chen, J.: ThunderSVM: a fast SVM library on GPUs and CPUs. J. Mach. Learn. Res. **19**(1), 797–801 (2018)
26. Yang, T., Li, Y.F., Mahdavi, M., Jin, R., Zhou, Z.H.: Nyström method vs. random fourier features: a theoretical and empirical comparison. In: Advances in Neural Information Processing Systems, pp. 476–484 (2012)
27. Zhang, K., Lan, L., Wang, Z., Moerchen, F.: Scaling up kernel SVM on limited resources: a low-rank linearization approach. In: Artificial Intelligence and Statistics, pp. 1425–1434. PMLR (2012)

# Automatic Generation of Product Concepts from Positive Examples, with an Application to Music Streaming

Kshitij Goyal[1]([✉])(iD), Wannes Meert[1](iD), Hendrik Blockeel[1](iD),
Elia Van Wolputte[1](iD), Koen Vanderstraeten[2], Wouter Pijpops[2],
and Kurt Jaspers[2]

[1] KU Leuven, Leuven, Belgium
{kshitij.goyal,wannes.meert,hendrik.blockeel,elia.wolputte}@kuleuven.be
[2] Tunify, Beringen, Belgium
{koen.vanderstraeten,wouter.pijpops,kurt.jaspers}@tunify.com

**Abstract.** Internet based businesses and products (e.g. e-commerce, music streaming) are becoming more and more sophisticated every day with a lot of focus on improving customer satisfaction. A core way they achieve this is by providing customers with an easy access to their products by structuring them in catalogues using navigation bars and providing recommendations. We refer to these catalogues as *product concepts*, e.g. product categories on e-commerce websites, public playlists on music streaming platforms. These *product concepts* typically contain products that are linked with each other through some common features (e.g. a playlist of songs by the same artist). How they are defined in the backend of the system can be different for different products. In this work, we represent product concepts using database queries and tackle two learning problems. First, given sets of products that all belong to the same unknown product concept, we learn a database query that is a representation of this product concept. Second, we learn product concepts and their corresponding queries when the given sets of products are associated with multiple product concepts. To achieve these goals, we propose two approaches that combine the concepts of PU learning with Decision Trees and Clustering. Our experiments demonstrate, via a simulated setup for a music streaming service, that our approach is effective in solving these problems.

**Keywords:** PU Learning · Machine Learning · Music Streaming

## 1 Introduction

Machine learning is used for various applications these days and more and more businesses are looking to use machine learning to improve their products. Recent advances in online consumer based businesses provide an opportunity to explore machine learning solutions to challenging problems. One such problem is generating dynamic product concepts that contain a selection of products that are linked

© The Author(s), under exclusive license to Springer Nature Switzerland AG 2023
T. Calders et al. (Eds.): BNAIC/Benelearn 2022, CCIS 1805, pp. 47–64, 2023.
https://doi.org/10.1007/978-3-031-39144-6_4

with each other through some common features. For example, in e-commerce a product category that contains similar items (e.g., 'cosmetic items') is a product concept, in music streaming services a public playlist is a product concept. Typically these kinds of product concepts are available for users to select from. There are benefits of having such product concepts in your system: 1. they provide a good way to structure the itinerary; 2. a user can use them to navigate the website; 3. they make it easy for users to discover new items.

Due to the lack of transparency behind how these product concepts are created for most services, we can not generalize their creation in the back-end of a system. However, in our work, we assume that a product concept is associated with a database query, which we term as the concept query, that filters that whole database of items (products, songs etc.) based on certain common features. This makes these product concepts dynamic in nature: they get automatically updated when new items are added to the database. This definition is inspired by our use case of a music streaming company called **Tunify**[1].

Tunify is a music streaming service that provides a predefined selection of playlists to businesses. Tunify has a database of songs where each song is represented by a fixed set of discrete valued features: *mood, popularity* etc. Tunify also maintains a set of database queries that define useful product concepts (the product concept defined by a query is a set of all songs that are returned when that query is run on the database). These products concepts are useful for generating playlists for businesses. A business can select a product concept based on a small description (e.g., 80's Rock) and a playlist based on the selected product concept is generated, the generated playlist is a sample of all the songs associated with the product concept. The database queries corresponding to product concepts are manually defined by music experts that Tunify employs. This query creation process has an obvious drawback: it requires a lot of time to fine tune the exact feature-values the query should contain. This motivates our first problem: can we automatically identify the database query corresponding to a product concept if we are provided with a set of playlists that the target product concept should generate? We argue that it is easier for an expert to manually create playlists that the target concept should generate compared to manually creating a database query.

Another interesting problem setting is when the provided playlists come from multiple target product concepts. Can we identify different concepts the playlists are coming from and their corresponding database queries? This problem is motivated by the fact that Tunify allows for customers to create their own playlists under one of their subscriptions. As these playlists come from multiple customers, we expect that: 1. not all of them contain similar songs; 2. there are multiple playlists that contain similar songs. We want to identify similar playlists and create product concepts based on them. There are two outcomes of this: either the identified product concepts are missing from Tunify's system, or the identified product concepts are already in the system but the customers didn't use them for whatever reasons. In the former case, we improve the database with

---

[1] https://www.tunify.com/nl-be/language/.

new concepts, and in the later case, Tunify could reach out to the customers that created their own playlists and recommend the already existing concepts.

Even though we motivate these problems based on our use case of Tunify, these problems are generally applicable for any business where such product concepts are used. Consider the example of an e-commerce company, here the product concepts are the product categories (e.g., *cosmetics, menswear*). The customers interact with the product concept in this case differently from Tunify: in Tunify, a playlist is generated when a customer selects a product concept, but in the case of e-commerce a customer can view all the products associated with a product concept. In the context of our two learning problems, however, this difference does not have any impact. For the first learning problem, instead of experts making a playlist of songs, the experts create a set of items. For the second problem, instead of using playlists of songs created by customers, we can use the items the customers purchased together.

To summarize, we consider two learning problems: 1. learning the product concept query given a collection of itemsets that are associated with it, 2. learning product concepts and their corresponding queries given a collection of itemsets that may or may not be associated with a single product concept. For the first problem, we use a combination of PU learning (Positive and Unlabelled Learning) [4] techniques with decision tree learning to learn the product concept queries as the rules from the decision tree. In addition to this, we also study the effect of noise in the provided itemsets on the final query and propose a way to deal with it. For the second problem, we combine the approach of task one with clustering to identify new product concepts from data generated by customers.

We design and test our experiments on the dataset provided to us by Tunify. With a simulated experimental setup, we demonstrate that our approaches are able to learn good quality concept queries with small number of items, even when there is noise in the set, and we are able to effectively identify product concepts using the customer data. We additionally show that our proposed algorithm for the first problem is robust to noise in the provided set of items.

The paper is structured in the following way: first we introduce some terminologies and explain the problem statements in Sect. 2, secondly we present our approach in Sect. 3, then we present the experimental results in Sect. 4 before the related works and a discussion in Sects. 5 and 6 respectively. Section 7 concludes.

## 2    Framework

In this section, we first give an overview of some concepts from logic and satisfiability which we use in our work before explaining our problem statement.

### 2.1    Propositional Logic

Propositional Logic formulas contain literals which are Boolean formulas, their negation and logical connectives, e.g., $(a \lor (b \land \neg(c)))$. An assignment $x$ of variables $\{a, b, c\}$ satisfies a formula $\phi$ if $x$ makes the formula $\phi$ True. Any logical formula can be rewritten in a normal form such as Conjunctive Normal Form (CNF) or Disjunctive Normal Form (DNF). A CNF formula consists of conjunction of disjunction of literals and a DNF formula contains disjunction of conjunction of literals, where conjunction is the logical 'AND' ($\wedge$) operator and disjunction is the logical 'OR' ($\vee$) operator.

## 2.2   Problem Statement

We now formally define our learning problems. The dataset of instances is represented by $\mathcal{D}$. We assume that an instance is represented by a fixed set of discrete valued features $\mathcal{F}$ and takes a single value for each feature. For a feature $f \in \mathcal{F}$, the discrete set of values $f$ can take is represented by $V(f)$.

**Definition 1. *Product Concept*.** *A product concept is a collection of instances. A product concept is associated with a concept query that defines which instances belong to it.*

A product concept can be a union of multiple 'sub-concepts'. For example, in e-commerce, a category can have many different sub categories; in Tunify, there are a number of product concepts that combine the music from multiple different product concepts to generate a playlist that contains songs from all the combined product concepts (e.g., 'Fitness Center' product concept combines product concepts 'Dance Workout' and 'Rock Dynamic'). Keeping this in mind, we formally define a concept query as follows:

**Definition 2. *Conjunctive Concept Query*.** *Given a set of attributes $F \subseteq \mathcal{F}$ and sets of values $V^f \subseteq V(f)$ for each $f \in F$. A conjunctive concept query $Q$, for an arbitrary input $x \in \mathcal{D}$, is defined as the following rule-based query in a conjunctive normal form:*

$$Q : \bigwedge_{f \in F} \bigvee_{v \in V^f} (x_f = v)$$

**Definition 3. *Concept Query*.** *A concept query is defined as:*

*1. A conjunctive concept query is a concept query.*
*2. A disjunction of two or more conjunctive concept queries is a concept query.*

In the case where a concept query is a disjunction of two or more conjunctive concept queries, each conjunctive concept query and all the items that make it true are said to be associated with a sub-concept of the parent product concept (where the parent product concept is the disjunctive combination of the sub-concepts). Any item that is associated with any of the sub-concepts is said to belong to the parent product concept. By definition, a sub-concept is also a product concept. We will refer to the concept query corresponding to a product concept $C$ as $Q_C$ in the text from now on. Also, for a given query $Q$, the items from the database $\mathcal{D}$ that are filtered by the query are denoted by $Q(\mathcal{D})$.

We now define our learning problems. The first problem we consider is the problem of learning the concept query for a target concept given a collection of set of instances that are associated with it. Note that this problem can be simplified: given that all the provided sets of instances correspond to the same target concept, we can combine them into one set of instances. This is the standard PU learning setting [4], where we want to learn just from positive instances. Formally we define the first learning problem as:

**Definition 4. _Learning Problem 1._** _Given a set of positive instances $S \subset C$, for a target concept $C$, find the corresponding concept query._

For the second learning problem, we want to learn product concepts and their corresponding queries provided a collection of sets of instances. The difference from problem 4 is that the sets do not necessarily belong to a single target concept. We do not know how many product concepts are to be learned. Different sets may belong to the same concept, or to different ones; we do not know which sets belong to the same concept. The task is still to learn a concept query for each concept. Note that problem 2 reduces to problem 1 once we find out which sets belong to the same concept: merging all sets belonging to one concept yields the set of positive instances for that concept. Formally, the second problem is:

**Definition 5. _Learning Problem 2._** _Given a collection of sets of instances $P_j$, $j = 1, \ldots, m$, find a partition of the collection into equivalence classes $K_i$ and corresponding instance sets $S_i = \bigcup_{P \in K_i} P$ such that $S_i \subset C_i$ for each concept $C_i$ to be learned; and find the concept query associated with each concept._

## 3 Approach

We present our approaches for the two learning problems in Sects. 3.1 and 3.2.

### 3.1 Problem 1: Learning Concept Query from a Set of Items

For the first learning problem, we observe that a concept query is essentially a binary classifier that predicts if a given item belongs to a product concept or not. From this perspective, since we are only provided with a small number of positive instances, the learning setting is of PU learning (Positive and Unlabelled Learning) [4]. Following a standard approach in PU learning, we approach this problem by generating the so called _reliable negatives_ [4] from the full data $\mathcal{D}$, which is discussed in more detail later in this section. Once we have generated the data, we fit a binary classifier that separates the positive instances from the negatives. Finally, we extract the rule based query from the classifier that can be used as the concept query in the form described in Definition 3. Next subsections provide a more detailed discussion. The pseudo code is available in Algorithm 1.

---

**Algorithm 1.** ConceptQueryLearner

**input:** initial set **S**, all items $\mathcal{D}$, discard threshold **d**
1: $Query = \{\}$
2: $N = \text{GetReliableNegatives}(S, \mathcal{D})$
3: $\mathcal{T} = \text{DecisionTree}(S, N)$
4: **for** each positive leaf $L$ in $\mathcal{T}$ **do**
5:     **if** $Size(L) \geqslant d * Size(S)$ **then**
6:         q = GetQuery(L)
7:         $Query = Query \cup q$
8:     **end if**
9: **end for**
10: **return** $Query$

---

**Getting Reliable Negatives:** Getting reliable negatives is a standard app-roach for a PU learning problem. The core assumption behind this is that the data point that are very different from the provided positive instances are likely to be negative examples. There are a number of approached proposed for this in the literature [4]. We employ two approaches for this purpose: First one is a novel probabilistic approach which we call the **likelihood approach** and the second one is the standard **rocchio approach** [14].

In the first approach, we calculate the probabilities for each value for each feature based on $S$. For a feature $f \in \mathcal{F}$ and a given value of the feature $v \in V(f)$, the probability is simply calculated as:

$$P(f = v|S) = \sum_{s \in S} 1_{\{s_f = v\}} / |S| \tag{1}$$

We assume these probabilities to be the marginal probabilities of the distribution of the target context. For an item $x \in \mathcal{D} \setminus S$, we calculate the probability that $x$ was sampled from the distribution defined by $S$. Let's assume that item $x$ is defined as $\{color = red, material = m_1, ...\}$, we write the probability as:

$$P(x) = P(color = red, material = m_1, ...) \tag{2}$$

This probability is always smaller than or equal to the marginal probabilities:

$$P(x) \leqslant P(color = red); P(x) \leqslant P(material = m_1), ... \tag{3}$$

If any of the feature values in $x$ has a marginal probability 0, this would imply that the $P(x) = 0$ according to Eq. 3. Hence, all the items $x \in \mathcal{D} \setminus S$ that have $P(x) = 0$ are chosen to be reliable negatives. Important to note that the set $S$ is a subset of the items in the target concept $C$, and the marginal probabilities based on $S$ are just an approximation of the true marginal. A larger initial set $S$ would lead to better approximation which in turn would lead to better quality of reliable negatives. We will study the impact of the size of $S$ on the learned context queries in the next section.

**Table 1.** Example of items in a leaf, for a music streaming service

| song id | decade | emotion | popularity | |
|---------|--------|---------|------------|-----|
| 1 | 2020s | excited | 6 | ... |
| 2 | 2010s | neutral | 4 | ... |
| 3 | 2000s | excited | 5 | ... |

The second approach we use is the existing *Rocchio* approach [14] which is based on the rocchio classification [8]. This method builds prototypes for the labelled ($S$) and the unlabelled data ($\mathcal{D} \setminus S$). The prototype in our implementation is the centroid of the data points in a binarized version of the dataset $\mathcal{D}$ where each feature value pair is replaced with a binary feature. The method then iterates over the unlabelled examples: if an unlabelled example is closer to the unlabelled prototype than the labelled prototype, it is chosen to be a reliable negative example. Euclidean distance is used in our implementation to calculate the distance between a data point and a prototype.

**Learning the Classifier and Extracting the Concept Query:** Once we have a set of reliable negatives, we fit a binary classifier. As the concept query can only be in a logical query form, our choice is limited to either a rule based classifier or a classifier which can be used to extract a rule based query. For our approach, we decide to use a decision tree classifier [23] because it is trivial to extract logical rules from these models and there are efficient open source implementations for learning decision trees[2]. In decision trees, positive instances are typically assigned to multiple leafs unless the tree is of depth 1. Different positive leafs can be considered as sub-concepts of the target concept. Hence, the final concept query is the disjunctive combination of the logical query corresponding to each positive leaf. Also, we want the positive leafs to be pure (containing only positive instances) because queries corresponding to impure leafs would lead to predictions that would contain a lot of false positives, this impacts the quality of the learned concept in terms of customer satisfaction. There are two possible options for creating a query corresponding to a positive leaf: 1. Use conjunction of each split from root to the selected leaf; 2. Use the instances in the positive leafs to generate the query.

Extracting the first type of query is straight forward: for each branch that leads to a positive leaf, all the tests at the splits can be combined in a conjunction to form a logical query in the conjunctive normal form, which can then be transformed into the form of Definition 3. The predictions made by final concept query created with this approach is equivalent to the predictions made by the decision tree. For the second type of query, we use the examples in a positive leaf to generate the most specific query that contains all the examples in the leaf. To create the most specific query, we use the logical formulation of the query from Definition 3 and add a literal for each feature value that occurs in the set of examples. For example, for a music streaming application, assume a leaf

---

[2] https://scikit-learn.org/stable/modules/classes.html.

contains the examples in Table 1. The most specific query for this leaf would be: $\{(decade = 2000s \vee decade = 2010s \vee decade = 2020s) \wedge (emotion = excited \vee emotion = neutral) \wedge (popularity = 4 \vee popularity = 5 \vee popularity = 6) \wedge ...\}$. The final concept query is the disjunction of query for each positive leaf.

We refer to the first type as $dt$-$query$ - $Q_d = \bigvee_l q_{dl}$, and the second type as $items$-$query$ - $Q_s = \bigvee_l q_{sl}$ where $q_{dl}$ and $q_{sl}$ are the queries corresponding to the leaf $l$. Interesting to note that for a given leaf $l$, $q_{sl}(\mathcal{D}) \subset q_{dl}(\mathcal{D})$. Using the example from Table 1, let's assume that $q_{dl} : (decade = 2020s \vee decade = 2010s \vee decade = 2000s) \wedge (popularity \neq 7)$, any item (song) $s \in q_{sl}(\mathcal{D})$ will satisfy the query $q_{dl}$ because the values of the features $decade$ and $popularity$ in $q_{sl}(\mathcal{D})$ are limited by the the instances in the leaf which all must satisfy the query $q_{dl}$. Hence, we expect that the $Q_d$ leads to a bigger set of examples compared to $Q_s$, implying that $Q_d$ will lead to low precision compared to $Q_s$ when compared to the target concept. We explore this in more detail in Sect. 4.

Another thing to consider is the quality of the positive examples in the set $S$. Since $S$ is curated by human experts, it can have noisy data. There may be many reasons for this: the expert is not experienced enough, or the selection of positive examples is based on a general criterion (e.g., all items from a brand $x$ should be in $S$). The concept query based on noisy positives would lead to larger amounts of noise in the items filtered by the query from $\mathcal{D}$, which compromises a good customer experience. Hence, it is important to be robust against such noisy positives. For this purpose, instead of generating a query based on each positive leaf, we only do it if the size of the leaf is bigger than a threshold (line 5 in Algorithm 1). For this, we introduce a parameter called $discard\ threshold$. The assumption here is that noisy positives would not be similar to each other or to the positive examples and they would be scattered across the tree in different small positive leafs, discarding those leafs would remove their impact.

### 3.2 Problem 2: Learning Concepts from a Collection of Itemsets

In the following, in the interest of conciseness, we refer to instances and sets of instances as items and itemsets, respectively. The second problem (Definition 5) then boils down to identifying product concepts using a collection of itemsets. The number of target product concepts is not known. We solve this problem with a two step approach: first we employ an unsupervised clustering approach to cluster different itemsets that contain 'similar' items together, secondly we use each identified cluster to create a product concept based on our approach for the first problem. For clustering, we use the k-means clustering [26] approach which partitions the data such that each data point is assigned to the cluster with the nearest mean. K-means clustering uses a distance measure between data-points to assign observation to the clusters. In our approach, however, as we want to cluster itemsets and not data points, we use a data-point representations of the itemsets which are the input to the clustering algorithm. We represent each itemset with a centroid, which is calculated based on the binarized version of the data points in the itemset. Clustering is performed on these centroids.

---

**Algorithm 2.** ConceptLearner

---

    **input:** set of itemsets $\mathcal{I}$, all items $\mathcal{D}$, discard threshold **d**,

1:  $Centroids = \{\}$; $Queries = \{\}$
2:  **for** each itemset $P$ in $\mathcal{I}$ **do**
3:     $Centroids = Centroids \cup MakeCentroid(P)$
4:  **end for**
5:  $Clusters = MakeClusters(\text{Centroids})$
6:  **for** each cluster $C$ in $Clusters$ **do**
7:     $S = \bigcup_{p \in C} GetOriginalInstances(p)$
8:     $Queries = Queries \cup ConceptQueryLearner(S, \mathcal{D}, d)$
9:  **end for**
10: **return** $Queries$

---

Once we have the clusters of centroids, we map the centroids back to the corresponding itemsets. For each cluster, the itemsets are then combined together in a bigger itemset which makes the input $S$ for the leaning problem Algorithm 1. We learn a product concept for each of the learned clusters. Importantly, we expect the clusters generated after the k-means approach to be noisy because we use a distance based approach on a simplified representation of the itemsets. Noise robust version of approach for problem 1 can be helpful in dealing with this noise, we study this in Sect. 4. The pseudo-code is available in Algorithm 2.

## 4  Experiments

Our experiments are based on the use case of a streaming company called *Tunify*. We first given an overview of Tunify before explaining our experiments. The code for the experiments is publicly available[3].

### 4.1  Use Case: Tunify

Tunify is a music streaming service for commercial clients, where the customers are businesses looking to play music with a commercial licence. Business places (like restaurants) often want to play music that fits the ambience of the place. Tunify provides users with a predefined selection of playlists (called *musical contexts*) which contain songs that generate different listening atmospheres (e.g., 'Hit Parade' contains hit songs being played on the radio). These musical contexts are the product concept in our work and from now on we refer to them as such for consistency. Our two learning problems in the context of Tunify are explained in the introduction. Tunify maintains a large corpus of songs and defines around 1000 product concepts which are all encoded in database queries using .xml files. We are provided with the full songs database along with the songs that belong to each product concept. Tunify uses a set of important attributes to define the concept queries, we use the same set of features for learning.

---

[3] https://github.com/kgoyal40/automatic-generation-of-product-concepts.

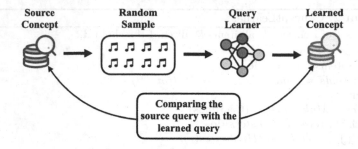

**Fig. 1.** The experimental setup to evaluate the problem 1. We select a concept from the tunify database and sample songs from this concept which becomes our initial set $S$. We learn the query based on this set $S$ and compare it with the source concept.

### 4.2 Experiments

The experimental setup in our case is not straightforward. Ideally, for the first learning problem, we would want the music experts to curate a number of initial samples that we can learn concept queries on and then manually evaluate the learned queries and for the second problem, we would like the music experts to manually evaluate all the identified product concepts. This, however, was infeasible in practice. Hence, we simulate the experimental setting by using the data provided to us by Tunify. Next two subsections explain the experimental setup and the evaluation of both learning problems separately. Experiments were run on an Intel Xeon Gold 6230R CPU@2.10GHz machine with 128 GB RAM.

### 4.3 Problem 1: Learning Concept Query from a Set of Items

For the first learning problem, we aim to answer the following research questions:

- **Q1:** Is it possible to learn good quality concept query with our approach?
- **Q2:** What is the impact of size of the initial set $S$ on the quality of the learned concept query?
- **Q3:** Is the dt-query more general than the items-query?
- **Q4:** Do the noisy positives in initial set impact the quality of the learned query negatively? If yes, can we curtail its impact?

**Experimental Setup:** The experimental design for task 1 is detailed in Fig. 1. For this task, we select a total of 184 target product concepts from the Tunify database. The size $s$ of the initial sample $S$ is varied from 20 to 1000. After sampling the songs from a target concept $C$, we add some noise by sampling songs from the rest of the database $(\mathcal{D} \setminus Q_C(\mathcal{D}))$, where $Q_C(\mathcal{D})$ represents the full set of songs corresponding to concept $C$. Amount of noise is controlled by a parameter noise ratio (**n**) which is selected from $[0, 0.1, 0.2]$ in our experiments ($n = 0.1$ means that there are $n * s$ noisy songs in the initial sample), $n = 0$ is the case where there's no noise in the initial sample. To curtail the effect of the noisy positives, we use the discard threshold (**d**), which is selected from $[0, 0.1, 0.2]$. For reliable negatives, we employ two approaches: the likelihood approach which we denote using 'l' and the rocchio approach which we denote using 'r'. We extract two types of queries from the trees: *dt-query* and *items-query*. For each target concept and every possible configuration of the parameters, the experiment is repeated 5 times and the average value is reported.

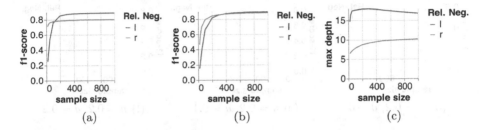

(a)                          (b)                          (c)

**Fig. 2.** Performance of the query learner when noise ratio = 0. (a) **dt-query**: Rocchio approach performs better than likelihood approach when the number of samples is small but performs worse when the number of samples increases; (b) **items-query**: Rocchio approach consistently performs better than the likelihood approach; (c) the tree learned with rocchio is smaller the tree learned with likelihood approach.

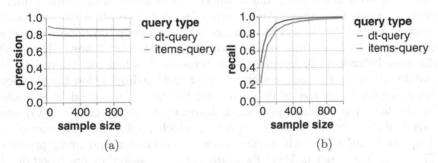

(a)                                      (b)

**Fig. 3.** (a) Precision of dt-query is lower than the items-query; (b) Recall for dt-query is higher than the items-query

**Evaluation:** We compare the target product concept $C$ with the learned query $Q$ by comparing the sets of songs $Q_C(\mathcal{D})$ with $Q(\mathcal{D})$ using the f1-score[4]. Higher value of f1-score implies higher quality of the learned query $Q$.

---

[4] https://en.wikipedia.org/wiki/F-score.

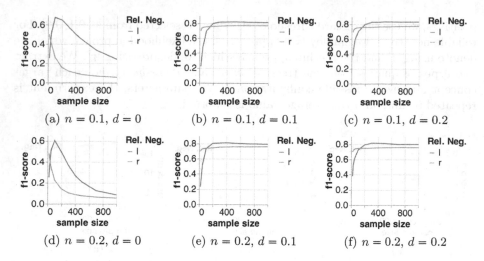

**Fig. 4.** Performance of the query learner for dt-query when noise ratio $n > 0$

## Results:

1. **Learning when there's no noise:** In our base configuration, we select the noise ratio $n = 0$ and discard threshold $d = 0$. Figure 2 represents the f1 score for different sample sizes with different choices for the reliable negative approach, for both items-query and dt-query. Performance of the learned queries improve when the sample size becomes larger before plateauing when size reaches around 200 instances, this answers the research question **Q2**. Rocchio is able to learn from smaller number of instances, however it exhibits different behaviour for dt-query and items-query when compared with the likelihood based approach: performance for rocchio drops below the likelihood approach for larger size of initial set, for dt-query. This could be explained by the fact that rocchio approach is learning smaller trees (Fig. 2(c)) compared to the likelihood based approach, which implies that the size of the dt-query is smaller which implies more generalization and lower precision. The effect would not be there for items-query because they are based on the song instances. Additionally, each configuration of reliable negative approach and the query type is able to learn a query with an f1-score of greater than 0.8 even for small sample size, with items-query performing better than the dt-query, this answers the **Q1** positively. The reason for items-query performing better than dt-query is because the dt-query generalizes the leaf more than the items-query does, we can check this by looking at precision and recall of the dt-query vs items-query in Fig. 3. Low precision and high recall for dt-query compared to items-query implies that dt-query predicts more song for a leaf than the corresponding items-query, this positively answers the research question **Q3**.

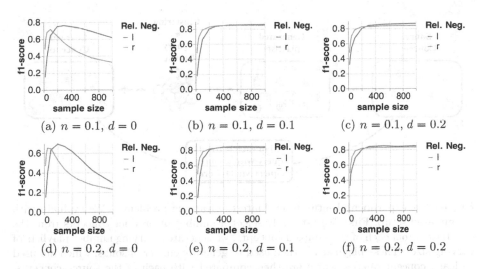

**Fig. 5.** Performance of the query learner for items-query when noise ratio > 0

2. **Learning with noisy positives:** In the configurations where there are noisy positives, we use the discard thresholds to discard the leafs with small cardinality. Figures 4 and 5 reports f1-scores for different noise ratio $n > 0$ and discard threshold $d$ for dt-query and items-query respectively. As expected, when there are noisy positives we see that the learned queries are not of good quality if the discard threshold is 0: there's a steep decline in f1-score when the data size is increased, this is because more instances lead to more noise which leads to lower precision. This behaviour is the same for different query types and reliable negative approaches. With non zero discard threshold, our approach is able to treat the impact of the noisy positives on the learned query and we achieve performance similar to the no noise case (f1-score $\geqslant 0.8$). This answers the research question **Q4** positively. An interesting behaviour to note here is that even when the noise ratio is 0.2, best performance is reached at a discard threshold of 0.1, suggesting that more noisy positives doesn't imply bigger noisy leafs.

### 4.4   Problem 2: Learning Concepts from a Collection of Itemsets

For the second learning problem, we aim to answer the following questions: **Q1:** Are the learned clusters noisy?; **Q2:** Do the clusters lead to product concepts?

**Experimental Setup:** Experimental design for task 2 is detailed in Fig. 6. 40 source product concepts are randomly selected from the already selected 184 tunify product concepts. For each selected source concept, somewhere between 5 to 15 playlists are generated randomly. Each playlist contains somewhere between 15 to 40 songs. The values discard threshold($d$) is selected from is the

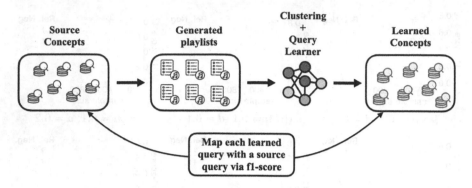

**Fig. 6.** The experimental setup to evaluate the learning problem 2. We evaluate with a simulated setup. First, we randomly select a number of product concepts from the database. From each of the sampled concepts, we generate a varying number playlists of varying sizes. These playlists are then used to generate cluster of songs, which are used to learn concept queries which are then compared with each of the source concepts. The aim is to map a learned concept to one of the source concepts.

same as the previous problem. We don't induce noise manually because we expect the final learned clusters to be already noisy. We repeat the experiments 10 times and the reported values are the average over all the experiments. For clustering, we use k-means [26] with the number of clusters same as the number of source concepts (40). In cases where the number of clusters is not known, approaches like the elbow [5] or silhouette distance [15] can be used to deduce it.

**Evaluation:** For the evaluation, we use the f1-score to compare the learned concepts and the source concepts. We compare a learned concept with all of the source concepts and select the source concept with the highest f1-score. The selected source concept is said to be the mapping of the learned concept. Then for a given configuration, across all experiments, we calculate the percentage of learned concepts where the f1-score of the mapped source concept is greater than 0.7. We term this ratio as **'overlap accuracy'**, higher overlap accuracy implies that more learned concepts can be mapped to a source concept.

**Results:** Results in Fig. 7 demonstrate that the discard threshold has a negative impact on the performance as we get the best results for $d = 0$, this implies that, the learned clusters are not noisy after all. This negatively answers the research question **Q1**. For the dt-query, likelihood approach performs better than rocchio, and for items-query, rocchio performs better than likelihood approach. This is consistent with our findings in the previous problem. Overall, we are able to learn a mapping from the learned concept to the source concept in more than 85% of cases for $d = 0$, which positively answers question **Q2**.

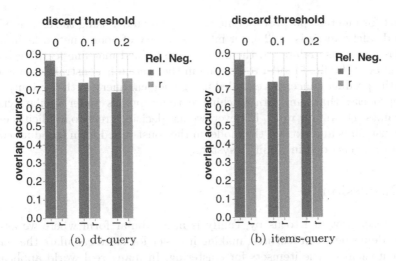

**Fig. 7.** Overlap Accuracy for different configurations of reliable negative approach and discard threshold for both **dt-query** and **items-query**

## 5 Related Work

The idea of learning playlists automatically using machine learning approaches has been around for many years. In [22], the authors propose a Gaussian regression based approach to generating music playlists using a few seed songs. A probabilistic approach for learning playlists was proposed in [17]. There are a number of works that use deep learning approaches for music generation [7]. In addition to this, machine learning has also been used in various other application involving music data, like music recommendation systems [1], automatic music generation [25], music lyrics generation [18], automatic music annotation [2] and so on. Based on the application, machine learning can be applied on different aspects of music data like deep learning on audio signals [6], music consumption data for recommender systems [9]. In contrast to deep learning models, tree based models have also been explored in music applications [3,13]. However, our proposed learning setting, to the best of our knowledge, has not been explored in any of the existing works. Also, our framework is general enough to be used in any application where such product concepts are used.

In terms of the approach, we rely on existing methods like rocchio [4] for generating reliable negatives and decision trees [23] for building the binary classifier. There's a lot of existing research in PU learning community for generating reliable negatives like 1-dnf [28], PNLH [10] and many more [4]. These methods can also be explored for the reliable negative generation in our approach for concept query generation. Additionally, for binary classification, other rule based approaches like association rule mining [12] can be explored instead of decision trees. Another important part of our approach is extracting the decision rules from the decision trees. This approach has been used in many applications in the past for different purposes. Some examples include: using the extracted rules for road safety analysis in [20], for interpretability of neural networks in [24].

This paper also relates to the field of constrained machine learning because the syntax of the final model to be used in the system is constrained in a logical form (the product concept is encoded using a logical query in the system). There are approaches that can learn machine learning models under similar syntactic constraints [11]. In our work, however, we use decision trees to implicitly enforce such constraints and extract the model in the constrained form (product concept query) to be encoded in Tunify's system.

## 6  Discussion

The dataset provided to us by Tunify is in a tabular form where we assumed independence between features, making it easier for us to calculate the centroid representations of the itemsets for clustering. In many real world applications, however, this may not be the case. Applications might be working with highly relational data, graph data and other complex representations of items. Centroid and prototype representations used in the clustering algorithm will be tricky to calculate in such cases. There is, however, a lot of research in representing relational data using embeddings [19,21]. These techniques could be explored in such scenarios. Additionally, there are special approaches for clustering in a relational domain, like in [16,27], which can be used for our second learning problem. We leave this as a possible direction for future work.

Another important thing to note here is that our problem setting is very well defined because of the clearly defined product concepts in Tunify. The simulated experimental setup makes it relatively easy for us to evaluate the proposed learning problems. In real world situations, however, a more thorough qualitative evaluation is needed before such a system can be deployed, either via product experts, or via constant user interaction and feedback using methods like A/B testing[5]. This was, however, out of the scope of this paper.

## 7  Conclusion

We proposed a decision tree based approach to learning queries defining product concepts from a small number of positive examples. Additionally, we proposed a clustering based approach to identifying relevant target concepts from a collection of itemsets. Using our experiments on a real dataset, we demonstrate, for the first task, that the presented approach is able to learn concepts with a high confidence. Our approach is robust enough to treat the noise in the system and can be used in conjunction to clustering based approaches to identify new product concepts from the data. For the second task, our simulated experiments show that if the curated itemsets have items that are similar, they will be identified and clustered together in a product concept. Even though we evaluate on

---

[5] https://en.wikipedia.org/wiki/A/B_testing.

one real world use case of a music streaming service, we believe that this kind of approach can be of interest in various other online businesses where users interact with the systems by using such product concepts.

**Acknowledgement.** We thank the reviewers for their constructive input, which helped improve the paper. This work was jointly supported by the Flanders Innovation & Entrepreneurship (VLAIO project HBC.2019.2467), Research Foundation - Flanders under EOS No. 30992574, and the Flemish Government (AI Research Program). We want to thank Tunify for providing us with their data and guidance throughout this project.

# References

1. Ayata, D., Yaslan, Y., Kamasak, M.E.: Emotion based music recommendation system using wearable physiological sensors. IEEE Trans. Consum. Electron. **64**(2), 196–203 (2018)
2. Bahuleyan, H.: Music genre classification using machine learning techniques. arXiv preprint arXiv:1804.01149 (2018)
3. Bai, B., Fan, Y.: Incorporating field-aware deep embedding networks and gradient boosting decision trees for music recommendation. In: The 11th ACM International Conference on Web Search and Data Mining (WSDM) (2017)
4. Bekker, J., Davis, J.: Learning from positive and unlabeled data: a survey. Mach. Learn. **109**(4), 719–760 (2020)
5. Bholowalia, P., Kumar, A.: EBK-means: a clustering technique based on elbow method and k-means in WSN. Int. J. Comput. Appl. **105**(9) (2014)
6. Briot, J.P., Hadjeres, G., Pachet, F.D.: Deep learning techniques for music generation-a survey. arXiv preprint arXiv:1709.01620 (2017)
7. Briot, J.P., Pachet, F.: Deep learning for music generation: challenges and directions. Neural Comput. Appl. **32**(4), 981–993 (2020)
8. Ceri, S., Bozzon, A., Brambilla, M., Valle, E.D., Fraternali, P., Quarteroni, S.: An introduction to information retrieval. In: Ceri, S., Bozzon, A., Brambilla, M., Valle, E.D., Fraternali, P., Quarteroni, S (eds.) Web Information Retrieval, pp. 3–11. Springer, Heidelberg (2013). https://doi.org/10.1007/978-3-642-39314-3_1
9. Chen, H.C., Chen, A.L.: A music recommendation system based on music and user grouping. J. Intell. Inf. Syst. **24**(2), 113–132 (2005)
10. Fung, G.P.C., Yu, J.X., Lu, H., Yu, P.S.: Text classification without negative examples revisit. IEEE Trans. Knowl. Data Eng. **18**(1), 6–20 (2005)
11. Goyal, K., Dumancic, S., Blockeel, H.: Sade: Learning models that provably satisfy domain constraints. arXiv preprint arXiv:2112.00552 (2021)
12. Kotsiantis, S., Kanellopoulos, D.: Association rules mining: a recent overview. GESTS Int. Trans. Comput. Sci. Eng. (2006)
13. Lavner, Y., Ruinskiy, D.: A decision-tree-based algorithm for speech/music classification and segmentation. EURASIP J. Audio Speech Music Process. **2009**, 1–14 (2009)
14. Li, X., Liu, B.: Learning to classify texts using positive and unlabeled data. In: IJCAI, vol. 3, pp. 587–592. Citeseer (2003)
15. Lletı, R., Ortiz, M.C., Sarabia, L.A., Sánchez, M.S.: Selecting variables for k-means cluster analysis by using a genetic algorithm that optimises the silhouettes. Anal. Chim. Acta **515**(1), 87–100 (2004)

16. Long, B., Zhang, Z., Wu, X., Yu, P.S.: Relational clustering by symmetric convex coding. In: Proceedings of the 24th International Conference on Machine Learning, pp. 569–576 (2007)

17. Maillet, F., Eck, D., Desjardins, G., Lamere, P., et al.: Steerable playlist generation by learning song similarity from radio station playlists. In: ISMIR. Citeseer (2009)

18. Malmi, E., Takala, P., Toivonen, H., Raiko, T., Gionis, A.: Dopelearning: a computational approach to rap lyrics generation. In: Proceedings of the 22nd ACM SIGKDD International Conference on Knowledge Discovery and Data Mining (2016)

19. Narayanan, A., Chandramohan, M., Venkatesan, R., Chen, L., Liu, Y., Jaiswal, S.: graph2vec: learning distributed representations of graphs. arXiv preprint arXiv:1707.05005 (2017)

20. de Oña, J., López, G., Abellán, J.: Extracting decision rules from police accident reports through decision trees. Accid. Anal. Prev. **50**, 1151–1160 (2013)

21. Perozzi, B., Al-Rfou, R., Skiena, S.: Deepwalk: online learning of social representations. In: Proceedings of the 20th ACM SIGKDD International Conference on Knowledge Discovery and Data Mining, pp. 701–710 (2014)

22. Platt, J., Burges, C.J., Swenson, S., Weare, C., Zheng, A.: Learning a gaussian process prior for automatically generating music playlists. In: Advances in Neural Information Processing Systems, vol. 14 (2001)

23. Quinlan, J.R.: Induction of decision trees. Mach. Learn. **1**(1), 81–106 (1986)

24. Sato, M., Tsukimoto, H.: Rule extraction from neural networks via decision tree induction. In: IJCNN 2001. International Joint Conference on Neural Networks (2001)

25. Sturm, B.L., et al.: Machine learning research that matters for music creation: a case study. J. New Music Res. **48**(1), 36–55 (2019)

26. Teknomo, K.: K-means clustering tutorial. Medicine **100**(4), 3 (2006)

27. Tsitsulin, A., Palowitch, J., Perozzi, B., Müller, E.: Graph clustering with graph neural networks. arXiv preprint arXiv:2006.16904 (2020)

28. Yu, H., Han, J., Chang, K.C.: PEBL: web page classification without negative examples. IEEE Trans. Knowl. Data Eng. **16**(1), 70–81 (2004)

# A View on Model Misspecification in Uncertainty Quantification

Yuko Kato[1(✉)], David M. J. Tax[1], and Marco Loog[1,2]

[1] Delft University of Technology, Delft, The Netherlands
{y.kato,d.m.j.tax}@tudelft.nl
[2] Radboud University, Nijmegen, The Netherlands
marco.loog@ru.nl

**Abstract.** Estimating uncertainty of machine learning models is essential to assess the quality of the predictions that these models provide. However, there are several factors that influence the quality of uncertainty estimates, one of which is the amount of model misspecification. Model misspecification always exists as models are mere simplifications or approximations to reality. The question arises whether the estimated uncertainty under model misspecification is reliable or not. In this paper, we argue that model misspecification should receive more attention, by providing thought experiments and contextualizing these with relevant literature.

**Keywords:** Uncertainty quantification · Model misspecification · Epistemic and Aleatoric uncertainty

## 1 Introduction

In fields such as biology, chemistry, engineering, and medicine [1–4], having an accurate estimate of prediction uncertainty is of great importance to guarantee safety and prevent unnecessary costs. In this regard, uncertainty quantification (UQ) is a vital step in order to safely apply Machine Learning (ML) models to real world situations involving risk. It is well-known, however, that these ML models are generally poor at quantifying these uncertainties [5,6].

Generally, depending on the exact source, the type of uncertainty can be categorized as being epistemic or aleatoric [7,8]. Epistemic uncertainty refers to the uncertainty of the model and arises due to lack of data used to train the model and lack of domain knowledge. This type of uncertainty is considered to be reducible by an appropriate selection of the model and increasing data size. On the contrary, aleatoric uncertainty is a consequence of the random nature of data and is therefore considered to be irreducible [9].

Although total uncertainty (the combination of epistemic and aleatoric uncertainty) can be estimated using different methods, some articles have focused on the separate estimation of aleatoric uncertainty and epistemic uncertainty [10–14]. Given the fact that only epistemic uncertainty is reducible, separation

T. Calders et al. (Eds.): BNAIC/Benelearn 2022, CCIS 1805, pp. 65–77, 2023.
https://doi.org/10.1007/978-3-031-39144-6_5

into the two types of uncertainty can help to guide model development [12]. For example, during active learning, Nguyen and colleagues [15] concluded that quantifying epistemic uncertainty separately has the potential to provide useful information to learners of the model and can potentially improve the performance of the learning process.

Notwithstanding, due to model misspecification, a question remains whether the estimated aleatoric and epistemic uncertainty are reliable or not [16,17]. Model misspecification exists when the best model differs from the truth and the associated hypothesis space does not include the truth. It is important to realize that model misspecification always exists without any exceptions [18]. As there is no uniquely prescribed way to deal with model misspecification, it has been treated differently among researchers. Some do not mention it at all in their papers [11,14], while others consider it to be part of epistemic uncertainty [19]. These variable interpretations of model misspecification make it difficult to compare the different estimated epistemic uncertainties.

In this paper, we argue that model misspecification should receive more attention. We start by defining model misspecification and propose three possible ways to see model misspecification in relation to epistemic uncertainty. The paper proceeds with a brief investigation of how model misspecification is recognized among researchers and how they relate to our proposed views. In addition, we assess the possible consequences of mistreating model misspecification qualitatively and conclude with a brief discussion.

## 2     Model Misspecification

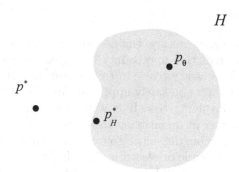

**Fig. 1.** Model misspecification: The truth $p^*$ is not included in the hypothesis space $H$ (shaded blue area) due to model misspecification. (Color figure online)

### 2.1     Definition of Model Misspecification

Whether the ML-method is applied in a regression or classification setting, the first step is to choose a model $p_\theta$ parameterized by $\theta$. Let $H = \{p_\theta : \theta \in \Theta\}$

denote the hypothesis space defined by the chosen model class and the associated parameters $\theta$ in the set $\Theta$. We denote the truth $p^*$ and the best possible model in $H$ by $p_H^*$. Now, model misspecification exists when the best model $p_H^*$ differs from the truth $p^*$ and $p^* \notin H$. This is illustrated in Fig. 1.

## 2.2   Example of Model Misspecification: Regression

Let us consider a simple regression problem using a dataset of $n$ observations $\mathcal{D} = (x_i, y_i)$ with $i = 1, ..., n$ and additive noise. Let us assume, in addition, that the true additive noise follows a heavy-tailed distribution (see Fig. 2a). The typical aim is to approximate the unknown underlying true data distribution $p^*(y|x)$ at a new test point $x$. Now, a typical model choice $\hat{p}_n(y|x)$ is to assume the additive noise to be Gaussian. This means that the assumption on the noise distribution is misspecified. Since $p^*(y|x)$ is not in the hypothesis space $H$ due to model misspecification (i.e., the assumed noise does not match the true one), we will never be able to reach the true distribution $p^*(y|x)$ even if we use an infinite amount of data to train the model $\hat{p}_\infty(y|x)$ (See Fig. 2b).

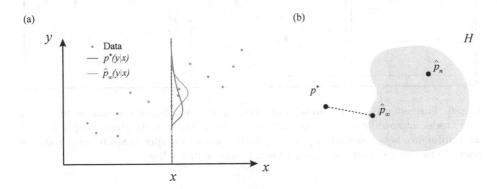

**Fig. 2.** Model misspecification in a regression example: (a) the true data distribution $p^*(y|x)$ (blue line) at a test point $x$ and the estimated data distribution $\hat{p}_\infty(y|x)$ (red line) which is trained using an infinite amount of data at a test point $x$ (b) $\hat{p}_\infty$ will never reach the truth $p^*$ – even when optimizing for a proper loss, due to model misspecification. (Color figure online)

## 2.3   Contextualizing Model Misspecification

When looking at model misspecification, a key uncertainty we consider is epistemic uncertainty which is related to the model choice [18]. Figure 3 shows three perspectives on model misspecification and its relation to epistemic uncertainty for regression setting.

The first two scenarios (Fig. 3a and Fig. 3b) illustrate the most common perspective where model misspecification is ignored. Ignoring it could be acceptable if the hypothesis space was sufficiently large and, therefore, model misspecification does not exist in principle (Fig. 3a). Even though most practitioners disregard model misspecification as illustrated in this Fig. 3a, in reality this is rarely the case. The most common circumstance in the literature is shown in Fig. 3b, where model misspecification exists despite being unintentionally ignored. As a result, for both scenarios, epistemic uncertainty does not contain model misspecification. In the third scenario (Fig. 3c), model misspecification is explicitly included as part of epistemic uncertainty. In this case, epistemic uncertainty consists of two parts: model misspecification (green line in Fig. 3c) and approximation uncertainty (blue line in Fig. 3c) as Hüllermeier and Waegeman [9] define it. In this scenario, model misspecification directly influences epistemic uncertainty estimates [20].

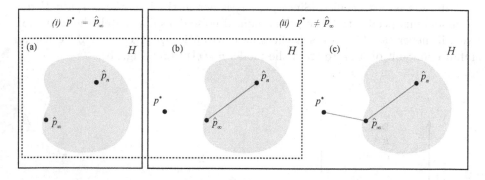

**Fig. 3.** Three views on model misspecification when a model class is assumed: In (a) and (b), model misspecification is ignored and epistemic uncertainty (blue line) is defined as a difference between $\hat{p}_\infty(y|x)$ and $\hat{p}_n$. In (c), model misspecification is treated as a part of epistemic uncertainty (green line). (Color figure online)

## 3   Effect of Model Misspecification on Uncertainty Estimates

We cover, in brief, the connection between model misspecification and epistemic uncertainty in different ML-methods and discuss possible consequences of model misspecification on uncertainty estimation and decision making. Although we mainly focus on neural network models in this section, the same principle applies to other methods as long as these models that require any distributional assumptions.

### 3.1   Model Misspecification and Uncertainty Estimates

Bayesian ML-methods are widely used for UQ [21]. Specifically, Bayesian neural networks (BNNs) are receiving a lot of attention due to their potential to model both epistemic and aleatoric uncertainty [10, 11, 14, 22]. The definition of uncertainty varies among researchers and BNN articles rarely include the effect of model misspecification. For instance, Gustafsson and colleagues [14] explain that epistemic uncertainty is uncertainty in the deep neural network model parameters, which ignores the fact that the model is not necessarily correctly specified. This definition of epistemic uncertainty is very common in the literature [9, 10, 23, 24].

Without loss of generality, consider once again the regression setting from Subsect. 2.2. In BNNs, the total uncertainty is modelled by the posterior $p(\theta|\mathcal{D})$, where $\mathcal{D}$ symbolizes data. At test time, predictions are made via the posterior predictive distribution (PPD):

$$p(\mathbf{y}|\ \mathbf{x}, \mathcal{D}) = \int p(\mathbf{y}|\ \mathbf{x}, \theta)p(\theta|\mathcal{D})d\theta. \tag{1}$$

In [14], both epistemic and aleatoric uncertainties are obtained assuming a Gaussian distribution with mean $\hat{\mu}$ and variance $\hat{\sigma}^2$ on PPD:

$$p(\mathbf{y}|\ \mathbf{x}, \mathcal{D}) \approx N(\mathbf{y}; \hat{\mu}(\mathbf{x}), \hat{\sigma}^2(\mathbf{x})). \tag{2}$$

It is safe to say that no true distribution is exactly Gaussian. The possible effects on UQ of such assumption are neither quantified nor discussed in this work; not as part of epistemic uncertainty itself, nor as a separate uncertainty. In the literature, the (implicit) assumption of a PPD with a Gaussian distribution seems to be made more generally when creating Bayesian ML-models [9, 10, 23, 24].

Another popular approach for UQ is the use of ensemble methods, such as Monte Carlo dropout (MC-dropout) [24], where predictive uncertainty is estimated using Dropout [24] at test time, and Deep ensembles [5] which rely on retraining the same network many times with different weight initializations. Both methods can be considered a simple alternative to Bayesian methods. It is known that ensemble methods can provide an estimation of the (epistemic) uncertainty of a prediction [9], meaning that the variance of the predictions can be used to estimate epistemic uncertainty. By increasing the number of ensemble members, improved estimation of epistemic uncertainty is possible [9, 25, 26].

Liu and colleagues pointed out two issues when performing uncertainty estimation (both epistemic and aleatoric) using ensemble methods [27]. Similar to Bayesian methods, currently existing ensemble methods typically assume that the ground-truth data distribution $p(y|x)$ follows a Gaussian distribution [5]. Furthermore, ensemble methods perform uncertainty estimation using base models of the same class, meaning in the same hypothesis space $H$ [5]. The consequence is that the creation of these models (that are all potentially misspecified) might result in a hypothesis space that still does not include the true distribution. Therefore epistemic uncertainty estimates from ensemble methods do not include model misspecification.

## 3.2    Consequences of Ignoring Model Misspecification

The central question that remains is what are the consequences of not taking model misspecification into account?

If we do not include model misspecification into epistemic uncertainty, we can only trust the estimated epistemic uncertainty when the model is correctly specified. As a result, we may significantly underestimate total uncertainty, which can be problematic in risk-involving tasks. Therefore, ignoring model misspecification usually leads to the scenario in Fig. 3b which can overestimate or underestimate the total uncertainty [16]. Specifically for Bayesian methods, when the distributional assumption on PPD is not correctly specified, the probability of the true distribution lying outside hypothesis space increases [16,28–32]. The consequences of ignoring model misspecification in real-world tasks are illustrated in Fig. 4, which is based on an example from [16].

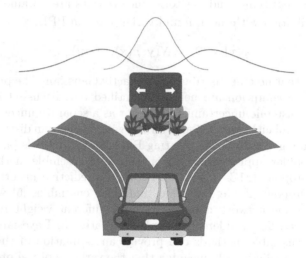

**Fig. 4.** A real-world example of model misspecification: In a decision making process at a split road, assuming a Gaussian distribution on the output distribution (red line) can cause a serious accident (Color figure online)

In Fig. 4, a lane splits in two directions, i.e., we have two outputs. In order to capture the multimodality, our output distribution has to follow a bi-modal distribution. However, by assuming a Gaussian distribution on the output distribution instead, the model predicts the mean of the two possible outcomes and the car goes in between lanes [33]. Although this can lead to a fatal accident, this possibility cannot be captured by estimating epistemic uncertainty with such model.

# 4    Discussion

In this paper, we highlighted the importance of considering model misspecification when performing UQ. Reviewing the literature, it should be noted that model misspecification is often not explicitly described or strong assumptions are imposed on the underlying data distributions. This can lead, in turn, to models that provide unreliable uncertainty estimates. These findings raise an important question: how should we handle model misspecification? As for the definition of different uncertainty types (i.e., aleatoric and epistemic uncertainty), the question remains whether epistemic uncertainty should contain model misspecification or not. These issues are discussed in the following Subsect. 4.1 and Subsect. 4.2.

## 4.1    How to Handle Model Misspecification

It is not possible to entirely avoid model misspecification when modeling real-world phenomena, mainly due to the imposed model assumptions. This means that we have to consider the impact of model misspecification and to explore ways to deal with it in various scenarios.

In principle, model misspecification can be reduced by expanding the initial hypothesis space $H_1$ (i.e., changing the associated model) (Fig. 5a). As a result, the impact of model misspecification can be reduced subsequently. Expanding the hypothesis space can be done, for instance, by easing the imposed assumptions. In the most favorable situation, the expanded hypothesis space $H_3$ includes the truth $p^*$. However, there is a possibility that we increase model misspecification when changing hypothesis space (Fig. 5b). As a result, we would never be able to reach the $p^*$ in $H_3$. This situation can be avoided by assigning a hierarchy to the expanded hypotheses spaces as follows, $H_1 \subset H_2 \subset H_3$. Under this assumption, structural risk minimization (SRM) [34], which is strongly universally consistent [35], can be arbitrary close to the $p^*$ in $H_3$. SRM uses the size of hypothesis space as a variable and tries to minimize the guaranteed risk over each hypothesis space [36,37]. This can reduce model misspecification.

Therefore, in either way (Fig. 5a or Fig. 5b), the impact of model misspecification can be minimized. This fact is important since it is not always clear if we change our hypothesis space inclusively (Fig. 5a) or exclusively (Fig. 5b).

Additionally, it is theoretically possible to reduce model misspecification completely according to the universal approximation theorem [38,39]. The theorem guarantees a neural network to represent any function (e.g., input-output relationship in regression) generically on its associated function space [40]. However, the theorem cannot be applicable to most practical situations due to the following reasons. Firstly, the theorem does not guarantee the network to learn the model [41]. Therefore, the chosen network can overfit to the training data, resulting in a poor generalization. Secondly, the network can require an exponential number of hidden units, which are often not desirable in practical situations [41]. These concerns lead us to the next question; What are the consequences when we attempt to reduce model misspecification during UQ?

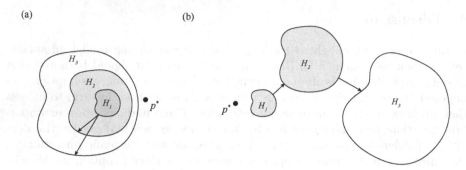

**Fig. 5.** Reducing model misspecification: By changing the initial hypothesis space $H_1$, model misspecification is either (a) reduced by including the truth $p^*$ in the new hypothesis space $H_3$ or (b) increased.

In order to consider the question, let us go back to the scenario where model misspecification is considered to be part of epistemic uncertainty (Fig. 3c). Lahlou and colleagues [19] state that model misspecification can be considered as a form of bias while approximation uncertainty can be a form of variance. With the use of this concept, we can think about a bias-variance tradeoff with respect to the size of hypothesis space, which is illustrated in Fig. 6. Although bias-variance decomposition has been studied for a long time, to our best knowledge, no paper has considered this bias-variance trade-off with respect to uncertainty quantification. It is important to emphasize the following points: 1) by considering this bias-variance trade-off, we cannot guarantee to choose the model with the lowest total error in contrast to the original concept (i.e. the model class with the lowest total uncertainty does not necessarily provide the lowest total error.), 2) increasing the size of the hypothesis space does not make the model more complex (instead, it would be less complex with fewer assumptions).

In Fig. 6, we can see the effect of model misspecification in relation to total uncertainty. Assume that we have an infinite amount of data, then every hypothesis space shares the same amount of aleatoric uncertainty (red shaded area in Fig. 6). Depending on the model choice, the size of hypothesis space can vary. If we choose the initial hypothesis space $H_1$, there is a high possibility that $p^*$ is not included in the hypothesis space, potentially increasing model misspecification and therefore bias of the model. On the contrary, if we choose an expanded hypothesis space $H_3$, model misspecification can be decreased due to the fact there is a higher possibility that $p^*$ lies in $H_3$. However, at the same time, it will be harder to find an optimal model in an expanded hypothesis space. Therefore, the variance which represents approximation uncertainty increases when hypothesis space expands. This means that there is trade-off between bias (model misspecification) and variance (approximation error). In this example, hypothesis space $H_2$ has an optimal size. In this case, $H_2$ results in the best trade-off between model misspecification and its size. Using this concept, we can choose the best possible model and the associated hypothesis space, even if we do not know $p^*$.

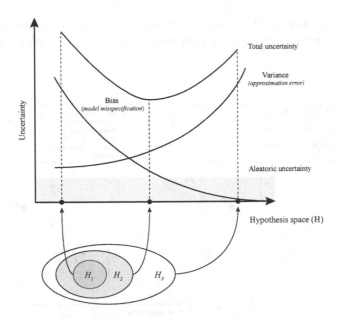

**Fig. 6.** Intuition for bias (model misspecification) variance (approximation error) trade-off with respect to the size of hypothesis space. Red shaded area represents aleatoric uncertainty. (Color figure online)

However, whether the approximation error and model misspecification can be estimated in practical scenarios is not entirely clear yet. This means that how to handle model misspecification still remains an open question.

## 4.2 Conflicting Views on Uncertainty Definitions

There are conflicting views and significant terminology diversity about the different types of uncertainty in the literature. In particular, model misspecification has been included as part of epistemic uncertainty by some authors while others do not [27,28]. This is problematic since it prevents a direct comparison regarding the performance of different methods. A uniform view on how to treat model misspecification (either being part of epistemic uncertainty or as a separate uncertainty type) should be made to make such comparison possible. Furthermore, it is not very clear which type of uncertainty is estimated in some situations. For example, Valdenegro-Toro and colleagues [30] claim that there is a clear connection between epistemic and aleatoric uncertainty. This would mean that underestimating or overestimating epistemic uncertainty can have an effect on the quality of aleatoric uncertainty. Therefore, a true possibility for such a separation can be doubted in this case. Additionally, there is another issue related to the definition of uncertainty, which is inconsistent naming of uncertainties. This variability in naming of epistemic uncertainty is illustrated in Fig. 7. Note that this figure does not reflect an exhaustive literature search, so there is even more diversity in terminology than what is illustrated there.

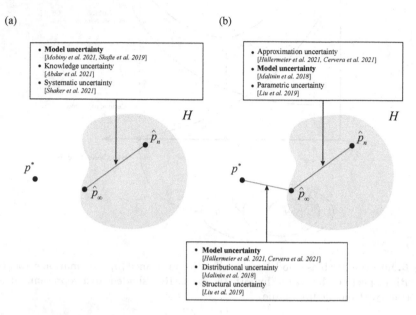

**Fig. 7.** Example of variability in naming of epistemic uncertainty: (a) Model misspecification is ignored. (b) Model misspecification is considered as part of epistemic uncertainty (a green line). Model uncertainty represents different concepts depending on literature. (Color figure online)

Epistemic uncertainty is called as, for instance, model uncertainty [23,42], knowledge uncertainty [8], systematic uncertainty [43] (Fig. 7a). In other work, model uncertainty is considered to be part of epistemic uncertainty (Fig. 7b), representing model misspecification [9,16]. Malinin and colleagues [44] call model misspecification as distributional uncertainty. This inconsistency can be confusing and leading to wrong interpretation of published work.

## 5   Conclusion

There are a number of concerns when it comes to model misspecification in relation to uncertainty estimation that can considerably influence the accuracy by which uncertainty estimation can be performed. No general definition of both epistemic and aleatoric uncertainty currently exists. Additionally, researchers treat model misspecification differently. Since model misspecification influences the reliability of uncertainty estimates, we would argue that model misspecification, and the ways to measure and control it, should receive more attention in the current UQ research. Furthermore, we propose directions for future work to minimize model misspecification, for instance, by looking into bias-variance trade-offs.

# References

1. Hie, B., Bryson, B.D., Berger, B.: Leveraging uncertainty in machine learning accelerates biological discovery and design. Cell Syst. **11**, 461–477 (2020)
2. Vishwakarma, G., Sonpal, A., Hachmann, J.: Metrics for benchmarking and uncertainty quantification: quality, applicability, and best practices for machine learning in chemistry. Trends Chem. **3**, 146–156 (2021)
3. Begoli, E., Bhattacharya, T., Kusnezov, D.: The need for uncertainty quantification in machine-assisted medical decision making. Nat. Mach. Intell. **1**, 20–23 (2019)
4. Michelmore, R., Kwiatkowska, M., Gal, Y.: Evaluating Uncertainty Quantification in End-to-End Autonomous Driving Control. arXiv: 1811.06817 (2018)
5. Lakshminarayanan, B., Pritzel, A., Blundell, C.: Simple and scalable predictive uncertainty estimation using deep ensembles. In: Advances in Neural Information Processing Systems, vol. 30 (2017)
6. Maddox, W.J., Garipov, T., Izmailov, P., Vetrov, D., Wilson, A.G.: in Proceedings of the 33rd International Conference on Neural Information Processing Systems, pp. 13153–13164. Curran Associates Inc., Red Hook (2019)
7. Kiureghian, A.D., Ditlevsen, O.: Aleatory or epistemic? Does it matter? Struct. Saf. **31**, 105–112 (2009)
8. Abdar, M., et al.: A review of uncertainty quantification in deep learning: techniques, applications and challenges. Inf. Fusion **76**, 243–297 (2021)
9. Hüllermeier, E., Waegeman, W.: Aleatoric and epistemic uncertainty in machine learning: an introduction to concepts and methods. Mach. Learn. **110**, 457–506 (2021)
10. Depeweg, S., Hernandez-Lobato, J.-M., Doshi-Velez, F., Udluft, S.: Decomposition of uncertainty in Bayesian deep learning for efficient and risk-sensitive learning. In: International Conference on Machine Learning, pp. 1184–1193 (2018)
11. Kendall, A., Gal, Y.: What uncertainties do we need in Bayesian deep learning for computer vision? In: Guyon, I., et al. (eds.) Advances in Neural Information Processing Systems, vol. 30. Curran Associates Inc. (2017)
12. Senge, R., et al.: Reliable classification: learning classifiers that distinguish aleatoric and epistemic uncertainty. Inf. Sci. **255**, 16–29 (2014)
13. Prado, A., Kausik, R., Venkataramanan, L.: Dual Neural Network Architecture for Determining Epistemic and Aleatoric Uncertainties. arXiv: 1910.06153 (2019)
14. Gustafsson, F.K., Danelljan, M., Schon, T.B.: Evaluating scalable Bayesian deep learning methods for robust computer vision. In: 2020 IEEE/CVF Conference on Computer Vision and Pattern Recognition Workshops (CVPRW), pp. 1289–1298 (2020)
15. Nguyen, V.-L., Shaker, M.H., Hüllermeier, E.: How to measure uncertainty in uncertainty sampling for active learning. Mach. Learn. **111**, 89–122 (2022)
16. Cervera, M.R., et al.: Uncertainty estimation under model misspecification in neural network regression. arXiv: 2111.11763 (2021)
17. Lv, J., Liu, J.S.: Model selection principles in misspecified models. J. R. Stat. Soc. Series B Stat. Methodol. **76**, 141–167 (2014)

18. Aydogan, I., Berger, L., Bosetti, V., Ning, L.I.U.: Three Layers of Uncertainty and the Role of Model Misspecification. Working Papers (2020)
19. Lahlou, S., et al.: DEUP: Direct Epistemic Uncertainty Prediction. arXiv:2102.08501 (2021)
20. Xu, A., Raginsky, M.: Minimum excess risk in Bayesian learning. IEEE Trans. Inf. Theory **68**(12), 7935–7955 (2022)
21. Tipping, M.E.: Bayesian inference: an introduction to principles and practice in machine learning. In: Bousquet, O., von Luxburg, U., Rätsch, G. (eds.) ML -2003. LNCS (LNAI), vol. 3176, pp. 41–62. Springer, Heidelberg (2004). https://doi.org/10.1007/978-3-540-28650-9_3
22. Scalia, G., Grambow, C.A., Pernici, B., Li, Y.-P., Green, W.H.: Evaluating scalable uncertainty estimation methods for deep learning-based molecular property prediction. J. Chem. Inf. Model. **60**, 2697–2717 (2020)
23. Mobiny, A., et al.: DropConnect is effective in modeling uncertainty of Bayesian deep networks. Sci. Rep. **11**, 5458 (2021)
24. Gal, Y., Ghahramani, Z.: Dropout as a Bayesian approximation: representing model uncertainty in deep learning. In: Balcan, M.F., Weinberger, K.Q. (eds.) Proceedings of the 33rd International Conference on Machine Learning, vol. 48, pp. 1050–1059. PMLR, New York (2016)
25. Charpentier, B., Senanayake, R., Kochenderfer, M., Günnemann, S.: Disentangling Epistemic and Aleatoric Uncertainty in Reinforcement Learning. arXiv: 2206.01558 (2022)
26. Caldeira, J., Nord, B.: Deeply uncertain: comparing methods of uncertainty quantification in deep learning algorithms. Mach. Learn. Sci. Technol. **2**, 015002 (2020)
27. Liu, J.Z., Paisley, J., Kioumourtzoglou, M.-A., Coull, B.A.: in Proceedings of the 33rd International Conference on Neural Information Processing Systems, pp. 8952–8963. Curran Associates Inc., Red Hook (2019)
28. Masegosa, A.: Learning under model misspecification: applications to variational and ensemble methods. In: Advances in Neural Information Processing Systems (2020)
29. Jewson, J., Smith, J.Q., Holmes, C.: Principles of Bayesian inference using general divergence criteria. Entropy **20**, 442 (2018)
30. Valdenegro-Toro, M., Mori, D.S.: A deeper look into aleatoric and epistemic uncertainty disentanglement. In: Proceedings of the IEEE/CVF Conference on Computer Vision and Pattern Recognition, pp. 1509–1517 (2022)
31. Hansen, L.P., Sargent, T.J.: Structured uncertainty and model misspecification. University of Chicago, Becker (2019)
32. Ramamoorthi, R.V., Sriram, K., Martin, R.: On Posterior Concentration in Misspecified Models, vol. 10, pp. 759–789 (2015)
33. Cerreia-Vioglio, S., Hansen, L.P., Maccheroni, F., Marinacci, M.: Making Decisions under Model Misspecification (2020)
34. Guyon, I., Vapnik, V., Boser, B., Bottou, L., Solla, S.A.: Structural risk minimization for character recognition. In: Moody, J., Hanson, S., Lippmann, R.P. (eds.) Advances in Neural Information Processing Systems, vol. 4. Morgan-Kaufmann (1991)
35. Lugosi, G., Zeger, K.: Concept learning using complexity regularization. In: Proceedings of 1995 IEEE International Symposium on Information Theory, Whistler, BC, Canada. IEEE (2002)
36. Corani, G., Gatto, M.: Structural risk minimization: a robust method for density-dependence detection and model selection. Ecography **30**, 400–416 (2007)

37. Zhang, X.: Structural risk minimization. In: Sammut, C., Webb, G.I. (eds.) Encyclopedia of Machine Learning, pp. 929–930. Springer, Boston (2010). https://doi.org/10.1007/978-0-387-30164-8_793
38. Hornik, K., Stinchcombe, M., White, H.: Multilayer feedforward networks are universal approximators. Neural Netw. **2**, 359–366 (1989)
39. Cybenko, G.: Approximation by superpositions of a sigmoidal function. Math. Control Signals Syst. **2**, 303–314 (1989)
40. Kratsios, A.: The universal approximation property. Ann. Math. Artif. Intell. **89**, 435–469 (2021)
41. Goodfellow, I., Bengio, Y., Courville, A.: Deep Learning. MIT Press, Cambridge (2016)
42. Skafte, N., Jo rgensen, M., Hauberg, S.R.: Reliable training and estimation of variance networks. In: Wallach, H., et al. (eds.) Advances in Neural Information Processing Systems, vol. 32. Curran Associates Inc. (2019)
43. Shaker, M.H., Hüllermeier, E.: Ensemble-based Uncertainty Quantification: Bayesian versus Credal Inference. arXiv: 2107.10384 (2021)
44. Malinin, A., Gales, M.: Predictive uncertainty estimation via prior networks. In: Proceedings of the 32nd International Conference on Neural Information Processing Systems, Montréal, Canada, pp. 7047–7058. Curran Associates Inc. (2018)

# A Comparative Study of Sentence Embeddings for Unsupervised Extractive Multi-document Summarization

Salima Lamsiyah$^{(\boxtimes)}$ (ID) and Christoph Schommer (ID)

Department of Computer Science, University of Luxembourg,
Esch-sur-Alzette, Luxembourg
{salima.lamsiyah,christoph.schommer}@uni.lu

**Abstract.** Obtaining large-scale and high-quality training data for multi-document summarization (MDS) tasks is time-consuming and resource-intensive, hence, supervised models can only be applied to limited domains and languages. In this paper, we introduce unsupervised extractive methods for both generic and query-focused MDS tasks, intending to produce a relevant summary from a collection of documents without using labeled training data or domain knowledge. More specifically, we leverage the potential of transfer learning from recent sentence embedding models to encode the input documents into rich semantic representations. Moreover, we use a coreference resolution system to resolve the broken pronominal coreference expressions in the generated summaries, aiming to improve their cohesion and textual quality. Furthermore, we provide a comparative analysis of several existing sentence embedding models in the context of unsupervised extractive multi-document summarization. Experiments on the standard DUC'2004-2007 datasets demonstrate that the proposed methods are competitive with previous unsupervised methods and are even comparable to recent supervised deep learning-based methods. The empirical results also show that the SimCSE embedding model, based on contrastive learning, achieves substantial improvements over strong sentence embedding models. Finally, the newly involved coreference resolution method is proven to bring a noticeable improvement to the unsupervised extractive MDS task.

**Keywords:** Unsupervised Multi-Document Summarization · Sentence Embeddings · Transfer Learning · Contrastive Learning · Coreference Resolution

## 1 Introduction

Automatic Text Summarization (ATS) is the task of automatically condensing long documents into shorter version that covers the main themes of those documents. There are two main approaches for ATS: *extractive approach* and *abstractive approach*. In the former, summaries are produced by identifying and

T. Calders et al. (Eds.): BNAIC/Benelearn 2022, CCIS 1805, pp. 78–95, 2023.
https://doi.org/10.1007/978-3-031-39144-6_6

extracting the most relevant sentences from the source documents, while in the latter, summaries are generated by reformulating and fusing ideas and often by using a new lexicon. Abstractive methods may produce coherent and less redundant summaries based on natural language generation, while extractive methods enjoy better factuality and efficiency [4]. Motivated by the latter, we propose to improve the extractive approach by incorporating text understanding methods as well as coreference resolution techniques.

More precisely, we focus on multi-document summarization (MDS) that aims to produce a summary from a collection of thematically related documents. We consider both *generic* (G-MDS) and *query-focused* (QF-MDS) tasks. G-MDS systems produce summaries that represent all relevant facts of the source documents without considering the users' information needs. Besides, QF-MDS systems generate summaries that answer specific users' queries [19,20]. Furthermore, we adopt an *unsupervised approach* that does not require labeled training data or domain knowledge. Multi-document summarization task has received significantly less attention compared to single-document summarization, partly due to the scarcity of suitable data required for learning models [23]. Human annotation for summarization tasks, especially MDS, is a substantial time-requiring, and costly manual effort. It is also unrealistic to expect that large-scale and high-quality labeled datasets will be created for different styles, domains, and languages. Additionally, summarizing multiple documents presents additional challenges and difficulties. For instance, the extracted sentences may contradict each other because there is more diverse and conflicting information among documents. Moreover, information redundancy is omnipresent in MDS and has a significant impact on the information diversity of the generated summaries. The complexities of all these issues make the multi-document summarization a challenging task.

Furthermore, generating a relevant summary is a cognitive process that requires a deep understanding of the source documents as well as linguistic competence. Thus, creating an internal representation to understand and analyze the semantic information of the source documents is a cornerstone step in text summarization methods. Bag-of-words and word embedding representations have shown promising results in text summarization [28,36]. However, they do not consider the ordering of words in sentences as well as the semantic and syntactic relationships between them, and thus they may map semantically similar sentences into different vectors. Therefore, we need more accurate text representation methods that capture the semantic content of the source documents.

Recently, contextual pre-trained sentence embedding models, including inferSent [9], BERT encoder [10], simCSE [16], sentence-BERT [32], and others have demonstrated impressive performance in various NLP tasks [9,10,16,32]. In this work, we apply several existing sentence embedding models to represent the documents' sentences as dense vectors in a low dimensional vector space and determine how well they capture relevant information to the unsupervised extractive multi-document summarization tasks (G-MDS and QF-MDS). Furthermore, we assess their performance, using the ROUGE method [22], on the standard DUC'2003-2004 and DUC'2005-2007 datasets for the G-MDS and

QF-MDS tasks, respectively. The experimental results show that the simCSE embedding model [16], based on contrastive learning [8], brings substantial improvement over several other strong sentence embedding models.

Meanwhile, despite countless successes of the extractive methods, the generated summaries may contain incoherent sentences, as pronominal coreference expressions may appear unbound [1]. To alleviate this issue, we use a coreference resolution system (i.e. NeuralCoref[1]) to detect the broken pronominal coreference expressions in the selected sentences, and then rewrite those sentences by substituting with correct mentions. Advantageously, the proposed methods have achieved encouraging results, as the final summaries reached better ROUGE scores. We find also that our unsupervised extractive methods (G-MDS and QF-MDS) yield promising performance compared to the best-performing systems, including recent supervised deep learning-based methods.

The paper consists of the following sections: In Sect. 2, we briefly review the recent existing sentence embedding models. In Sect. 3, we present our generic and query-focused multi-document summarization methods. In Sect. 4, we analyze and compare the strengths and weaknesses of the described models and methods. Finally, in Sect. 5, we conclude the paper and outline some future directions in the field.

## 2   Related Work

The main objective of this work is to assess the performance of recent sentence embeddings in the context of unsupervised extractive multi-document summarization, considering both *generic* and *query-focused* tasks. To make the paper self-contained for reading, we briefly introduce the sentence embedding models exploited in this work. However, for readers who are interested in an overview of text summarization methods, they may refer to these recent surveys [12,15].

Several sentence embedding methods exist that aim to encode sentences into dense vectors, which accurately capture the semantic and syntactic relationships between these sentences' constituents. Early work mostly concentrate on weighting and averaging words embedding vectors to construct the sentence embedding vector. In this context, the author in [13] has introduced the unsupervised smoothed inverse frequency (uSIF) model, which uses a pre-trained word vector model, tuned on the ParaNMT-50 dataset [38], to generate word embedding vectors. Then, it creates sentence embedding vectors using the weighted average of word embedding vectors followed by a modification with singular vector decomposition and an unsupervised random walk algorithm.

In recent years, learning universal sentence embeddings using pre-trained models has gained much attention in NLP and tackled extensively in the literature [7,9,10,16,32]. For instance, Cer et al. [7] have introduced the universal sentence encoder DAN (USE-DAN) based on a deep average network [17]. It takes the average of word embeddings and bi-grams as input, which are then passed

---

[1] https://github.com/huggingface/neuralcoref.

through a feed-forward neural network to produce the final sentence embedding vector. It is trained using unlabeled data selected from Wikipedia, web news, web question-answer pages, and discussion forums. Then, it is fine-tuned on the natural language inference task using the Stanford Natural Language Inference (SNLI) dataset [2], which has shown promising performance in various NLP tasks [7]. Besides, other embedding models use recurrent neural networks for learning universal sentences' representations. In this context, the supervised InferSent [9] trains a bi-directional long short-term memory network with max-pooling on the SNLI dataset. It has proven the suitability of natural language inference for transfer learning to other NLP tasks.

Furthermore, pre-trained sentence embedding models based on the Transformer architecture [37] have shown tremendous success in text encoding [7,10, 16,32]. In this context, Cer et al. [7] have introduced the universal sentence encoder (USE-Transformer) that uses the encoding sub-graph of the Transformer for sentence representation learning. Similarly to the USE-DAN model, the USE-Transformer is also trained on unlabeled data from Wikipedia, web news, web question-answer pages and discussion forums. Then, it is fine-tuned on the SNLI and the question-answering SQuAD datasets [2,29]. In the same vein, other researchers have introduced the Bidirectional Encoder Representations from Transformers (BERT) model [10], which is based on a multi-layer bidirectional transformer encoder with attention mechanisms. BERT is trained on a large amount of unlabeled data selected from English Wikipedia and Book-Corpus, using two unsupervised tasks: masked language modeling and the next sentence prediction. Then, the pre-trained BERT can be fine-tuned on new NLP tasks using task-specific data. It has achieved impressive performance in a wide range of NLP tasks, including single text summarization [24].

Nevertheless, other researchers have introduced the Sentence-BERT (SBERT) model [32], a modified version of the original pre-trained BERT model, which is mainly based on the siamese neural networks [3]. SBERT combines two BERT encoders into a siamese architecture to process two sentences in the same way, simultaneously. These two sub-networks derive semantically meaningful sentence embeddings[2], which can be then compared using the cosine similarity metric. It is trained on the combination of the SNLI [2] and Multi-Genre NLI [39] using the *classification*, *regression*, and *triplet* objective functions, depending on the available training data. Indeed, SBERT has shown state-of-the-art performance on the common STS benchmark [6] and transfer learning tasks.

More recently, the SimCSE embedding model [16], based on contrastive learning [8], has greatly advanced state-of-the-art sentence embedding methods. Contrastive learning [8] is a machine learning paradigm that aims to learn effective representation by pushing semantically close neighbors towards each other in the embedding space while pulling non-neighbors against each other. In conjunction with this, Gao et al. [16] have introduced two variants of SimCSE: 1) The *unsupervised SimCSE* that simply takes an input sentence and predicts itself in a contrastive learning framework, with only standard dropout used as

---

[2] *Semantically meaningful* means similar sentences are close in the vector space.

noise; 2) The *supervised SimCSE* that incorporates annotated pairs from the NLI datasets [2,39] into contrastive learning by using entailment pairs as positives and contradiction pairs as hard negatives. The authors have demonstrated that the contrastive learning objective can be extremely effective when coupled with pre-trained language models such as BERT [10].

Sentence embedding models are often evaluated at the time of their introduction with regard to the current state-of-the-art methods. Hence, it is rare when a single work presents a comparison of several embedding models for a specific task, we need to gather the results from numerous individual contributions. To the best of our knowledge, this is the first work that presents a comparative study of sentence embedding models for unsupervised generic and query-focused multi-document summarization tasks.

## 3   Multi-document Summarization Methods

An extractive multi-document summarization method aims to identify and extract the most relevant sentences from a cluster of documents and adequately assemble them to form the final summary. Generally, the process of an extractive method involves the following main steps: text pre-processing, text representation, sentence scoring and selection, and possibly additional sentence-level operations like reordering or coreference resolution [1]. Our proposed extractive G-MDS and QD-MDS methods follow these same steps, which we describe in detail in the rest of this section.

### 3.1   Text Pre-processing

Given a cluster $D$ consisting of $n$ documents, we first split each document $d_i$ into a set of sentences using the spaCy library[3], in particular, the pre-trained model "en_core_web_md". Then, we use the NLTK library[4] and regular expressions to perform tokenization, lowercasing, stemming, and to remove special characters (e.g. XML/HTML tags, URLs, email addresses, and redundant white-space). Hence, we obtain a cluster $D$ of $N$ sentences, denoted as $D = \{S_1, S_2, ..., S_N\}$. It is worth mentioning that for the query-focused summarization task, we also need to pre-process the pre-given user's query and represent it as a simple sentence $Q$.

### 3.2   Text Representation

Text representation plays a central role in extractive multi-document summarization methods to understand the content of the source documents. Thus, we leverage the potential of sentence embedding models (described in Sect. 2) to convert the documents' sentences into numeric fixed-length vectors that capture their semantic. They are two main approaches to use pre-trained sentence

---

[3] https://spacy.io/.
[4] https://www.nltk.org/.

embedding models, namely 1) *feature-based approach* and 2) *fine-tuning app-roach*. In the former, the pre-trained model is used to extract fixed features for the input documents' sentences, which can be used as input to the task at hand without any other modification. In the latter, the pre-trained model is fine-tuned on the downstream task where parameters of some layers are fixed and others are learned using the task-specific data.

Since we introduce in this paper *unsupervised* extractive methods, we opt for the first approach (*feature-based approach*). More precisely, given the cluster $D = \{S_1, S_2, ..., S_N\}$, we use a sentence embedding model (e.g. BERT, SBERT, and others) to map each sentence $S_i$ in $D$ into an embedding vector $\overrightarrow{S_i^D}$. Note that for the QF-MDS task, we also map the user's query into an embedding vector $\overrightarrow{Q}$ using the same sentence embedding models.

### 3.3 Sentence Scoring and Selection

Sentence scoring methods assign a score for each sentence in the cluster of documents to decide which sentences are most relevant to be selected as summary. For the generic G-MDS task, we measure the relevance of each sentence $S_i$ in the cluster $D$ without taking account of the user's specific need, while for the query-focused QF-MDS task, we score each sentence $S_i$ in $D$ based on its relevance to the input user's query $Q$. Our G-MDS and QF-MDS sentence scoring methods are successively described in the following.

**Generic-MDS Task.** Given a cluster $D = \{S_1, S_2, ..., S_N\}$ of $N$ sentences, we assign a score for each sentence $S_i$ in $D$ by linearly combining three metrics, namely sentence content relevance, sentence novelty, and sentence position.

– **Sentence content relevance score**, formally defined in Eq. 1, is computed using the cosine similarity between the sentence embedding vector $\overrightarrow{S_i^D}$ and the centroid embedding vector of the cluster of documents $\overrightarrow{C_D}$ (defined in Eq. 2).

$$score^{contRelevance}(S_i, D) = \frac{\overrightarrow{S_i^D}.\overrightarrow{C_D}}{\| \overrightarrow{S_i^D} \| . \| \overrightarrow{C_D} \|} \tag{1}$$

$$\overrightarrow{C_D} = \frac{1}{N} \sum_{i=1}^{N} \overrightarrow{S_i^D} \tag{2}$$

where $\overrightarrow{C_D}$ is the centroid embedding vector of the cluster $D$, $N$ is the number of sentences in $D$, and $\overrightarrow{S_i^D}$ is the embedding vector of the sentence $S_i$. The $score^{contRelevance}$ is bounded in [0,1] where sentences with higher scores are considered more relevant.

- **Sentence novelty score**, denoted as $score^{novelty}(S_i, D)$, is explicitly used to deal with redundancy and produce summaries with good information diversity [20]. More precisely, for each sentence $S_i$ in the cluster $D$, we compute its similarity with all the other sentences in $D$ using the cosine similarity between their corresponding embedding vectors. Then, if the maximum of the obtained similarities is below a given threshold $\tau$, then the sentence $S_i$ is considered novel. However, when the similarity between two sentences is greater than the given threshold, the sentence with the higher content relevance score gets the higher novelty score
- **Sentence position** assigns a score for each sentence based on its position in the document, assuming that the first sentences of a document are more relevant to the summary [20]. Given $D$ a cluster of $n$ documents where each document $d$ consists of $M$ sentences $d = \{S_1, S_2, ..., S_M\}$, we compute the sentence position score of each sentence $S_j$ in $d$ using the following equation:

$$score^{position}(S_j) = \max(0.5, \exp(\frac{-p(S_j)}{3\sqrt{M}})) \tag{3}$$

where $M$ is the number of sentences in the document $d$, and $p(S_j)$ function is the relative position of the $j^{th}$ sentence $S_j$ in the document $d$ with $p(S_j) = 1$ for the first sentence and so on. The $score^{position}(S_j)$ is bounded between 0.5 and 1. It is higher for sentences located at the beginning of the document, while it gets stable at a value of 0.5 after a given number of sentences depending on the total number of sentences $M$ in the document.

Finally, we linearly combine these three metrics to get the final score of each sentence $S_i$ in the cluster $D$, formally defined in the following equation:

$$score^{final}(S_i, D) = \alpha * score^{contRelevance} + \beta * score^{novelty} + \lambda * score^{position} \tag{4}$$

where, $\alpha + \beta + \lambda = 1$ with $\alpha, \beta, \lambda \in [0, 1]$ with constant steps of 0.1. The top-ranked sentences are iteratively selected to form the summary w.r.t. the constraint on summary length $L$.

**Query-Focused-MDS Task.** Given a cluster $D = \{S_1, S_2, ..., S_N\}$ of $N$ sentences and a user's query $Q$, we measure the relevance of each sentence $S_i$ in $D$ according the query $Q$ using the cosine similarity between their embedding vectors $\overrightarrow{S_i^D}$ and $\overrightarrow{Q}$, respectively. Then, based on the obtained scores, we iteratively select the top-$k$ ranked sentences such as $k \in \{50, 100\}$, formally denoted as top-$k = \{S_1, S_2, ..., S_k\}$. Next, we use a modified Maximal Marginal Relevance method [5,19] that incorporates sentence embeddings to re-rank the top-$k$ selected sentences intending to produce summaries that are relevant to the query $Q$ and less redundant.

Finally, based on the obtained MMR sentences' scores, we apply a greedy search algorithm to select the relevant sentences to the input user's query, where a new sentence is added to the current summary if the constraint on the length limit $L$ is not reached and the semantic similarity between this sentence and the already selected summary sentences is below a threshold $\tau$.

## 3.4 Post-processing

As previously stated, extractive methods have proven to be effective for text summarization tasks, however, the generated summaries may lack cohesiveness since they sometimes contain unresolved pronouns. To address this issue, we use the NeuralCoref[5] model to detect each unresolved pronoun in the generated summary and then replace it with its corresponding entity. Nevertheless, as illustrated in the following example $S_1$, the simple strategy of replacing every pronoun may cause redundant information and repetitive entity references in the generated summary.

- **Example $S_1$:** On primary and secondary education, Mrs Gillian Shephard, the education secretary, announced tougher standards for teaching English in England and Wales, she (Mrs Gillian Shephard) launched an initiative to raise public consciousness about the need for good communication skills.

To deal with this issue, we apply a rule-based heuristic that for each sentence in the generated summary, it keeps the pronoun if it appears after its referents in the same sentence; otherwise, the pronoun is unbound and must be replaced by its entity. The idea is straightforward: do not replace the same pronoun twice in the same sentence.

# 4 Experiments

In this work, we are more interested in the degree to which the different sentence embedding models capture contextual and relevant information for solving unsupervised multi-document summarization tasks. Therefore, we present in this section all the experiments that are carried out to investigate the performance of the exploited models w.r.t the G-MDS and QF-MDS tasks.

## 4.1 Evaluation Datasets and Metrics

The experiments are carried out using the standard DUC'2003-2007 benchmarks[6], created essentially for evaluating multi-document summarization tasks. Table 1 summarizes some basic statistics of the used datasets.

For the evaluation measures, we use ROUGE (Recall-Oriented Understudy for Gisting Evaluation) method [22], in particular ROUGE-N (R-1, R-2, R-4) and ROUGE-SU4, adopting the same ROUGE settings[7] used for evaluating multi-document summarization methods.

---

[5] https://github.com/huggingface/neuralcoref
[6] https://duc.nist.gov/data.html.
[7] ROUGE-1.5.5 with parameters "-n 4 -m -l 100 -c 95 -r 1000 -f A -p 0.5 -t 0" (G-MDS), "-a -c 95 -m -n 2 -2 4 -u -p 0.5 -l 250" (QF-MDS).

**Table 1.** A description of DUC'2003-2007 datasets [19,20]. *Num docs* is the number of docs in each cluster. *Sum length* is the number of words in gold summaries.

| Dataset | Clusters | Num docs | Sentences | Queries | Sum Length | Task |
|---------|----------|----------|-----------|---------|------------|--------|
| DUC'2003 | 30 | 10 | 7691 | – | 100 | G-MDS |
| DUC'2004 | 50 | 10 | 13135 | – | 100 | G-MDS |
| DUC'2005 | 50 | 32 | 45931 | 50 | 250 | QF-MDS |
| DUC'2007 | 45 | 25 | 24282 | 45 | 250 | QF-MDS |

### 4.2   Experimental Setup

The introduced G-MDS and QF-MDS methods have been developed using PyTorch and a set of python tools, including the TrecTools[8] library and the available implementation of sentenc embedding models in Hugging Face[9], TensorFlow Hub[10], and GitHub[11] Each model is designed to embed a sentence into a fixed dimensional length vector. For BERT, SBERT, and SimCSE-BERT, we used $BERT_{base}$ model that produces embeddings vectors of 712 dimensions. The universal sentence encoders USE-DAN and USE-Transformer generate embeddings vectors of 512 dimensions, while the supervised InferSent-GloVe model produces embeddings vectors of 4090 dimensions.

For the G-MDS task, we need to optimize the hyper-parameters $\alpha$, $\beta$, $\lambda$, and the threshold $\tau$. Thus, we built a small held-out set by shuffling and randomly sampling 20 clusters from DUC'2002 dataset. Then, we performed a grid search on the held-out set under the condition $\alpha+\beta+\lambda = 1$, which gave us a total of 330 feasible combinations. Accordingly, the obtained values of the hyperparameters are 0.6, 0.2, 0.2, and 0.95 for $\alpha$, $\beta$, $\lambda$, and $\tau$, respectively.

For the QF-MDS task, we follow the same approach to optimize the three used hyper-parameters (i.e. the number of top ranked sentences $k$, the interpolation coefficient $\lambda$, and the threshold $\tau$). We create a small held-out set by shuffling and randomly sample 20 clusters from DUC'2006 dataset. Then, we apply a grid search on the held-out set that gave us a total of 200 feasible combinations. Accordingly, the optimized values of $\lambda$, $\tau$, and $k$ are 0.9, 0.85, and 50, respectively.

Furthermore, for the statistical significance test, we used the *paired t-test* [11] to determine whether there is a significant difference in performance among all the evaluated models. Our choice is motivated by the fact that the authors in [31] have demonstrated that the *paired t-test* is more powerful than the equivalent unpaired test when applied to compare the outputs of two automatic text summarization systems. We attached a superscript to the performance number in the tables when the $p - value < 0.05$.

---

[8]  https://pypi.org/project/trectools/.
[9]  https://huggingface.co/.
[10]  https://tfhub.dev/google.
[11]  https://github.com/facebookresearch/InferSent, https://github.com/kawine/usif.

## 4.3  Results

**Comparison of the Different Sentence Embeddings w.r.t to the Unsupervised G-MDS and QF-MDS Tasks.** The main objective of this paper is to examine the influence of transfer learning from sentence embedding models on the unsupervised multi-document summarization, considering both G-MDS and QF-MDS tasks. Tables 2 and 3 summarize the evaluation results of the different used text representation methods on G-MDS and QF-MDS tasks, including: a) Bag-of-words representation based on TF-IDF weighting scheme [30]; b) Word embeddings using the average of GloVe embeddings [27]; c) Unsupervised sentence embedding models using the average of BERT embeddings [10] and uSIF model [13]; d) Semi-supervised models using the universal sentence encoders (USE-Transformer, USE-DAN) [7]; e) Finally, supervised sentence embedding methods using InferSent [9], Sentence-BERT [32], and SimCSE [16] models.

**Table 2.** Comparison results of the used sentence embeddings w.r.t to the **G-MDS** task based on ROUGE recall scores. The superscripts *number* indicates significant improvement ($p$ − value $< 0.05$) over the sentence embedding model that has the same superscript *number* attached.

| MODELS | DUC'2003 | | | DUC'2004 | | |
|---|---|---|---|---|---|---|
| | R-1 | R-2 | R-4 | R-1 | R-2 | R-4 |
| BOW and Word Embedding Models | | | | | | |
| TF-IDF[1] | $35.83^3$ | $7.62^3$ | $1.01^3$ | $36.41^3$ | $7.97^3$ | $1.21^3$ |
| Avg. GloVe Embedding[2] | $36.72^{1,3}$ | $8.45^{1,3}$ | $1.12^3$ | $37.10^{1,3}$ | $8.80^{1,3}$ | $1.32^3$ |
| Unsupervised Models | | | | | | |
| BERT Embedding[3] | 28.03 | 4.48 | 0.45 | 28.92 | 4,43 | 0.59 |
| uSIF[4] | $38.29^{1-3}$ | $9.27^{1-3}$ | $1.48^{1,3}$ | $39.72^{1-3}$ | $9.79^{1-3}$ | $1.65^{1-3}$ |
| Semi-Supervised Models | | | | | | |
| USE-DAN[5] | $38.35^{1-3}$ | $9.06^{1-3}$ | $1.28^{1,3}$ | $40.14^{1-3,7}$ | $9.85^{1-3}$ | $1.58^{1-3}$ |
| USE-Transformer[6] | $38.56^{1-3,7}$ | $9.36^{1-3}$ | $1.52^{1-3}$ | $40.32^{1-3,7}$ | $9.94^{1-3}$ | $1.67^{1-3}$ |
| Supervised Models | | | | | | |
| InferSent-GloVe[7] | $37.59^{1-3}$ | $9.01^{1-3}$ | $1.47^{1,3}$ | $38.71^{1-3}$ | $9.17^{1-3}$ | $1.38^{1,3}$ |
| SBERT[8] | $39.24^{1-7}$ | $9.72^{1-3}$ | $1.68^{1-3}$ | $40.58^{1-3,7}$ | $10.04^{1-3}$ | $1.84^{1-3}$ |
| SimCSE[9] | $40.32^{1-8}$ | $9.98^{1-7}$ | $1.92^{1-3,5}$ | $40.96^{1-8}$ | $10.23^{1-7}$ | $1.96^{1-7}$ |

As shown in Table 2, the average of GloVe embeddings has significantly outperformed the TF-IDF model and BERT embeddings on the two used datasets and for most of the evaluation measures (R-1, R-2, and R-4). Noticing that using BERT model adopting the *feature-based approach* leads to rather poor performance, which is worse than computing the average of GloVe embeddings and TF-IDF model. The results show also that uSIF, USE-DAN, and USE-Transformer models have shown promising performance and outperformed the

supervised InferSent-GloVe model for most of evaluation measures. However, the
difference between them is not statistically significant. Moreover, the SBERT
model, based on siamese architecture, has outperformed all the other models
except the SimCSE-BERT model, which has shown the best performance for all
the evaluation metrics and on the two used datasets.

**Table 3.** Comparison results of the used sentence embeddings w.r.t to the **QF-MDS**
task based on ROUGE recall scores. The superscripts *number* indicates significant
improvement ($p$ − value < 0.05) over the sentence embedding model that has the same
superscript *number* attached.

| MODELS | DUC'2005 | | | DUC'2007 | | |
|---|---|---|---|---|---|---|
| | R-1 | R-2 | R-SU4 | R-1 | R-2 | R-SU4 |
| BOW and Word Embedding Models | | | | | | |
| TF-IDF[1] | 35.02 | 7.25 | 13.16 | 36.32 | 9.22 | 13.88 |
| Avg. GloVe Embedding[2] | 37.66[1,3] | 7.67[1,3] | 14.05[1,3] | 40.22[1,3] | 9.62[3] | 15.23[1,3] |
| Unsupervised Models | | | | | | |
| BERT Embedding[3] | 35.15 | 6.64 | 12.62 | 36.63 | 7.74 | 13.24 |
| uSIF[4] | 37.81[1,3] | 7.68[1,3] | 14.31[1,3] | 41.54[1-3] | 10.08[3] | 17.05[1-3] |
| Semi-Supervised Models | | | | | | |
| USE-DAN[5] | 38.55[1-4] | 7.62[1,3] | 14.76[1-3] | 42.54[1-4] | 10.41[1-3] | 17.84[1-4] |
| USE-Transformer[6] | 39.65[1-4,7] | 8.21[1-4,7] | 15.5[1-4], 7 | 43.37[1-4,7] | 11.10[1-4,7] | 18.11[1-4,7] |
| Supervised Models | | | | | | |
| InferSent-GloVe[7] | 38.03[1-3] | 7.75 | 14.47[1,3] | 42.06[1-3] | 9.96[3] | 17.37[1-3] |
| SBERT[8] | 40.07[1-5,7] | 8.57[1-5,7] | 15.72[1-5,7] | 43.75[1-5,7] | 11.27[1-5,7] | 17.96[1-4] |
| SimCSE[9] | 40.92[1-8] | 8.70[1-7] | 16.19[1-7] | 44.23[1-8] | 12.06[1-7] | 18.65[1-4,7] |

As regards the QF-MDS task, the trend is similar. From Table 3, it seems clear
that the SBERT and SimCSE-BERT models have achieved the best performance
and led to significant improvement over most other models for all the evaluation measures (R-1, R-2, R-SU4). Furthermore, the universal sentence encoder
USE-Transformer model has achieved better results than the USE-DAN and significantly outperformed the other models on both DUC'2005-2007 datasets and
for most evaluation measures.

Therefore, the overall comparison of the exploited sentence embedding models has drawn the same conclusions on all the used datasets with regard to both
G-MDS and QF-MDS tasks. More precisely, directly using BERT with no fine-
tuning provides sentence embeddings, which are not suitable for the unsupervised
multi-document summarization tasks; they yield slightly worse results than all
the other models, including bag-of-words and word embeddings representations.
Moreover, even though the supervised InferSent model is based on bidirectional
LSTM networks and trained on the human-labeled SNLI dataset [2], it achieves

comparable performance to the unsupervised uSIF model. This proves the effectiveness of uSIF sentence embeddings for the unsupervised multi-document summarization tasks.

Furthermore, the universal sentence encoder USE-Transformer has shown better performance that the USE-DAN. This can be due to their different architectures as well as the used training datasets. In fact, the USE-Transformer is further fine-tuned on the question-answering SQuAD dataset [29], and thus the knowledge gained from this related learning task helps boost the performance of the unsupervised MDS task. Additionally, we find that SBERT, based on siamese architecture and fine-tuning mechanisms, performs better than all the other previous models. Noticing that the SimCSE embedding model, based on the contrastive learning [8], has shown the best performance for both G-MDS and QF-MDS tasks.

**Comparison with State-of-the-Art Methods.** To prove the effectiveness of the introduced methods, we compare their performance with the best-performing supervised and unsupervised state-of-the-art systems. ROUGE recall scores of the different systems used for comparison are summarized in Tables 4 and 5. It is worth mentioning that for the state-of-the-art methods, we report the results presented in their corresponding papers on DUC'2004 and DUC'2007, considered as the most used datasets for evaluating extractive G-MDS and QF-MDS systems. However, for our methods, we report the results obtained using the **SimCSE** embedding model, which achieves the best performance.

**Table 4.** ROUGE score of the G-MDS systems on DUC'2004 dataset.

| System | R-1 | R-2 | R-4 |
|---|---|---|---|
| DPP [18] | **39.79** | 9.62 | 1.57 |
| ConceptBased_ILP [26] | 38.65 | **10.02** | **1.67** |
| PG-MMR [21] | **36.42** | **9.36** | – |
| Hi-MAP [14] | 35.78 | 8.9 | – |
| GMDS-SimCSE (ours) | **40.96*** | **10.23*** | **1.96*** |

The first set of analyses is performed to compare our **GMDS-SimCSE** method with unsupervised systems, including the DPP [18] and the Concept-Based_ILP [26], which are considered as the best-performing extractive generic MDS systems on DUC'2004 dataset. As shown in Table 4, our method has achieved the best performance for all the evaluation measures (R-1, R-2, and R-4). More precisely, it achieves an increment of 1.17% w.r.t the DPP system for the R-1 measure and an improvement of 0.21% and 0.29% w.r.t the Concept-Based_ILP system for R-2 and R-4, respectively.

To further investigate the effectiveness of the introduced method, we compare its performance with recent supervised systems, including the PG-MMR [21] and the Hi-MAP [14] that are mainly based on the pointer-generator networks with the maximal marginal relevance method [5]. As depicted in Table 4, our method GMDS-SimCSE has shown better performance than both the PG-MMR and HI-MAP methods. In particular, it has achieved an increment of 4.54% and 0.87% with respect to PG-MMR for R-1 and R-2 respectively. This can be explained by the fact that both PG-MMR and HI-MAP methods have been trained on the CNN/ DailyMail datasets, mainly created for single-document summarization, where documents are very short compared to a cluster of documents.

The second set of analyses is conducted to evaluate the performance of our query-focused multi-document summarization method (**QFMDS-SimCSE**) using DUC'2007 dataset. We compare it against the best-performing state-of-the-art methods, including 1) the unsupervised Dual-CES [35] and USE-Transformer-Sum [19] systems, and 2) the supervised CRSum-SF [33] and SRSum [34] systems, which are based on convolutional neural networks with attention mechanisms. Therefore, as shown in Table 5, in terms of R-1 and R-2 our method has achieved comparable performance to all the other systems except Dual-CES, which has yielded very high performance w.r.t R-1 score. This can be because the Dual-CES system better handles the tradeoff saliency and focus in the summarization process. However, in terms of R-SU4 evaluation measure, our method has achieved the best performances.

**Table 5.** ROUGE recall score of the QF-MDS systems on DUC'2007 dataset.

| System | R-1 | R-2 | R-SU4 |
|---|---|---|---|
| Dual-CES [35] | **46.02\*** | 12.53 | 17.91 |
| USE-Transformer-Sum [19] | 43.54 | 11.42 | 18.54 |
| CRSum-SF [33] | 44.6 | 12.48 | – |
| SRSum [34] | 45.01 | **12.8\*** | – |
| QFMDS-SimCSE (ours) | 44.23 | 12.06 | **18.65\*** |

The overall obtained results show that our unsupervised extractive multi-document summarization methods, based on sentence embeddings and coreference resolution, achieve promising results for both generic and query-focused tasks. Moreover, they yield far better performance than the state-of-the-art methods that are based on bag-of-words and word embeddings representations. A concrete example of gold summary and our **QFMDS-SimCSE** system's output is presented in Table 6 in Appendix A. It can be seen from this example that replacing the broken pronoun "**They**" in sentence "$S_3$" by its entity "**Richard Roberts and Phillip Sharp**" has improved the cohesion of the generated summary. Furthermore, this example shows also that the produced summary is relevant to the input query.

# 5    Conclusion and Future Directions

Different from other natural language processing applications, text summarization is a challenging task that is highly subjective and dependent on the content. Determining the relevance of information included in documents requires a deep understanding of the source documents. Therefore, the main objective of this paper was to investigate the performance of deep understanding methods, namely recent sentence embedding models, on the unsupervised extractive multi-document summarization, considering both generic and query-focused tasks. The results have shown that models based on the Transformer architecture and fine-tuned on the NLI datasets lead to strong results compared to other models. This proves the effectiveness of transfer learning from pre-trained sentence embedding models, which allows benefiting from knowledge learned from other related natural language understanding tasks to improve the performance of the target task. Additionally, the results have also shown that the SimCSE embedding model, based on contrastive learning, has demonstrated substantial improvement in extractive unsupervised MDS task.

Furthermore, as previously mentioned, supervised multi-document summarization methods require high-quality labeled training data, which is of immense importance for the success of these methods. However, acquiring such data for MDS is a cumbersome task, especially for specific domains, where experts are required to annotate the data. Thus, the recent focus of deep learning research is to reduce the requirement for supervision in model training. In fact, fine-tuning deep pre-trained language models has set state-of-the-art performance on a wide range of NLP applications, however, their generalization performance drops under domain shift. To mitigate this issue, several s*elf-supervised learning* methods have been introduced in the literature, which are based for instance on *unsupervised domain adaptation* or *contrastive learning* approaches.

Unsupervised domain adaptation methods aim to generalize well on the target domain by learning from both labeled samples from the source domain and unlabeled samples from the target domain, while contrastive learning methods learn to contrast between pairs of similar and dissimilar data points [8]. These methods have shown impressive performance in several NLP tasks [25]; they facilitate data-efficient learning, especially when training data is not abundantly available. Motivated by these findings, we plan to investigate the potential of self-supervised learning methods, based on unsupervised domain adaptation and contrastive learning, to improve the *abstractive* multi-document summarization tasks.

Finally, we believe that our unsupervised G-MDS and QF-MDS methods that do not require labeled training data nor domain knowledge can be used as strong baselines for evaluating *extractive* multi-document summarization systems.

# A   Example of Our QFMDS-SimCSE Output's Summary

**Table 6.** Example of the generated summary for **Cluster D374a** from DUC'2005 dataset using our **QFMDS-SimCSE** method.

---

**Query**

- $S_1$ Who are the Nobel Prize winners in the sciences and in economics and what are their prize-winning achievements? What are common factors in their backgrounds?

---

**Generated summary**

- $S_1$ THE WINNERS of the Nobel prizes, announced in Stockholm, made discoveries which helped to uncover some of the most fundamental processes in science
- $S_2$ The Nobel Prize in chemistry is shared by Thomas Cech, 41, of the University of Colorado, and Sidney Altman, 50, of Yale University
- $S_3$ Richard Roberts and Phillip Sharp(They) have just jointly been awarded the Nobel prize in medicine
- $S_4$ Jerome I. Friedman and Henry W. Kendall of the Massachusetts Institute of Technology and Canadian Richard E. Taylor of Stanford University will share the $700,000 Nobel Prize in physics
- $S_5$ Murray Gell-Mann won the Nobel prize for physics in 1969, and later helped establish the Santa Fe Institute, an interdisciplinary foundation devoted to the study of 'complex systems' as various as quantum mechanics, the human body, and international economics
- $S_6$ MR GARY BECKER, named as this year's winner of the Nobel prize for economics, is proof that economists have more to offer than dubious forecasts, indecipherable equations and contradictory conclusions about the behavior of money and markets
- $S_7$ THE Nobel prize for economics was awarded to Robert Fogel of the University of Chicago and Douglass North of Washington University in St Louis for pioneering work on the causes of economic and institutional change
- $S_8$ The Nobel Prize for Economics was awarded to three 'game theorists': John Harsanyi, John Nash and Rheinhard Selten
- Norman Ramsey of Harvard University will receive half the physics prize for his discovery of the atomic clock
- $S_9$ The announcements completed a near-sweep of the science Nobel's by U.S. researchers this year, continuing U.S. dominance of the prizes.

---

**Gold summary**

- Nobel prizes are award each year for achievements in the physical sciences − physics, chemistry, medicine, economics, literature and for peace
- Winners in physics include Norman Ramsey, Wolfgang Paul and Hans Delmelt in 1989 for work leading to the cesium atomic clock; Jerome Friedman, Henry Kendall and Richard Taylor in 1990 for first detecting quarks; Georges Charpak in 1992 for particle detectors; and Betran Brockhouse and Clifford Shull in 1994 for work on neutron scattering
- Chemistry winners include Sidney Altman and Thomas Cech in 1989 for work on RNA; Elias Cory in 1990 for work on organic synthesis; and Rudolph Marcus in 1992 for electron transfer theory
- Winners in medicine include J. Michael Bishop and Harold Varmus in 1989 for contributions to cancer research; Joseph Murray and E. Donnall Thomas in 1990 for work on organ transplants; Richard Roberts and Phillip Sharp in 1993 for cancer research; and Alfred Gilman and Martin Rodbell in 1994 for work on proteins
- Among winners in economics are Robert Fogel and Douglas North in 1993 for work on causes of economic change; Gary Becker in 1992 for work on the economics of discrimination and human capital theory; and John Harsanyi, John Nash and Rheinhard Selten in 1994 for work on game theory
- Winners share some common background factors, One is that generally took five and 20 years between a discovery and its recognition
- Another is that most winners in certain fields were Americans − of 142 medicine prizes awarded, 69 were to Americans

# References

1. Antunes, J., Lins, R.D., Lima, R., Oliveira, H., Riss, M., Simske, S.J.: Automatic cohesive summarization with pronominal anaphora resolution. Comput. Speech Lang. **52**, 141–164 (2018)
2. Bowman, S.R., Angeli, G., Potts, C., Manning, C.D.: A large annotated corpus for learning natural language inference. In: Proceedings of the 2015 Conference on Empirical Methods in Natural Language Processing, pp. 632–642 (2015)
3. Bromley, J., et al.: Signature verification using a "siamese" time delay neural network. Int. J. Pattern Recognit. Artif. Intell. **7**(04), 669–688 (1993)
4. Cao, Z., Wei, F., Li, W., Li, S.: Faithful to the original: fact aware neural abstractive summarization. In: Thirty-Second AAAI Conference on Artificial Intelligence (2018)
5. Carbonell, J., Goldstein, J.: The use of MMR, diversity-based reranking for reordering documents and producing summaries. In: Proceedings of the 21st Annual International ACM SIGIR Conference on Research and Development In Information Retrieval, pp. 335–336 (1998)
6. Cer, D., Diab, M., Agirre, E., Lopez-Gazpio, I., Specia, L.: SemEval-2017 task 1: semantic textual similarity multilingual and crosslingual focused evaluation. In: Proceedings of the 11th International Workshop on Semantic Evaluation (SemEval-2017), pp. 1–14 (2017)
7. Cer, D., et al.: Universal sentence encoder for English, pp. 169–174 (2018)
8. Chen, T., Kornblith, S., Norouzi, M., Hinton, G.: A simple framework for contrastive learning of visual representations. In: International Conference on Machine Learning, pp. 1597–1607 (2020)
9. Conneau, A., Kiela, D., Schwenk, H., Barrault, L., Bordes, A.: Supervised learning of universal sentence representations from natural language inference data. In: Proceedings of the 2017 Conference on Empirical Methods in Natural Language Processing, EMNLP, pp. 670–680 (2017)
10. Devlin, J., Chang, M.W., Lee, K., Toutanova, K.: BERT: pre-training of deep bidirectional transformers for language understanding, pp. 4171–4186 (2019)
11. Dietterich, T.G.: Approximate statistical tests for comparing supervised classification learning algorithms. Neural Comput. **10**(7), 1895–1923 (1998)
12. El-Kassas, W.S., Salama, C.R., Rafea, A.A., Mohamed, H.K.: Automatic text summarization: a comprehensive survey. Expert Syst. Appl. **165**, 113679 (2020)
13. Ethayarajh, K.: Unsupervised random walk sentence embeddings: a strong but simple baseline. In: Proceedings of the Third Workshop on Representation Learning for NLP, pp. 91–100 (2018)
14. Fabbri, A., Li, I., She, T., Li, S., Radev, D.: Multi-news: a large-scale multi-document summarization dataset and abstractive hierarchical model. In: Proceedings of the 57th Annual Meeting of the Association for Computational Linguistics, pp. 1074–1084 (2019)
15. Gambhir, M., Gupta, V.: Recent automatic text summarization techniques: a survey. Artif. Intell. Rev. **47**(1), 1–66 (2017)
16. Gao, T., Yao, X., Chen, D.: SimCSE: simple contrastive learning of sentence embeddings. In: Proceedings of the 2021 Conference on Empirical Methods in Natural Language Processing, pp. 6894–6910 (2021)
17. Iyyer, M., Manjunatha, V., Boyd-Graber, J., Daumé III, H.: Deep unordered composition rivals syntactic methods for text classification. In: Proceedings of the 53rd Annual Meeting of the Association for Computational Linguistics and the 7th International Joint Conference on Natural Language Processing, pp. 1681–1691 (2015)

18. Kulesza, A., Taskar, B., et al.: Determinantal point processes for machine learning. Found. Trends® Mach. Learn. **5**(2–3), 123–286 (2012)
19. Lamsiyah, S., El Mahdaouy, A., El Alaoui, S.O., Espinasse, B.: Unsupervised query-focused multi-document summarization based on transfer learning from sentence embedding models, BM25 model, and maximal marginal relevance criterion. J. Ambient Intell. Humaniz. Comput. 1–18 (2021)
20. Lamsiyah, S., El Mahdaouy, A., Espinasse, B., Ouatik, S.E.A.: An unsupervised method for extractive multi-document summarization based on centroid approach and sentence embeddings. Expert Syst. Appl. **167**, 114152 (2021)
21. Lebanoff, L., Song, K., Liu, F.: Adapting the neural encoder-decoder framework from single to multi-document summarization. In: Proceedings of the 2018 Conference on Empirical Methods in Natural Language Processing, pp. 4131–4141 (2018)
22. Lin, C.Y.: ROUGE: a package for automatic evaluation of summaries. In: Text Summarization Branches Out, pp. 74–81 (2004)
23. Liu, Y., Lapata, M.: Hierarchical transformers for multi-document summarization. In: Proceedings of the 57th Annual Meeting of the Association for Computational Linguistics, pp. 5070–5081 (2019)
24. Liu, Y., Lapata, M.: Text summarization with pretrained encoders. In: Proceedings of the 2019 Conference on Empirical Methods in Natural Language Processing and the 9th International Joint Conference on Natural Language Processing (EMNLP-IJCNLP), pp. 3730–3740 (2019)
25. Long, Q., Luo, T., Wang, W., Pan, S.: Domain confused contrastive learning for unsupervised domain adaptation. In: Proceedings of the 2022 Conference of the North American Chapter of the Association for Computational Linguistics: Human Language Technologies, pp. 2982–2995 (2022)
26. Oliveira, H., Lins, R.D., Lima, R., Freitas, F., Simske, S.J.: A concept-based ilp approach for multi-document summarization exploring centrality and position. In: 2018 7th Brazilian Conference on Intelligent Systems (BRACIS), pp. 37–42 (2018)
27. Pennington, J., Socher, R., Manning, C.: Glove: global vectors for word representation. In: Proceedings of the 2014 Conference on Empirical Methods in Natural Language Processing (EMNLP), pp. 1532–1543 (2014)
28. Radev, D.R., Jing, H., Styś, M., Tam, D.: Centroid-based summarization of multiple documents. Inf. Process. Manag. **40**(6), 919–938 (2004)
29. Rajpurkar, P., Zhang, J., Lopyrev, K., Liang, P.: SQuAD: 100,000+ questions for machine comprehension of text. In: Proceedings of the 2016 Conference on Empirical Methods in Natural Language Processing (2016)
30. Ramos, J., et al.: Using TF-IDF to determine word relevance in document queries. In: Proceedings of the First Instructional Conference on Machine Learning, vol. 242, pp. 29–48 (2003)
31. Rankel, P.A., Conroy, J., Slud, E., O'leary, D.P.: Ranking human and machine summarization systems. In: Proceedings of the 2011 Conference on Empirical Methods in Natural Language Processing, pp. 467–473 (2011)
32. Reimers, N., Gurevych, I.: Sentence-BERT: sentence embeddings using Siamese BERT-networks. In: Proceedings of the 2019 Conference on Empirical Methods in Natural Language Processing and the 9th International Joint Conference on Natural Language Processing (EMNLP-IJCNLP), Hong Kong, China, pp. 3982–3992 (2019)
33. Ren, P., Chen, Z., Ren, Z., Wei, F., Ma, J., de Rijke, M.: Leveraging contextual sentence relations for extractive summarization using a neural attention model. In: Proceedings of the 40th International ACM SIGIR Conference on Research and Development in Information Retrieval, pp. 95–104 (2017)

34. Ren, P., et al.: Sentence relations for extractive summarization with deep neural networks. ACM Trans. Inf. Syst. (TOIS) **36**, 1–32 (2018)
35. Roitman, H., Feigenblat, G., Cohen, D., Boni, O., Konopnicki, D.: Unsupervised dual-cascade learning with pseudo-feedback distillation for query-focused extractive summarization. In: WWW 2020: The Web Conference 2020, Taipei, Taiwan, 20–24 April 2020, pp. 2577–2584 (2020)
36. Rossiello, G., Basile, P., Semeraro, G.: Centroid-based text summarization through compositionality of word embeddings. In: Proceedings of the MultiLing 2017 Workshop on Summarization and Summary Evaluation Across Source Types and Genres, pp. 12–21 (2017)
37. Vaswani, A., et al.: Attention is all you need. In: Advances in Neural Information Processing Systems, pp. 5998–6008 (2017)
38. Wieting, J., Gimpel, K.: ParaNMT-50M: pushing the limits of paraphrastic sentence embeddings with millions of machine translations. In: Proceedings of the 56th Annual Meeting of the Association for Computational Linguistics (Volume 1: Long Papers), pp. 451–462 (2018)
39. Williams, A., Nangia, N., Bowman, S.: A broad-coverage challenge corpus for sentence understanding through inference. In: Proceedings of the 2018 Conference of the North American Chapter of the Association for Computational Linguistics: Human Language Technologies, Volume 1 (Long Papers), pp. 1112–1122 (2018)

# On-device Deep Learning Location Category Inference Model

Gadzhi Musaev[1,3](✉)(iD), Kevin Mets[2](iD), Rokas Tamošiūnas[3](iD),
Vadim Uvarov[3](iD), Tom De Schepper[2](iD), and Peter Hellinckx[4](iD)

[1] IDLab - Faculty of Applied Engineering, University of Antwerp - imec,
Sint-Pietersvliet 7, 2000 Antwerp, Belgium
[2] Department of Computer Science, University of Antwerp - imec,
Sint-Pietersvliet 7, 2000 Antwerp, Belgium
{kevin.mets,tom.deschepper}@uantwerpen.be
[3] Sentiance, Korte Lozanastraat, 20-26, Antwerp, Belgium
{gadzhi.musaev,rokas.tamosiunas,vadim.uvarov}@sentiance.com
[4] Faculty of Applied Engineering, University of Antwerp, Antwerp, Belgium
peter.hellinckx@uantwerpen.be

**Abstract.** We define Location Category Inference (LCI) as a task of predicting the category of a visited venue, such as *bar*, *restaurant* or *university*, given user location GPS coordinates and a set of venue candidates. LCI is an essential part of the hyper-personalization systems as its output provides deep insights into user lifestyle (has children, owns a dog) and behavioral patterns (regularly exercises, visits museums). Due to such factors as signal obstruction, especially in urban canyons, the GPS positioning is inaccurate. The noise in the GPS signal makes the problem of LCI challenging and requires researchers to explore models that incorporate additional information such as the time of day, duration of stay or user lifestyle in order to overcome the noise-induced errors. In this paper we propose an embeddable on-device LCI model which fuses spatial and temporal features. We discuss how initial clustering of locations helps limiting the GPS noise. Then, we propose a multi-modal architecture that incorporates socio-cultural information on when and for how long people typically visit venues of different categories. Finally, we compare our model with one nearest neighbor, a simple fully connected neural network and a random forest model and show that the multi-modal neural network achieves f1 score of 73.2% which is 6.6% better than the best of benchmark models. Our model outperforms benchmark models while being almost 180 times smaller in size at around 1.9Mb.

**Keywords:** Location Category Inference · Deep Learning · On-device Machine Learning

---

Supported by Sentiance.

T. Calders et al. (Eds.): BNAIC/Benelearn 2022, CCIS 1805, pp. 96–111, 2023.
https://doi.org/10.1007/978-3-031-39144-6_7

# 1   Introduction

A system that maps raw mobile user location coordinates to a semantic meaning of that location is a rich source of knowledge and insights for a variety of applications. We can broadly define two categories of insights that an LCI system might provide: user profiles and contextual moments. The main function of a user profiling model is to get insights into *who* the users are: parents, students, office workers, etc. Contextual moment inference models are designed to give insights into *what they are busy with at certain moments*: commute, lunch, shopping, leisure, vacation, etc. Context-aware advertisement [17], personalized next point-of-interest recommendation [9], behavior change [13] and other applications rely explicitly or implicitly on such models in order to deliver most appropriate messages to the right users in timely manner.

Despite the undeniable progress in both mobile hardware and software during the last years, this problem is still challenging due to such technical problems as signal obstruction, signal reflection in densely built-up areas such as city centers, the trade off between GPS accuracy and battery consumption, etc. The uncertainty in the GPS location estimation leads researchers to explore additional sources of information. It has been shown that incorporating time of events and socio-cultural clues on how venues of different categories are typically used has significant impact on the accuracy of the LCI predictions [4,5]. Other studies also show that the impact of the GPS noise can be reduced by applying clustering on the set of all locations visited by a user and grouping the visits that correspond to the same location together [15,16].

Additional challenges arose recently with the growing concerns about privacy in location-based services. A number of recent studies explore geoprivacy issues and potential solutions [10,19,20]. This problem is not merely of academic interest, but is also critical for the industry. Today, businesses are expected to handle their users location-based data with full responsibility and limit the data storage and processing to the minimum required to provide the service. Thanks to the recent advances in mobile hardware and emergence of on-device deep learning frameworks such as tensorflow-lite, one of the practical steps to improve user experience with location-based services is to build on-device models and to guarantee that the location data never leave user devices. Unfortunately, this requires new research since many models proposed earlier were not designed to run in restricted mobile environments.

In this paper we address the problem of building an LCI model that satisfies both requirements: it must be lightweight and embeddable into mobile applications while incorporating additional temporal features and ensuring best performance in terms of accuracy metrics. We use one nearest neighbour model as a baseline that shows the lower bound of an LCI model performance. We also compare our model against a random forest which has been successfully applied to the same task [2,12]. Finally, we train a simple fully connected neural network and show that such a model would not achieve performance of the random forest.

Main contributions of this paper are following:

- We present a lightweight on-device deep learning LCI model embeddable into mobile applications that outperforms larger cloud-based models.
- We present a novel method of encoding spatial data on positions of an arbitrary number of venues in the neighbourhood as a spatial histogram of a fixed size. In order to combine the spatial histogram with temporal features we propose a multi-modal architecture.
- The data set we collected for our model is unique. Next to well-known temporal models based on time of day, we also introduce duration-based models.

## 2   Background

The model we propose is intended to work as a component of mobile applications that require insights into the lifestyle of a user. Since the runtime of the inference is significantly different from the training runtime, we need to discuss these additional details and also establish terminology used in the following sections. In order to facilitate the discussion, the Journeys application [21, 22] is used as an example. Figure 1 presents a screen of the Journeys application which demonstrates the timeline of a user.

As a user moves around their area of living while carrying a mobile device, each moment of time can be considered as either a moment of staying at a fixed location or moving from one location to another. Thus, the timeline of the user unfolds into a sequence of being still connected with transportations between them. For example, if one leaves their home in the morning, takes a bus to the office, works till noon and then goes to a cafe nearby, their timeline can be represented as a sequence $S(home) \rightarrow T(bus) \rightarrow S(work) \rightarrow T(walk) \rightarrow S(cafe)$. We call each such event $S$ a *stationary* and each $T$ a *transport*. Describing specific algorithms that detect stationaries and transports

**Fig. 1.** The Journeys app. The timeline screen shows the timeline for an entire day of the user including each location they visited and transport modes they used to move around. Here we show a correctly identified visit to a lunch place in Antwerp. Using the insights from the LCI model we can compute the 'moments' of the user (*Lunch* in this case)

are out of scope of this paper. What is important is that a stationary contains all spatial and temporal variables our model needs to run the inference: $S = (lat, lon, start, stop)$. For each stationary, the LCI model is applied in order to classify the stationary into one of the supported categories, such as *drink-day*, *drink-evening*, etc. We derive the categories based on the OpenStreetMap (OSM) tags attached to each venue. The full list of supported categories together with a short description and an example of a corresponding OSM tag is given in the Table 3. For this project, 27 location categories have been defined according the business requirements of the downstream products and they are described in more details further.

In order to infer a category of a location, we also need to obtain a set of candidate venues in a certain radius around the location. We call a component that provides a service for executing such queries a *venue provider*. The representation of the set of venue candidates in a form of features is called the *environment fingerprint*. Describing an implementation of a venue provider is out of scope of this paper, but it is important to mention that in order to guarantee that the location data never leave the user device, the venue provider should also be on-device.

It is important to clarify that the proposed model itself cannot guarantee user privacy. It merely facilitates the development of the mobile applications by letting the developers run inference on-device. In case of Sentiance in combination with the on-device implementation of the venue provider, we can guarantee that only approximate user locations are shared between the mobile app and the server. For example, we need to know that the user is somewhere around Brussels in order to query the locations in this large area and store them on-device to be served by the location provider. The data exchanged between the Sentiance SDK and the client app is abstracted away even further. The exact GPS coordinates are used by the SDK to run the model and only sequences of moments (*shopping, training*, etc) and segments (*shopaholic, sportive*, etc) would be emitted for the client app.

## 3    Methodology

We propose an end-to-end system that receives raw stationary events, runs clustering on the entire timeline, builds spatial histogram of venues, incorporates temporal models and finally outputs the category of the visited location. In this section we describe each of the steps and models used in them. A high-level overview of the entire pipeline is presented in Fig. 2.

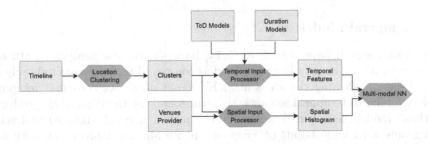

**Fig. 2.** Location category inference pipeline

### 3.1   Location Clustering

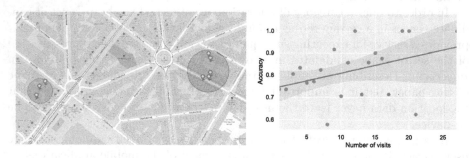

**Fig. 3.** Visualization of the location clustering action and its impact on the LCI model. We can see that as the cluster accumulates more repeated visits, the model has bigger chance to classify it correctly

A location clustering model should be able to answer a simple question: which of the stationary events in the user timeline correspond to visiting the same location. We hypothesise that by clustering separate locations and considering their centroids instead of raw GPS coordinates, we can average the noise out and get closer to the true location. In order to verify the anticipated relation, we studied how the accuracy of the LCI model changes depending on the size of the clusters on the same test set which we use for all the experiments described below. Figure 3 shows that there is indeed a positive correlation between the number of visits to the same location and the accuracy of the model.

Existing research on the topic of location clustering based on GPS coordinates shows that density-based clustering techniques work well for the task [3,15,16]. Following the ideas from these papers, we implement a version of DBSCAN compatible with tensorflow-lite and use the scikit-learn implementation of DBSCAN as a benchmark to make sure our model produces the same clusters on both synthetic and real-world data.

### 3.2   Temporal Models

Numerous research papers such as [5,14] have shown how temporal data can improve location category inference models compared to those that only rely on spatial data. Following the ideas of McKenzie et al. [5] we construct temporal models similar to temporal semantic signatures and use the likelihoods produced by these models as input features for the neural network. Instead of having histograms with wide bands of 1 day or 1 h, we aim for more granularity and fit a kernel density estimation (KDE) model per category. Each KDE model represents the likelihood of being at location of the corresponding category at the given time of day for each day and each time bin of 12 min. In Fig. 4 we

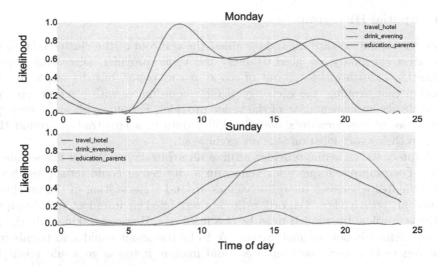

**Fig. 4.** Example of ToD models for Monday and Sunday for *drink-evening, education-parents* and *travel-hotel*

can see Monday and Sunday time of day models for 3 different categories *drink-evening, education-parents* and *travel-hotel*. We can clearly see that those models successfully captured the visiting patterns for each of the categories. For example, the *education-parents* on Monday has two spikes: one early in the morning and around 16:00. Those are typical hours of bringing children to school and picking them up once their classes finish. The corresponding curve on Sunday is almost flat which is expected as the schools are closed on Sunday.

Unlike with other check-in data sets [6,7], we have access to both start time and the duration of stay for each stationary event in the data set. Thus, we apply the same technique to build temporal signatures based on duration as well. Figure 5 shows an example of the duration models for the same three categories. A vivid example of its potential impact is the model for *travel-hotel*: it has a second spike around 8 h and it will yield much larger likelihood values for longer durations than the other two models.

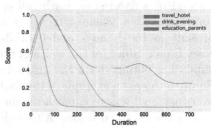

**Fig. 5.** Example of duration models for *drink-evening, education-parents* and *travel-hotel*. Duration is measured in minutes.

## 3.3    Spatial Histogram

Once we computed clusters and obtained the centroid of the cluster related to the latest stationary, we need to query the venue provider. Discussing implementation of such queries is out of scope of this paper, but it's important to mention that avoiding the exchange of GPS coordinates with a server requires an on-device implementation of the venue provider. For our application we populate a local on-device database with OSM data in a large radius around the user, so their exact location is never exchanged.

A query to the venue provider returns an arbitrary number of venue candidates. For example, a query for venues in a city center could return hundreds of candidates whereas a query for venues around a gas station in the outskirts would only return a few. Tensorflow-lite is a restricted environment and the input to the tensorflow-lite models must be of a fixed size. However, taking only the $N$ nearest venues is not optimal. Setting $N$ to be too small would lead to missing true venues in densely built-up areas and making it too large would result in unnecessary computations.

We solve this technical issue by encoding the venue candidates into a fixed-size table called spatial histogram. Every column in this table corresponds to a venue category and each row is a band of distances. Since the true venue is more likely to be among the candidates located closer to the centroid than those further away, a logarithmic scale is used instead of a fixed step. Each cell $c_{ij}$ contains 1 if a venue category $j$ is present in the band $i$ and 0 otherwise. Exact values for the width of the

**Fig. 6.** Example of encoding environment fingerprint of arbitrary size into a fixed-size spatial histogram

bands are obtained via the grid search at a hyper-parameter fine-tuning step. Figure 6 shows an example of the spatial histogram construction. Another option we considered was to count a number of venues per category per band and normalize the obtained values. Although intuitively it should provide richer context to the model, in reality our experiments did not show improvements compared to the indicator values described above. Conversely, this led to faster overfitting. We hypothesise that the main obstacle here is the size of the data set which makes each environment fingerprint constructed with counters rather unique and does not let the model generalise.

## 3.4   Location Category Inference Model

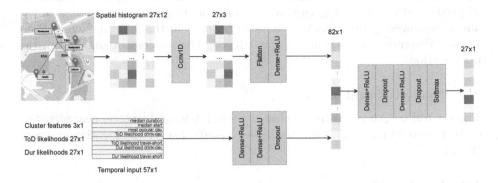

**Fig. 7.** Architecture of the Location Category Inference NN model

The output of the spatial histogram encoding procedure described above is passed to the neural network as it is. In order to complete the discussion of data preparation for the multi-modal NN model, we need to explain how the temporal input is constructed. We can think of each time of day model as a function that maps a triplet of $(category, day, hour)$ to the corresponding likelihood: $tod : (category, day, hour) \rightarrow \mathbb{R}$. The duration model can be defined similarly: $dur : (category, duration) \rightarrow \mathbb{R}$. We precomputed seven tables for time of day models per day of week and one table for the duration models. For each training sample we simply query the corresponding time of day table and the duration table to obtain 27 time of day and 27 duration likelihoods and concatenate them into a single vector together with cluster features. The resulting vector is visualized on the Fig. 7 as the 'Temporal Input'

Since temporal features are encoded as a one-dimensional vector and the spatial histogram is two-dimensional, we build a multi-modal neural network which has two separate inputs. Temporal features are processed with a small fully-connected neural network, whereas the spatial histogram is first processed with a 1D convolutional layer with 3 filters and then flattened. Vector representations of both temporal and spatial features are then concatenated into a single vector which is further processed by few more dense layers. The last layer is a softmax layer which represents probabilities assigned by the neural network to each of the supported categories. Figure 7 visualizes the architecture of the NN.

## 4   Experiments

The model is trained, fine-tuned and evaluated on a data set of 25709 clusters labelled via the feedback functionality of the Journeys app discussed above. The data set spans 64 different countries but is imbalanced and the majority of records come from the US and Europe. For the experiments we set a fixed 10%

subset of our data aside for evaluation. A stratified split was applied to ensure that the class imbalance in both training and evaluation are similar. We train and validate each model as a multi-class classifier that should predict one of the 27 predefined location categories. We use 4 metrics to judge the models: *accuracy* and macro-averaged *precision*, *recall* and *f1 score*. In the following subsections we will describe how each model was trained. The results are analysed in the next section.

## 4.1 Nearest Neighbor

The nearest neighbor is a trivial classifier which selects the venue nearest to the cluster centroid and uses it's category as a prediction for the location category (Fig. 8).

## 4.2 Random Forest

In order to compare our model against best models of other classes, Random Forest (RF) has been selected as the best candidate. RF as well as ensemble models based on gradient boosting, are known to perform well in classification tasks on tabular data in general and for the LCI task specifically. Alsudais et al. apply RF to infer categories of locations where users tweeted from [2]. In a more recent study Kim et al. apply RF to infer location categories based on a variety of personal data such as age, gender, hobby, etc. [12]. RF is also relevant for this study since it is widely adopted in the industry.

**Fig. 8.** Vector of features for the Random Forest model

The current cloud-based service used in production at Sentiance features a large RF model. To train our version of RF LCI model, we transform the data set into a tabular form where each row represents a cluster. For that, we transform the spatial histogram into a simplified version where we only keep the distance to the nearest venue of each category.

## 4.3 Simple Fully-Connected Neural Network

In order to verify that our multi-modal architecture justifies additional complexity, we also train a simple fully-connected network. We reuse the tabular dataset produced for the RF model, but we additionally apply standard feature normalization for *median-duration*, *median-start-hour*, *most-popular-day* and the distance-based features by dividing each feature by the corresponding maximal value. To address the problem of overfitting, aggressive regularization is applied. We use $l_2$ regularization with the $l_2$-weight $w = 0.01$ on each dense layer and also add dropout layers after each dense layer with the dropout-rate $\alpha = 0.4$ which is similar to the regularization used for the multi-modal NN. Early-stopping is used based on the value of the loss function on the dev set which is 15% of the training data set. Class weights are computed similar to the multi-modal NN model.

## 4.4  Multi-modal Neural Network

A series of experiments have been conducted to fine-tune hyperparameters and avoid overfitting. First, a model without any regularization has been trained and proved to overfit quickly. We searched for optimal values for the $l_2$-weight $w$ in range $[10^{-5}, 10^{-1}]$ and obtained best results with $w = 0.01$. For the dropout-rate hyperparameter we searched in range $[0.1, 0.5]$. Larger dropout-rates allow training larger models without overfitting and for our model the optimal value was $\alpha = 0.4$. Increasing it leads to overfitting whereas increasing the model size does not yield any improvements in terms of validation metrics. Finally, early stopping based on the value of the change of the loss on the validation dataset is applied with the patience factor of 100.

Location-based data with true labels for visited venues are imbalanced by nature: people visit venues of certain categories more often than others. Willingness to share personal visits is also biased towards more popular venues such as restaurants and bars. Table 1 shows the class imbalance in our data set. In order to overcome this issue, we compute the standard class weights computation procedure as defined in scikit-learn and specify these weights during the training.

**Table 1.** Each cell contains a category supported by the model and the number of examples of that category in the dataset. The classes are highly imbalanced and this problem will be discussed further.

| | | | | | |
|---|---|---|---|---|---|
| drink-day | 367 | leisure-museum | 213 | shop-short | 2481 |
| drink-evening | 830 | leisure-nature | 52 | sport | 946 |
| education-independent | 175 | leisure-park | 901 | sport-attend | 65 |
| education-parents | 618 | office | 2579 | travel-bus | 675 |
| health | 459 | religion | 247 | travel-conference | 6 |
| industrial | 32 | residential | 290 | travel-fill | 1395 |
| leisure-beach | 87 | resto-mid | 2446 | travel-hotel | 682 |
| leisure-day | 68 | resto-short | 363 | travel-long | 1123 |
| leisure-evening | 272 | shop-long | 3741 | travel-short | 1971 |

## 4.5  Post-training Quantization

Additionally, we investigated different options to optimise the size and the inference time of the model by applying various post-training quantization methods available in tensorflow-lite. We experimented with 3 methods: *dynamic range quantization, integer with float fallback quantization* and *float16 quantization*. In general, post-training quantization is a technique that aims to improve the runtime characteristics of models, such as size and time of inference, by representing weights of the model as simpler numeric types in exchange for less precision. Ideally, the goal is to reduce the size and the inference run time while the performance of the model is reduced only slightly.

Dynamic range quantization applies dynamic conversion to 8-bit integer precision for activations and weights manipulations while storing outputs with floating-point numbers. Full-integer quantization with float fallback further aims to guarantee to convert all mathematical operations to 8-bit precision. The *float fallback* is used only if a certain operation is not implemented for integer numeric types. Float16 quantization represents all numbers as float16 numbers, thus significantly reducing the size of the model while minimizing the performance reduction.

For each of the quantization techniques mentioned above we measured the mean run time of the tensorflow-lite *invoke()* method, the size of the data-only buffers and the f1-score on the test data set. Table 4 contains all measurements and can be found in the appendix. Although quantization would allow us significantly reduce the size of the model (up to 93%) and in the speed of the calculations (up to 51%), we also observe severe performance reductions. Given these results, we recommend using the unoptimized model for mobile applications targeting modern smartphones.

## 5   Results and Discussion

Table 2 shows the results for each model. Due to the class imbalance problem, the accuracy score alone is not enough to compare the models. A model that trades off recall on the less presented classes to increase its accuracy and precision, for example, would lead to poor user experience on each of the classes underrepresented in the training data set. For that reason, the f1 score is considered more important for the current study.

- 1-NearestNeighbor achieves 68.9% accuracy and 64.4% f1 score. To the best of our knowledge, this is significantly larger than in the previous research. For example, Shaw et al. report only 20%, although it is important to notice that in their research the exact venue is predicted and not only its category.
- As expected, Random Forest performs significantly better than the benchmark in terms of accuracy (+7.2%). It is important to notice, however, that the f1 score gain is much lower (+2.2%). Due to the imbalanced classes, Random Forest achieves the best precision of all the models, but the recall is significantly low.
- The naive NN fails to achieve the performance of Random Forest and shows performance similar to the baseline model.
- The multi-modal architecture we propose performs significantly better than the competitors. It is on par with the Random Forest model in terms of accuracy, while achieving the best recall score, which gives the f1 score of 73.2% which is 6.6% better than that of the Random Forest.
- The multi-modal NN model only weighs 1.9Mb whereas a serialized version of the random forest weighs 364Mb.

**Table 2.** Comparison of the models on accuracy, precision, recall and the f1 score. The latter is more important as it depends on both precision and recall.

| Model | Accuracy | Precision | Recall | F Score |
|---|---|---|---|---|
| 1-NearestNeighbor | 68.9 | 62.5 | 71.2 | 64.4 |
| Naive NN | 67.6 | 62.0 | 71.7 | 64.5 |
| RandomForest | 75.7 | 81.8 | 61.5 | 66.6 |
| Multi-modal NN | 76.4 | 75.2 | 72.2 | 73.2 |

## 6  Related Work

The problem addressed in this paper has many variations and is also known under different names. Yi et al. propose an LCI model that shows promising results [14]. The main difference of our model is that it is lightweight and can be used on-device. The authors also mention extremely high location estimation uncertainty in their data set, which is not the case for the data we collected. McKenzie et al. address the problem of mapping the user location to a specific venue under the name of 'reverse geocoding' [5]. We reused their ideas on constructing temporal signatures with some changes geared towards more granularity in time resolution and used KDE models instead of raw histograms to avoid having underrepresented time bands. Shaw et al. pose a similar problem as learning to rank [1]. The main difference is in the application domain: we are interested in fully autonomous prediction of a single category whereas [1] aim to select top-N candidates and let the user pick the correct one.

He et al. are solving a very similar problem but from a recommendation systems point of view [9]. PoI recommendation seems to be the most actively studied setting with respect to the LCI problem and Islam et al. [18] provide an overview of the most recent advancements in this field with deep learning techniques. Bao et al. also produced a survey on recommendations in location-based services without a specific focus on deep learning [4]. Duan et al. apply recurrent neural networks to build embeddings of user locations and predict the next visited PoI [11]. We also learn representations of user locations, but the main difference is that we only use geospatial data for that, whereas Duan et al. mix in some data on the user and textual data on the location. Another difference is that the nature of the data set available for our experiments does not allow us to benefit from the main strengths of RNNs. We only have access to the aggregated cluster-level data set where the sequential patterns of transitions between stationaries are lost.

Angmo et al. study the impact of clustering on identifying significant locations from spatio-temporal data and propose improvements for the classical DBSCAN algorithm [16]. Due to the specific features of the data set, authors use rather large values for the minimum number of points in a cluster - 50, 80, 100. For our model, we set this parameter to 1, since even a single visit to a location matters and we do not have any a-priori assumptions about this feature of the data set. Andrade et al. also study DBSCAN for location clustering and introduce a new variation of DBSCAN for spatio-temporal data that derives significant locations [15]. They also apply Gaussian Mixture Models on the obtained clusters in order to derive habits of the users. Given the success of density-based clustering techniques on this task, we also applied DBSCAN for location clustering.

Some researchers address the LCI problem but with the data sets enriched with data inaccessible to us. Kim and Song successfully apply random forest models to predict categories of visited venues based on fusion of location data and personal data such as *age, job, salary*, etc. [12]. Alsudais et al. also train random forest models for the same problem, but they mix in textual data from the tweets of the users. We take inspiration from these results and train our own version of a random forest model to challenge the multi-modal neural network.

Another interesting study related to building embeddings is DeepCity [8]. The authors propose a framework that can learn embeddings for both locations and users by utilizing task specific random walks on a bipartite graph. As one of the use cases, they consider location category prediction. The embeddings learned by the DeepCity model are passed to a task-specific classifier model. Unfortunately, the size of the embeddings table is prohibitively large for our use case.

## 7   Conclusion

In this paper we present an on-device multi-modal neural network model for the location category inference problem which outperforms large ensemble based models while being lightweight and embeddable into mobile applications. We present a simple yet effective method to incorporate both spatial and temporal features - temporal models and the spatial histogram. Due to this method, our model performs significantly better than a naive neural network which utilizes simpler representation for its input data.

# A    Appendix

**Table 3.** Full list of location categories.

| Category | Description | Example OSM tag |
|---|---|---|
| drink-day | Coffee bars and tea rooms | amenity:cafe |
| drink-evening | Bars and pubs | amenity:bar |
| education-independent | Educational centers for adults, universities | building:university |
| education-parents | Primary schools and kindergartens | amenity:kindergarten |
| health-long | Hospitals | amenity:hospital |
| health-short | Dentists and GP's | amenity:dentist |
| industrial | Factories and warehouses | building:industrial |
| leisure-beach | Beaches and resorts | leisure:beach |
| leisure-day | Day-time entertainments | sport:paintball |
| leisure-evening | Evening entertainments | amenity:cinema |
| leisure-museum | Museums | tourism:museum |
| leisure-nature | Nature reserves | leisure:fishing |
| leisure-park | City parks and gardens | leisure:park |
| office | Office buildings | building:office |
| religion | Monasteries, abbeys | building:cathedral |
| residential | Residential buildings, houses | building:apartments |
| resto-mid | Restaurants | amenity:food_court |
| resto-short | Fast food, sandwich bars | amenity:ice_cream |
| shop-long | Malls, shopping centers | shop:mall |
| shop-short | Small local shops, bakeries | shop:bakery |
| sport | Gyms, sport centers | leisure:fitness_center |
| sport-attend | Stadiums | building:stadium |
| travel-bus | Bus stops | highway:bus_stop |
| travel-conference | Conference halls | amenity:conference_centre |
| travel-fill | Gas stations | amenity:fuel |
| travel-hotel | Hotels and B&B's | building:hotel |
| travel-long | Airports | aeroway:airport |
| travel-short | Public transport stations | station:subway |

**Table 4.** Comparison of quantization techniques. We report the size of the data-only buffers in bytes, f1 score of the model and the mean run time of inference in milliseconds

| Quantization | Size | F1 score | Time |
|---|---|---|---|
| Unoptimized | 314513 | 73.2 | 0.035 |
| Dynamic range | 23143 | 65.7 | 0.018 |
| Integer with fallback | 23071 | 63.3 | 0.027 |
| Float16 | 44217 | 65.9 | 0.02 |

# References

1. Shaw, B., Shea, J., Sinha, S., Hogue, A.: Learning to rank for spatiotemporal search. In: WSDM 2013 (2013). https://doi.org/10.1145/2433396.2433485
2. Alsudais, A., Leroy, G., Corso, A.: We know where you are tweeting from: assigning a type of place to tweets using natural language processing and random forests. In: 2014 IEEE International Congress on Big Data, pp. 594–600 (2014). https://doi.org/10.1109/BigData.Congress.2014.91. ISSN 2379-7703
3. Sabatelli, M., Osmani, V., Mayora, O., Gruenerbl, A., Lukowicz, P.: Correlation of significant places with self-reported state of bipolar disorder patients. In: 2014 4th International Conference on Wireless Mobile Communication and Healthcare - Transforming Healthcare Through Innovations in Mobile and Wireless Technologies (MOBIHEALTH), pp. 116–119 (2014). https://doi.org/10.1109/MOBIHEALTH. 2014.7015923
4. Bao, J., Zheng, Yu., Wilkie, D., Mokbel, M.: Recommendations in location-based social networks: a survey. GeoInformatica **19**(3), 525–565 (2015). https://doi.org/ 10.1007/s10707-014-0220-8
5. McKenzie, G., Janowicz, K.: Where is also about time: a location-distortion model to improve reverse geocoding using behavior-driven temporal semantic signatures. Comput. Environ. Urban Syst. **54**, 1–13 (2015). https://doi.org/10.1016/ j.compenvurbsys.2015.05.003
6. Yang, D., Zhang, D., Chen, L., Qu, B.: NationTelescope: monitoring and visualizing large-scale collective behavior in LBSNs. J. Netw. Comput. Appl. **55**, 170–180 (2015). https://doi.org/10.1016/j.jnca.2015.05.010. ISSN 1084-8045
7. Yang, D., Zhang, D., Qu, B.: Participatory cultural mapping based on collective behavior data in location-based social networks. ACM Trans. Intell. Syst. Technol. **7**(3), 30:1–30:23 (2016). https://doi.org/10.1145/2814575. ISSN 2157-6904
8. Pang, J., Zhang, Y.: DeepCity: a feature learning framework for mining location check-ins. In: Eleventh International AAAI Conference on Web and Social Media (2017)
9. He, J., Li, X., Liao, L., Cheung, W.K.: Personalized next Point-of-Interest Recommendation via Latent Behavior Patterns Inference (2018). arXiv:1805.06316
10. Keßler, C., McKenzie, G.: A geoprivacy manifesto. Trans. GIS **22**(1), 3–19 (2018). https://doi.org/10.1111/tgis.12305. ISSN 1467-9671
11. Duan, Y., Lu, W., Xing, W., Bao, P., Wei, X.: PBEM: a pattern-based embedding model for user location category prediction. In: 2019 Twelfth International Conference on Mobile Computing and Ubiquitous Network (ICMU), pp. 1–6 (2019). https://doi.org/10.23919/ICMU48249.2019.9006662
12. Kim, Y.M., Song, H.Y.: Analysis of relationship between personal factors and visiting places using random forest technique. In: 2019 Federated Conference on Computer Science and Information Systems (FedCSIS), pp. 725–732 (2019). https:// doi.org/10.15439/2019F318. ISSN 2300-5963
13. Wongvibulsin, S., Martin, S., Saria, S., Zeger, S., Murphy, S.: An individualized, data-driven digital approach for precision behavior change. Am. J. Lifestyle Med. **14**, 155982761984348 (2019). https://doi.org/10.1177/1559827619843489
14. Yi, J., Lei, Q., Gifford, W.M., Liu, J., Yan, J., Zhou, B.: Fast unsupervised location category inference from highly inaccurate mobility data. In: Proceedings of the 2019 SIAM International Conference on Data Mining (SDM), Proceedings, pp. 55–63. Society for Industrial and Applied Mathematics (2019). https://doi.org/10.1137/ 1.9781611975673.7

15. Andrade, T., Cancela, B., Gama, J.: Mining human mobility data to discover locations and habits. In: Cellier, P., Driessens, K. (eds.) ECML PKDD 2019. CCIS, vol. 1168, pp. 390–401. Springer, Cham (2020). https://doi.org/10.1007/978-3-030-43887-6_32

16. Angmo, R., Aggarwal, N., Mangat, V., Lal, A., Kaur, S.: An improved clustering approach for identifying significant locations from spatio-temporal data. Wireless Pers. Commun. **121**(1), 985–1009 (2021). https://doi.org/10.1007/s11277-021-08668-w

17. De Maio, C., Gallo, M., Hao, F., Yang, E.: Who and where: context-aware advertisement recommendation on Twitter. Soft. Comput. **25**(1), 379–387 (2020). https://doi.org/10.1007/s00500-020-05147-5

18. Islam, M.A., Mohammad, M.M., Das, S.S.S., Ali, M.E.: A survey on deep learning based point-of-interest (POI) recommendations. Neurocomputing **472**, 306–325 (2022). https://doi.org/10.1016/j.neucom.2021.05.114. ISSN 0925-2312

19. McKenzie, G., Romm, D., Zhang, H., Brunila, M.: PrivyTo: a privacy-preserving location-sharing platform. Trans. GIS **26**(4), 1703–1717 (2022). https://doi.org/10.1111/tgis.12924

20. Zhang, H., McKenzie, G.: Rehumanize geoprivacy: from disclosure control to human perception. GeoJournal **88**(1), 189–208 (2022). https://doi.org/10.1007/s10708-022-10598-4. ISSN 1572-9893

21. Sentiance journeys app for android. https://play.google.com/store/apps/details?id=com.sentiance.journeys. Accessed 01 Apr 2023

22. Sentiance journeys app for IoS. https://apps.apple.com/be/app/journeys-by-sentiance/id984087229. Accessed 01 Apr 2023

# Specificity and Context Dependent Preferences in Argumentation Systems

Nico Roos[(⊠)]

Department of Advanced Computing Sciences, Maastricht University,
P.O.Box 616, 6200 MD Maastricht, The Netherlands
roos@maastrichtuniversity.nl
https://dke.maastrichtuniversity.nl/nico.roos/

**Abstract.** Dung and Son [6] argue that *specificity* as a criterion for resolving conflicts between arguments, is context dependent. They propose to use arguments to address the context dependency of specificity in combination with a new special argumentation semantics. Unfortunately, their solution is restricted to argumentation systems without undercutting arguments. This paper presents a more general solution which allows for undercutting arguments and allows for any argumentation semantics. Moreover, the solution is applicable to any form a context dependent preferences.

**Keywords:** specificity · argumentation · context dependent preferences

## 1 Introduction

*Specificity.* Dung and Son [6] argue that *specificity* as a criterion for resolving conflicts between arguments, is context dependent. They illustrate their point with the following example:

1. Students are normally not married.
2. Students are normally young adults.
3. Young adults are adults.
4. Adults are normally married.

The first and the fourth sentence support contradictory conclusions. Given that someone is a student, we can construct an argument for *being an adult*. Therefore, *being a student* is more specific than *being an adult*, implying that the first sentence is preferred to the fourth sentence [6,10,18,19]. However, knowing that someone *is a student and an adult but not a young adult*, the specificity preference should not be valid.

The solution that Dung and Son [6] propose, is:

1. to represent an argument by the defeasible sentences (the defeasible rules) used to derive a conclusion,

T. Calders et al. (Eds.): BNAIC/Benelearn 2022, CCIS 1805, pp. 112–132, 2023.
https://doi.org/10.1007/978-3-031-39144-6_8

2. to let an argument attack a defeasible rule instead of other arguments,
3. to register the argument for a rule to be more specific than another rule (the argument for the antecedent of the more general rule given the antecedent of the more specific rule), and
4. to attack the more general rule based on specificity.

Applying this solution to the above example, the second sentence forms the argument that the first sentence is more specific that the fourth sentence. If a student is an adult but not a young adult, the second sentence is not applicable (is attacked and defeated), and therefore the argument that the first sentence is more specific than the fourth sentence, is not valid. Note that the first and fourth sentence attack each other (rebuttal) and that the attack on the fourth sentence based on specificity, ensures that the more general sentence (rule) is defeated if the specificity argument is valid.

A problem with the solution of Dung and Son [6] is that it fails to handle undercutting attacks correctly. Suppose that the first sentence is not applicable for students from the country Utopia, and that we model this with an undercutting attack. Given a student from Utopia, the first sentence in not applicable, but because the first sentence is more specific than the fourth sentence, indirectly, it still successfully attacks the fourth sentence. This is not what we expect. The cause of the problem is that an attack based on specificity only considers whether the situation in the first sentence (the antecedent of the first rule) is more specific than the situation in the fourth sentence (the antecedent of the fourth rule). It does not consider whether the more specific sentence (rule) is applicable. Without undercutting attacks, this is not a problem because any attacking argument will support the opposite conclusion. Consider for instance the sentence: "Students from Utopia are normally married".

To address the above outlined problem, we will investigate the following solution:

– We use an argumentation system which handles arguments for inconsistencies by constructing undercutting arguments that attack the application of defeasible rules used in the arguments for inconsistencies [18,19]. This approach is in line with the solution of Dung and Son [6] where a set of defeasible rules represents the argument that attacks a defeasible rule. An advantage of this argumentation system is the existence of a semantic tableau method for generating arguments [21].
– We explicitly *assume the absence* of a preference when we construct undercutting arguments that resolve derived conflicts (inconsistencies). In case of the above example, we assume: "Students are normally not married" **is not preferred to** "Adults are normally married", and assume: "Adults are normally married" **is not preferred to** "Students are normally not married". In the absence of preferences, multiple undercutting arguments may be formulated, which may result in multiple extension [18,19].
– We use explicit arguments for (specificity based) preferences. For instance an argument for: "Students are normally not married" **is preferred to** "Adults

are normally married". These arguments may attack the assumptions mentioned in the previous item.

*Context Dependent Preferences.* Specificity is a special case of context dependent preferences. Since a specificity preference is essentially not different from other context dependent preferences, the above outlined approach may also be used for general context dependent preferences. It will offer an alternate for several approaches described in the literature [7,11,14]. These approaches have in common that they use special procedures for handling the derived preferences.

– Prakken and Sartor [14] focus on the grounded semantics. They make use of the property that the least fixed point of the characteristic function can be computed by repeatedly applying the characteristic function, starting from the empty set, to the result from the previous application. Each application monotonically extends the set of 'justified arguments'. The justified preferences after one iteration are used by the characteristic function to determine justified arguments of the next iteration.

– Modgil [11] proposes a more general approach. He extends Dung's is argumentation framework in order to incorporate defeasible preferences over arguments. The preferences are used to introduce a defeat relation, which is an attack relation that is consistent with preferences supported by a set of arguments. This definition has been criticized by Amgoud and Vesic [1], who propose a modified definition that solves the problem they identified. Beside introducing a defeat relation, Modgil adapts Dung's definition [5] of an argument that is acceptable w.r.t. a set of arguments. Other definitions of Dung's argumentation semantics are not changed. Modgil's approach leaves open how preferences over defeasible rules are mapped to preferences over arguments.

– Dung et al. [7] present a different approach to handling defeasible preferences. They allow an argument for a preference between two rules, to attack an attack relation between two arguments that use the two rules, which they call *preference attacks*. This approach makes it possible to use a standard argumentation framework [5] given a set of preference arguments that we accept. To select the set of preference arguments that we accept, Dung et al. [7] formulate postulates for preference attacks and select the smallest set of arguments supporting preferences satisfying these postulates.

The main difference between the approach investigated in this paper and several other approaches is in the view of an argument. Following Dung [5], an argument is often viewed as an atom. Although this offers important advantages, one should keep in mind that an argument is defeasible because it is build using defeasible elements, usually, defeasible rules [18,19]. Preferences are not about arguments but about these defeasible elements. Therefore, an approach that focuses on these defeasible elements may have benefits over other approaches.

*Outline.* The next section describes the preliminaries. It introduces the arguments and the argumentation system used in the paper. Section 3 describes the handling of context dependent (specificity) preferences and Sect. 4 evaluates the proposed approach. Section 5 concludes the paper.

## 2    Preliminaries

This section presents the argumentation system that will be used in the discussion of a general solution for context dependent preferences, including specificity.

We assume a standard logic such as propositional or predicate logic. The language of the logic will be denoted by $\mathcal{L}$. We also assume that the language $\mathcal{L}$ contains the symbols $\top$ denoting *true*, and $\bot$ denoting *false*. In case of predicate logic, the set of ground terms is denoted by $\mathcal{G}$.

Since this paper focuses on using context dependent preferences for resolving conflicts between arguments, we need a definition of an argument. Toulmin [23] views an argument as a support for some *claim*. The support is grounded in *data*, and the relation between the data and the claim is the *warrant*. Here, we use the following definition.

**Definition 1.** *A pair $A = (\mathcal{S}, \varphi)$ is called an argument where $\varphi$ is said to be its conclusion, and $\mathcal{S}$ is a set said to be its support; its elements are called supporting elements. It is worthwhile observing here that this definition is very general and a many pairs might be qualified as arguments.*

In case of propositional and predicate logic, the support $\mathcal{S}$ is a set of propositions from the language $\mathcal{L}$. Generally, $\mathcal{S}$ contains the set of premises used to derive the supported proposition $\varphi$. So, $\mathcal{S} \vdash \varphi$. In special applications, such as Model-Based Diagnosis, we may restrict $\mathcal{S}$ to assumptions about the normal behavior of components.

We may extend a standard logic with a set of defeasible rules. Defeasible rules are of the form:

$$\varphi \rightsquigarrow \psi$$

in case of propositional logic, and of the form:

$$\varphi(\mathbf{x}) \rightsquigarrow \psi(\mathbf{x})$$

in case of predicate logic. Here, $\varphi$ is propositions from the language $\mathcal{L}$, $\psi$ is either a proposition from the language $\mathcal{L}$ or a negated defeasible rule of the form: $\mathbf{not}(\eta \rightsquigarrow \mu)$, and $\mathbf{x}$ is a sequence of free variables. The free variables denote a set of ground instances of the defeasible rule $\varphi(\mathbf{x}) \rightsquigarrow \psi(\mathbf{x})$. We do not use the universal quantifier because the rule is not a proposition that belongs to the language $\mathcal{L}$. It is an additional statement that need not be valid for every ground instance.

The defeasible rules $\varphi \rightsquigarrow \mathbf{not}(\eta \rightsquigarrow \mu)$ and $\varphi(\mathbf{x}) \rightsquigarrow \mathbf{not}(\eta(\mathbf{x}) \rightsquigarrow \mu(\mathbf{x}))$ are called *undercutting defeaters* [12]. These undercutting defeaters specify the conditions $\varphi$ and $\varphi(\mathbf{x})$ under which the defeasible rules $\eta \rightsquigarrow \mu$ and $\eta(\mathbf{x}) \rightsquigarrow \mu(\mathbf{x})$ respectively, are not applicable.

We use $\Sigma \subseteq \mathcal{L}$ to denote the set of available information and we use $D$ to denote the set of available rules. Moreover, we use $\overline{D} = \{\varphi(\mathbf{t}) \rightsquigarrow \psi(\mathbf{t}) \mid \varphi(\mathbf{x}) \rightsquigarrow \psi(\mathbf{x}) \in D, \mathbf{t} \in \mathcal{G}^n\}$ to denote the set of ground instances of the defeasible rules with $n$ free variables in case of predicate logic, and $\overline{D} = D$ in case of propositional logic.

Defeasible rules are used in the construction of arguments. Whenever we have a support $\mathcal{S}'$ for the antecedent $\varphi$ of a defeasible rule $\varphi \leadsto \psi$, we can create a supporting element $(\mathcal{S}', \varphi \leadsto \psi)$, which can be used to support $\psi$. The arguments that can be constructed are defined as:

**Definition 2.** *Let $\Sigma \subseteq \mathcal{L}$ be the initial information and let $D$ be a set of defeasible rules. An argument $A = (\mathcal{S}, \psi)$ with premises $\bar{A}$, defeasible rules $\tilde{A}$, last defeasible rules $\vec{A}$, supported proposition (claim/conclusion) $\hat{A}$, and supporting propositions $\hat{S}$ of $\hat{A}$, is recursively defined as:*

- *If $\psi \in \Sigma$, then $A = (\{\psi\}, \psi)$ is an argument.*
  $\bar{A} = \{\psi\}$.    $\tilde{A} = \varnothing$.    $\vec{A} = \varnothing$.    $\hat{A} = \psi$.    $\hat{S} = \{\psi\}$.
- *If $A_1 = (\mathcal{S}_1, \varphi_1), \ldots, A_k = (\mathcal{S}_k, \varphi_k)$ are arguments and $\{\varphi_1, \ldots, \varphi_k\} \vdash \psi$, then $A = (\mathcal{S}_1 \cup \cdots \cup \mathcal{S}_k, \psi)$.*
  $\bar{A} = \bar{A}_1 \cup \cdots \cup \bar{A}_k$.    $\tilde{A} = \tilde{A}_1 \cup \cdots \cup \tilde{A}_k$.    $\vec{A} = \vec{A}_1 \cup \cdots \cup \vec{A}_k$.    $\hat{A} = \psi$.
  $\hat{S} = \hat{S}_1 \cup \cdots \cup \hat{S}_k$.
- *If $A' = (\mathcal{S}', \varphi)$ is an argument and $\varphi \leadsto \psi \in D$ is a defeasible rule, then $A = (\{(\mathcal{S}', \varphi \leadsto \psi)\}, \psi)$ is an argument.*
  $\bar{A} = \bar{A}'$.    $\tilde{A} = \{\varphi \leadsto \psi\} \cup \tilde{A}'$.    $\vec{A} = \{\varphi \leadsto \psi\}$.    $\hat{A} = \psi$.    $\hat{S} = \{\psi\}$.

$A = (\mathcal{S}, \psi)$ *is a* minimal argument *iff (1) $\mathcal{S}$ is a minimal set such that $\hat{S} \vdash \psi$, and (2) for every $(\mathcal{S}', \alpha \leadsto \beta) \in \mathcal{S}$, $(\mathcal{S}', \alpha)$ is a minimal argument.*

Note that for every argument, there exists a corresponding minimal argument supporting the same conclusion.

This abstract representation of arguments is based on the representation of arguments proposed in [18,19]. It assumes that the derivation relation $\vdash$ of the underlying logic is sound and complete. This ensures that inconsistencies do not remain hidden because of the chosen formulation. A reasoning process, called an argumentation tableau, which is based on the construction of a semantic tableau, has been proposed for this argumentation system [21].

We will use a graphical representation of an argument for human readability. The argument for an inconsistency:

$$A = (\{(\{(\{p \vee q, \neg q\}, p \leadsto r), (\{s\}, s \leadsto t)\}, r \wedge t \leadsto u), \\ (\{v\}, v \leadsto w), \neg(u \wedge w)\}, \bot)$$

is graphically represented as:

$$A = \begin{bmatrix} \begin{matrix} p \vee q \\ \neg q \end{matrix} \Big| p \leadsto r & & \\ & \Big| r \wedge t \leadsto u & \\ s \vdash s \leadsto t & & \Big| \bot \\ & v \vdash v \leadsto w & \\ & \neg(u \wedge w) & \end{bmatrix}$$

Here, $\hat{A} = \bot$, $\vec{A} = \{r \wedge t \leadsto u, v \leadsto w\}$, $\tilde{A} = \{p \leadsto r, s \leadsto t, r \wedge t \leadsto u, v \leadsto w\}$, $\bar{A} = \{p \vee q, \neg q, s, v, \neg(u \wedge w)\}$ and $\hat{S} = \{u, w, \neg(u \wedge w)\}$ with $A = (\mathcal{S}, \bot)$. Note that we use $\vdash$ in the graphical representation to denote standard deduction. We will use $\not\models$ instead of $\vdash$ for derivations that are neither deductive nor the result of applying a defeasible rule, as in Definitions 3, 4 and 5.

When an argument for an inconsistency is derived[1], one of the defeasible rules is not applicable in the current context. If no defeasible rule is involved in the argument for the inconsistency, one of the premises is invalid. In both cases we will use a strict partial order $<$ on the defeasible rules $D$ and on the information in $\Sigma$ to determine the rule and premise that is invalid, respectively. Note that context dependent preferences will be added in subsequent sections and $<$ can be an empty set of preferences. Following [15–19], we formulate an *undercutting* argument for the culprit. That is, an argument attacking every argument that uses the culprit.[2]

**Definition 3.** *Let $A = (\mathcal{S}, \perp)$ be an argument for an inconsistency. Moreover, let $< \subseteq (\Sigma \times \Sigma) \cup (D \times D)$ be a strict partial order over the information $\Sigma$ and over the defeasible rules $D$. Finally, let $A' = (\mathcal{S}', \mathbf{not}(\varphi \rightsquigarrow \psi))$ and $A' = (\mathcal{S}', \mathbf{not}(\sigma))$ denote the arguments for an undercutting attack of a defeasible rule in $\overline{D}$ and a proposition in $\Sigma$ respectively.*

- *If $\bar{A} \neq \varnothing$,* **defeat the weakest last rule.** *For every $\varphi \rightsquigarrow \psi \in min_<(\vec{A})$ with $(\mathcal{S}'', \varphi \rightsquigarrow \psi) \in \mathcal{S}$, $A' = (\mathcal{S} \backslash (\mathcal{S}'', \varphi \rightsquigarrow \psi), \mathbf{not}(\varphi \rightsquigarrow \psi))$ is an undercutting argument of $\varphi \rightsquigarrow \psi \in \overline{D}$.*
- *If $\bar{A} = \varnothing$,* **defeat the weakest premise.** *For every $\sigma \in min_<(\bar{A})$, $A' = (\mathcal{S} \backslash \sigma, \mathbf{not}(\sigma))$ is an undercutting argument of $\sigma \in \Sigma$.*

Note that $min_<(\cdot)$ need not be unique because $<$ is a strict partial order. Also note that all undercutting arguments for elements in $min_<(\cdot)$ attack each other. Finally, note that $\mathcal{S} \backslash (\mathcal{S}', \varphi \rightsquigarrow \psi)$ is an argument for $\neg \psi$, and that $\mathcal{S} \backslash \sigma$ is an argument for $\neg \sigma$.

The undercutting arguments define an attack relation over the arguments. We denote the attack relation over a set of arguments $\mathcal{A}$ by $\longrightarrow \subseteq \mathcal{A} \times \mathcal{A}$. An undercutting argument $A = (\mathcal{S}, \mathbf{not}(\varphi \rightsquigarrow \psi))$ attacks every argument $A'$ for which $\varphi \rightsquigarrow \psi \in \bar{A}'$ holds. Moreover, an undercutting argument $A = (\mathcal{S}, \mathbf{not}(\sigma))$ attacks every argument $A'$ for which $\sigma \in \bar{A}'$ holds. We denote the attack of $A$ on $A'$ by $A \longrightarrow A'$. The set of all derived arguments $\mathcal{A}$ and the attack relation over the arguments $\longrightarrow \subseteq \mathcal{A} \times \mathcal{A}$ determine an instance of an argumentation framework $(\mathcal{A}, \longrightarrow)$ as defined by Dung [5]. We can use one the semantics for argumentation frameworks to determine sets of valid arguments; i.e., the argument extensions. See for instance: [2–5, 8, 9, 20, 24].

---

[1] Arguments for inconsistencies cover rebutting attacks.

[2] Note the difference between an undercutting argument and an undercutting defeater. The former is an argument for not using a proposition or a defeasible rule, and the latter is a defeasible rule specifying a condition under which another defeasible rule should not be used [12].

## 3  Context Dependent Preferences

We first address *specificity*, which is a specific form of context dependent preferences. Next we discuss general context dependent preferences. We conclude with a description of the changes to the argumentation system described in the previous section.

### 3.1  Specificity

Specificity is the principle by which rules applying to situations that are more specific, override those applying to situations that are more general. In other words, what holds in a specific situation may represent an exception on what holds in the more general situation. To determine whether we have a specificity preference between two defeasible rules, we must determine whether the situation in which one rule is applicable, implies the situation in which the other rule is applicable. For this we may use the general knowledge described by the defeasible rules $D$ and by the background knowledge $\mathcal{K} \subseteq \mathcal{L}$. Therefore, to determine whether a rule $\varphi \rightsquigarrow \psi$ is preferred to a rule $\eta \rightsquigarrow \mu$ based on a specificity preference, we have to check whether we can construct an argument for the antecedent $\eta$ given the antecedent $\varphi$, using the defeasible rules $D$ and by the background knowledge $\mathcal{K}$ [6,10,13,19,22].

Suppose that we have the defeasible rules $D = \{\varphi \rightsquigarrow \psi, \eta \rightsquigarrow \mu, \varphi \rightsquigarrow \eta\}$ with $\{\psi, \mu\} \cup \mathcal{K} \vdash \perp$. Then, assuming $\varphi$, we can construct an argument for $\eta$:

$$A^\eta = [\varphi \vdash \varphi \rightsquigarrow \eta \vdash \eta]$$

This implies that the situation described by $\varphi$ is more specific than the situation described by $\eta$, and therefore, $\varphi \rightsquigarrow \psi$ must be preferred to $\eta \rightsquigarrow \mu$ because of specificity [6,10,13,18,19,22]. Of course, we must make sure that the situation described by $\varphi$ is *strictly* more specific than the situation described by $\eta$. Therefore, given $\eta$, we should not be able to derive an argument for $\varphi$.

There are two aspects that we need to consider using this approach. First, for no sub-argument $A' = (\mathcal{S}', \alpha)$ of $A^\eta$, $\hat{\mathcal{S}}'$ may be inconsistency [6]. If $\hat{\mathcal{S}}'$ is inconsistent, a rule in $\vec{A}'$, and therefore a rule in $\tilde{A}^\eta$ must be defeated. To give an illustration, the following specificity argument for $\eta$ is *not* allowed:

$$A^\eta = \left[ \begin{array}{c} \varphi \vdash \varphi \rightsquigarrow \alpha \vdash \alpha \rightsquigarrow \neg\beta \\ \varphi \vdash \varphi \rightsquigarrow \beta \end{array} \middle| \eta \right]$$

Second, the specificity argument $A^\eta$ supporting that $\varphi \rightsquigarrow \psi$ is preferred to $\eta \rightsquigarrow \mu$ may not be defeated by another argument [6]. Repeating the example mention in the Introduction, suppose that we have the defeasible rules: students are normally not married, students are normally young adults, and adults are normally married.

$$student \rightsquigarrow \neg married$$
$$student \rightsquigarrow young\ adult$$
$$adult \rightsquigarrow married$$

The first and the last rule support conflicting conclusions. Since being a student is more specific than being a young adult, which is more specific than being an adult, the first rule should be preferred to the last rule.

$$A = [student \vdash student \rightsquigarrow young\ adult \vdash adult]$$

However, if we know that someone is a student and an adult but not a young adult, then this specificity preference is no longer valid for this student.

The following definition specifies the argument for the specificity preference.

**Definition 4.** *Let $D$ be a set of defeasible rules, let $\mathcal{K} \subseteq \Sigma$ be the background knowledge, let $\varphi \rightsquigarrow \psi, \eta \rightsquigarrow \mu$ be two rules in $\overline{D}$, and let $A^\varphi = (S^\varphi, \varphi)$ be an argument for $\varphi$.*

*$A = (S, \eta \rightsquigarrow \mu < \varphi \rightsquigarrow \psi)$ is an argument for preferring $\varphi \rightsquigarrow \psi$ to $\eta \rightsquigarrow \mu$ based on specificity if and only if*

- *given the information $\{\varphi\} \cup \mathcal{K}$, there exists an argument $A^\eta = (S^\eta, \eta)$ (note that $\bar{A}^\eta \subseteq \{\varphi\} \cup \mathcal{K}$),*
- *for **no** sub-argument $A' = (S', \alpha)$ of $A^\eta$, $\hat{S}' \vdash \perp$,*
- *given the information $\{\eta\} \cup \mathcal{K}$, there **does not** exists an argument $A' = (S,' \varphi)$ (note that $\bar{A}' \subseteq \{\eta\} \cup \mathcal{K}$), and*
- *$S$ is the result of replacing every occurrence of $\varphi$ in the support $S^\eta$ by the support $S^\varphi$.*

Since $\varphi$ may not be part of the given information (i.e., $\varphi \notin \Sigma$), the last item in the above definition ensures that we have a proper argument for the specificity preference.

As an illustration, consider the defeasible rules $D = \{\alpha \rightsquigarrow \varphi, \varphi \rightsquigarrow \psi, \varphi \rightsquigarrow \eta, \eta \rightsquigarrow \neg\psi\}$ and the available information $\Sigma = \{\alpha\}$. Given $\varphi$, we can derive the argument $A^\eta = [\varphi \vdash \varphi \rightsquigarrow \eta \vdash \eta]$. Clearly, $\bar{A}^\eta \subseteq \{\varphi\} \cup \mathcal{K}$. Moreover, $A^\eta$ has no sub-arguments supporting an inconsistency, and we cannot derive an argument $A'$ for $\varphi$ with $\bar{A}' \subseteq \{\eta\} \cup \mathcal{K}$. Therefore, $\varphi \rightsquigarrow \psi$ is preferred to $\eta \rightsquigarrow \neg\psi$ based on specificity. Using the argument $A^\varphi = [\alpha \vdash \alpha \rightsquigarrow \varphi \vdash \varphi]$, we can construct the following argument for this preference:[3]

$$A = [\alpha \vdash \alpha \rightsquigarrow \varphi \vdash \varphi \rightsquigarrow \eta \,\flat\, \eta \rightsquigarrow \mu < \varphi \rightsquigarrow \psi]$$

There are two practical issue concerning Definition 4 that we need to address. Definition 4 contains a consistency test and a derivability test. Both tests can easily be carried out for proposition logic, for instance using the argumentation tableau [21]. However, since predicate logic is semi-decidable, these tests raise a problem. Fortunately, an argumentation based approach offers a solution. Because in the last item of Definition 4, we construct a proper argument $A = (S, \eta \rightsquigarrow \mu < \varphi \rightsquigarrow \psi)$ for the specificity preference of which the premises $\bar{A}$

---

[3] In argument $A$ we use the symbol $\flat$ to indicate that the preference $\eta \rightsquigarrow \mu < \varphi \rightsquigarrow \psi$ does not deductively follow from $\eta$ in the support: $S = [\alpha \vdash \alpha \rightsquigarrow \varphi \vdash \varphi \rightsquigarrow \eta]$.

are a subset of the given information $\Sigma$, for each sub-argument of $A^\eta$ supporting an inconsistency, there is a corresponding sub-argument of $A$ supporting an inconsistency. When this sub-argument is derived, Definition 3 is applied ensuring that this inconsistency is avoided, thereby addressing the consistency test.

The derivability test, needed to ensure that the specificity preference is strict, forms a bigger challenge. We can address it by adding to the definition of the preference argument $A$ in Definition 4, the *assumption*, denoted by the keyword **assume**, that there is no valid preference for the opposite. If we do derive an argument for such a preference, it will attack argument $A$. Based on the above suggested ways to handle the two issues, we modify Definition 4.

**Definition 5 (Definition 4 revised).** *Let $D$ be a set of defeasible rules, let $\mathcal{K} \subseteq \Sigma$ be the background knowledge, let $\varphi \rightsquigarrow \psi, \eta \rightsquigarrow \mu$ be two rules in $\overline{D}$, and let $A^\varphi = (S^\varphi, \varphi)$ be an argument for $\varphi$. Moreover, let **assume**$(X)$ denote the defeasible assumption that $X$ holds.*

$$A = (S \cup \{assume(\varphi \rightsquigarrow \psi \not< \eta \rightsquigarrow \mu)\}, \eta \rightsquigarrow \mu < \varphi \rightsquigarrow \psi)$$

*is an argument for preferring $\varphi \rightsquigarrow \psi$ to $\eta \rightsquigarrow \mu$ based on specificity if and only if*

- *given the information $\{\varphi\} \cup \mathcal{K}$, there exists an argument $A^\eta = (S^\eta, \eta)$ (note that $\bar{A}^\eta \subseteq \{\varphi\} \cup \mathcal{K}$), and*
- *$S$ is the result of replacing every occurrence of $\varphi$ in the support $S^\eta$ by the support $S^\varphi$.*

## 3.2 General Context Dependent Preferences

The previous subsection introduced arguments for specificity-based preferences. By allowing rules that specify preferences between defeasible rules in $\overline{D}$ or between initial information $\Sigma$, we enable the derivation of arguments supporting other types of preferences. There are different ways in which we can introduce rules that specify preferences. Here, we choose to extend the definition of a defeasible rule. Alternative choices are special strict rules, or even extending set of atomic propositions used to define the language $\mathcal{L}$ with special atomic propositions that specify preferences between rules in $D$ or between information in $\Sigma$. The first alternative is not considered here because it requires a new type of rules that is not a part of the recursive definition of the language $\mathcal{L}$, and the second alternative is not considered because it introduces more expressiveness than needed. So, we allow for additional defeasible rules in $D$ of the form:

$$\alpha \rightsquigarrow (\eta \rightsquigarrow \mu < \varphi \rightsquigarrow \psi) \quad \text{and} \quad \alpha(\mathbf{x}) \rightsquigarrow (\eta(\mathbf{x}) \rightsquigarrow \mu(\mathbf{x}) < \varphi(\mathbf{x}) \rightsquigarrow \psi(\mathbf{x}))$$

where $\{\eta \rightsquigarrow \mu, \varphi \rightsquigarrow \psi\} \subseteq D$ and $\{\eta(\mathbf{x}) \rightsquigarrow \mu(\mathbf{x}), \varphi(\mathbf{x}) \rightsquigarrow \psi(\mathbf{x})\} \subseteq D$ in case of propositional and predicate logic respectively. We also allow for defeasible rules of the form:

$$\alpha \rightsquigarrow (\varphi < \psi)$$

where $\{\varphi, \psi\} \subseteq \Sigma$. These additional defeasible rules allow us to construct arguments for preferences that are not based on specificity.

Since we are considering strict preferences, opposite preferences must be inconsistent. So given arguments $A = (\mathcal{S}, X < Y)$ and $A' = (\mathcal{S}', Y < X)$, we can construct a new argument $A'' = (\mathcal{S} \cup \mathcal{S}', \perp)$ for an inconsistency. This argument for an inconsistency is handled in the same way as other arguments for inconsistencies. Another point is the transitive closure of arguments. If desired, a rule for combining the arguments for preferences $X < Y$ and $Y < Z$, can be added.

### 3.3  The Argumentation System

The derivation of (specificity-based) arguments for preferences requires an adaptation of the argumentation system introduced in Sect. 2. Since preferences are used in resolving derived inconsistencies, Definition 3 must be adapted. A problem that we need to address is that an argument for an inconsistency can be derived before deriving argument for a relevant preference that can be used to resolve the inconsistency. For this reason we propose to resolve the inconsistency by *explicitly assuming* the absence of preferences between relevant defeasible rules or relevant pieces of information. If an argument for a preference is derived, it will attack the assumption of its absence. Therefore, we propose the following adaptation of Definition 3.

**Definition 6 (Definition 3 revised).** *Let $A = (\mathcal{S}, \perp)$ be an argument for an inconsistency. Moreover, let $< \subseteq (\Sigma \times \Sigma) \cup (D \times D)$ be a strict partial order over the information $\Sigma$ and over the defeasible rules $D$. Finally, let $A' = (\mathcal{S}', \mathbf{not}(\varphi \rightsquigarrow \psi))$ and $A' = (\mathcal{S}', \mathbf{not}(\sigma))$ denote the arguments for an undercutting attack of a defeasible rule in $\overline{D}$ and a proposition in $\Sigma$ respectively.*

- *If $\tilde{A} \neq \varnothing$, **defeat the weakest last rule**. Let $M = \min_<(\vec{A}^{\perp})$ be the set of least preferred last rules for the inconsistency given the fixed preference relation $<$. For every $\varphi \rightsquigarrow \psi \in M$ with $S = (\mathcal{S}'', \varphi \rightsquigarrow \psi) \in \mathcal{S}$,*

$$A' = \left(\mathcal{S}\backslash S \cup \{\mathbf{assume}(\eta \rightsquigarrow \mu \nless \varphi \rightsquigarrow \psi) \mid \eta \rightsquigarrow \mu \in M\backslash\varphi \rightsquigarrow \psi\}, \mathbf{not}(\varphi \rightsquigarrow \psi)\right)$$

  *is an undercutting argument of $\varphi \rightsquigarrow \psi \in \overline{D}$.*
- *If $\tilde{A} = \varnothing$, **defeat the weakest premise**. For every $\sigma \in \min_<(\bar{A})$,*

$$A' = \left(\mathcal{S}\backslash\sigma \cup \{\mathbf{assume}(\delta \nless \sigma) \mid \delta \in \min_<(\bar{A})\backslash\sigma\}, \mathbf{not}(\sigma)\right)$$

  *is an undercutting argument of $\sigma \in \Sigma$.*

## 4  Evaluation

We will evaluate the proposed approach for handling context dependent (specificity) preferences

1. by looking at formal properties of proposed approach,
2. by evaluating several problematic examples that have described in the literature,
3. by addressing the postulates of Dung et al. [7],
4. by comparing the proposed approach with related proposals.

## 4.1    Formal Properties

The approach proposed in this paper is based on the introduction of assumptions that no other last rule has a lower preference (Definitions 5 and 6). We can relate this to the original argumentation system described in Sect. 2. The following two proposition describe the relation. The first proposition addresses how the original argumentation system relates to the modified argumentation system.

**Proposition 1.** *The introduction of assumptions that no other last rule has a lower preference, does not change the original argumentation system if we ignore attacks on the assumption by arguments supporting preferences.*

*Proof.* If we remove the attack relation of arguments supporting preferences on assumptions, the assumptions about the absence of preferences have no function. They can therefore be removed from the arguments. This corresponds to replacing Definition 6 by Definition 3. Therefore, the same arguments extensions will be generated given an argumentation semantics.

The second proposition addresses the relation between a fixed preference order and a derived preference order.

**Proposition 2.** *In the absence of arguments attacking arguments for preferences, we can encode the specificity preference using the fixed preference relation $<$ over defeasible rules and use the original argumentation system instead of the new argumentation system. Both argumentation systems will give the same result.*

*Proof.* To prove the proposition, we will show that for every argument extension with undercutting arguments generated by Definition 3 there is corresponding argument extension with undercutting arguments generated by Definition 6, and vice versa.

In the absence arguments attacking assumptions in preference arguments, the preferences are strict. Moreover, in the absence of arguments attacking preference arguments, the preference arguments will all be justified and belong to every extension. Let $<$ encode the preferences supported by these justified preference arguments.

– Let $\mathcal{A}$ be a set of arguments and let arguments for inconsistencies be addressed by generating undercutting arguments using Definition 3. Moreover, let $\mathcal{E}$ be an argument extension for the set of arguments $\mathcal{A}$ according to one of the argumentation semantics. For every undercutting argument $A = (\mathcal{S}, \mathbf{not}(\varphi \rightsquigarrow$

$\psi)) \in \mathcal{E}$ that is not the result of applying an undercutting defeater, $\varphi \rightsquigarrow \psi$ must be a least preferred last rule in an argument $A^\perp$ for an inconsistency given the preference relation $<$. It is also al least preferred last rule given the original empty preference relation, and therefore there is an undercutting argument $A' = (\mathcal{S}', \mathbf{not}(\varphi \rightsquigarrow \psi))$ generated by Definition 6 such that $\tilde{A} = \tilde{A}'$. Let $\mathcal{E}'$ be the extension that is the result of replacing all arguments $A$ by $A'$ in $\mathcal{E}$. Because $\varphi \rightsquigarrow \psi$ is a least preferred last rule in an argument $A^\perp$ given $<$, there is no preference argument attacking an assumption in the undercutting argument $A'$. Hence, replacing $A$ by $A'$ does not affect the attack relation of the argumentation framework, and therefore, $\mathcal{E}'$ a valid extension of the adapted argumentation framework according to the chosen argumentation semantics, and $\mathcal{E}'$ supports the same conclusions as $\mathcal{E}$.

– Let $\mathcal{A}$ be a set of arguments and let arguments for inconsistencies be addressed by generating undercutting arguments using Definition 6. Moreover, let $\mathcal{E}'$ be an argument extension for the set of arguments $\mathcal{A}$ according to one of the argumentation semantics. For every undercutting argument $A' = (\mathcal{S}', \mathbf{not}(\varphi \rightsquigarrow \psi)) \in \mathcal{E}$ that is not the result of applying an undercutting defeater, $\varphi \rightsquigarrow \psi$ must be a last rule in an argument $A^\perp$ for an inconsistency. Since all arguments for preference arguments are justified, all preferences arguments belong to the argument extension $\mathcal{E}'$. Since $A'$ belongs to $\mathcal{E}'$ too, no preference argument attacks an assumption in $A'$. Therefore, for no other last rule $\eta \rightsquigarrow \mu$ of $A^\perp$, $\eta \rightsquigarrow \mu < \varphi \rightsquigarrow \psi$. Hence, there is an undercutting argument $A = (\mathcal{S}, \mathbf{not}(\varphi \rightsquigarrow \psi))$ generated by Definition 3 given the preference relations $<$ such that $\tilde{A} = \tilde{A}'$. Let $\mathcal{E}$ be the extension that is the result of replacing all arguments $A'$ by $A$ in $\mathcal{E}$. Replacing $A$ by $A'$ does not affect the attack relation of the argumentation framework, and therefore, $\mathcal{E}$ a valid extension of the adapted argumentation framework according to the chosen argumentation semantics, and $\mathcal{E}$ supports the same conclusions as $\mathcal{E}'$.

## 4.2   Problematic Examples

Approaches proposed in the literature use examples to motivate their proposal and to falsify previously proposed approaches.

*The Extended Example of Dung and Son.* We investigate Dung and Son's example of a context dependent specificity preference [6]. We use the defeasible rules $D$:

$$student \rightsquigarrow \neg married$$
$$student \rightsquigarrow young\ adult$$
$$adult \rightsquigarrow married$$

Given the information $\Sigma = \{student, young\ adult \rightarrow adult\}$, we can construct the following relevant arguments:

$A_1 = [student \vdash student \rightsquigarrow \neg married \vdash \neg married]$

$A_2 = [student \vdash student \rightsquigarrow young\ adult \vdash adult \rightsquigarrow married \vdash married]$

$A_3 = \left[ \begin{matrix} student \vdash student \rightsquigarrow \neg married \\ student \vdash student \rightsquigarrow young\ adult \vdash adult \rightsquigarrow married \end{matrix} \middle| \vdash \bot \right]$

$A_4 = \left[ \begin{matrix} student \vdash student \rightsquigarrow \neg married \\ \mathbf{assume}(student \rightsquigarrow \neg married \not< adult \rightsquigarrow married) \end{matrix} \middle| \circ \mathbf{not}(adult \rightsquigarrow married) \right]$

$A_5 = \left[ \begin{matrix} student \vdash student \rightsquigarrow young\ adult \vdash adult \rightsquigarrow married \\ \mathbf{assume}(adult \rightsquigarrow married \not< student \rightsquigarrow \neg married) \end{matrix} \middle| \circ \mathbf{not}(student \rightsquigarrow \neg married) \right]$

$A_6 = [\underline{student} \vdash student \rightsquigarrow young\ adult \vdash adult]$

$A_7 = [student \vdash student \rightsquigarrow young\ adult \,\flat\, adult \rightsquigarrow married < student \rightsquigarrow \neg married]$

Note that it is a coincident that the hypothesis *student* in arguments $A_6$ is an element of the information $\Sigma$. To indicate that *student* is a hypothesis that is used to derive an argument for the specificity preference, we underline *student*. Also note that $A_6$ is an auxiliary argument that is only used to derive $A_7$ and has no role in the final set of arguments.

Argument $A_4$ attacks arguments $A_2$, $A_3$ and $A_5$ ($A_4 \longrightarrow A_2, \ldots$), argument $A_5$ attacks arguments $A_1$, $A_3$ and $A_4$, and argument $A_7$ attacks argument $A_5$. Without the specificity argument $A_7$, both the stable and the preferred semantics give us two argument extensions: $\{A_1, A_4\}$ and $\{A_2, A_5\}$. The two extension indicate that *we do not know whether the student is married*. After deriving the specificity argument $A_7$, we have only one argument extension: $\{A_1, A_4, A_7\}$. The latter extension indicates that *the student is not married*.

If we also know that the student is an adult but not a young adult: $\Sigma' = \{student, adult, \neg young\ adult, t, young\ adult \rightarrow adult\}$, we can derive the following additional arguments:

$A_8 = [adult \vdash adult \rightsquigarrow married \vdash married]$

$A_9 = \left[ \begin{matrix} student \vdash student \rightsquigarrow \neg married \\ adult \vdash adult \rightsquigarrow married \end{matrix} \middle| \vdash \bot \right]$

$A_{10} = \left[ \begin{matrix} student \vdash student \rightsquigarrow \neg married \\ \mathbf{assume}(student \rightsquigarrow \neg married \not< adult \rightsquigarrow married) \end{matrix} \middle| \circ \mathbf{not}(adult \rightsquigarrow married) \right]$

$A_{11} = \left[ \begin{matrix} adult \vdash adult \rightsquigarrow married \\ \mathbf{assume}(adult \rightsquigarrow married \not< student \rightsquigarrow \neg married) \end{matrix} \middle| \circ \mathbf{not}(student \rightsquigarrow \neg married) \right]$

$A_{12} = \left[ \begin{matrix} \neg young\ adult \\ student \vdash student \rightsquigarrow young\ adult \end{matrix} \middle| \vdash \bot \right]$

$A_{13} = [\neg young\ adult \,\flat\, \mathbf{not}(student \rightsquigarrow young\ adult)]$

These additional arguments extend the attack relation. Arguments $A_4$ and $A_{10}$ both attack arguments $A_2$, $A_3$, $A_5$, $A_8$, $A_9$ and $A_{11}$, argument $A_5$ and $A_{11}$ both attack arguments $A_1$, $A_3$, $A_4$, $A_9$, $A_{10}$, argument $A_7$ attacks arguments $A_5$ and $A_{11}$, and argument $A_{13}$ attacks arguments $A_2$, $A_3$, $A_5$, $A_7$, and $A_{12}$. Given these attack relations both the stable and the preferred semantics give us two argument extensions: $\{A_1, A_4, A_{10}, A_{13}\}$ and $\{A_2, A_5, A_8, A_{11}, A_{13}\}$. The two extensions indicate that *we do not know whether the student is married*.

Extending the information $\Sigma$ with *Utopia student* and the defeasible rules $D$ with *Utopia student* $\rightsquigarrow \mathbf{not}(student \rightsquigarrow \neg married)$, we can derive the argument:

$A_{14} = [Utopia\ student \vdash Utopia\ student \rightsquigarrow \mathbf{not}(student \rightsquigarrow \neg married)$
$\vdash \mathbf{not}(student \rightsquigarrow \neg married)]$

This argument attacks arguments $A_1$, $A_3$, $A_4$. As a result we have only one argument extension: $\{A_2, A_5, A_{14}\}$. This extension indicates that *the student is married*. Note that we do not consider arguments $A_8, \ldots, A_{13}$ here because we do not use the information that the student is an adult but not a young adult.

*The Example of Modgil.* Modgil formulates his motivating example in terms of natural language sentences with which he associates arguments and attack relations [11]. We first need to reformulate his example in the language of a logic. We choose propositional logic to keep things simple.

- Today will be dry in London since the BBC forecast sunshine: $bs \leadsto d$.
- Today will be wet in London since CNN forecast rain: $cr \leadsto w$.
- additional information: $bs$, $cr$ and $\neg(d \wedge w)$.
- The BBC is more trustworthy than CNN: $bt \leadsto (cr \leadsto w < bs \leadsto d)$
- Statistically CNN is a more accurate forecaster than the BBC:
  $ca \leadsto (bs \leadsto d < cr \leadsto w)$
- additional information: $bt$ and $ca$.
- Basing a comparison on statistics is more rigorous and rational than basing a comparison on your instincts about their relative trustworthiness:
  $\top \leadsto (bt \leadsto (cr \leadsto w < bs \leadsto d) < ca \leadsto (bs \leadsto d < cr \leadsto w))$.

Using the formulation of the problem in propositional logic, we can derive the following arguments:

$$A_1 = [bs \vdash bs \leadsto d \vdash d]$$
$$A_2 = [cr \vdash cr \leadsto w \vdash w]$$
$$A_3 = \begin{bmatrix} bs \vdash bs \leadsto d \\ cr \vdash cr \leadsto w \\ \neg(d \wedge w) \end{bmatrix} \vdash \bot$$
$$A_4 = \begin{bmatrix} bs \vdash bs \leadsto d \\ \neg(d \wedge w) \circ \mathbf{not}(cr \leadsto w) \\ \mathbf{assume}(bs \leadsto d \not< cr \leadsto w) \end{bmatrix}$$
$$A_5 = \begin{bmatrix} cr \vdash cr \leadsto w \\ \neg(d \wedge w) \circ \mathbf{not}(bs \leadsto d) \\ \mathbf{assume}(cr \leadsto w \not< bs \leadsto d) \end{bmatrix}$$
$$A_6 = [bt \vdash bt \leadsto (cr \leadsto w < bs \leadsto d) \vdash cr \leadsto w < bs \leadsto d]$$
$$A_7 = [ca \vdash ca \leadsto (bs \leadsto d < cr \leadsto w) \vdash bs \leadsto d < cr \leadsto w]$$
$$A_8 = \begin{bmatrix} bt \vdash bt \leadsto (cr \leadsto w < bs \leadsto d) \\ ca \vdash ca \leadsto (bs \leadsto d < cr \leadsto w) \end{bmatrix} \vdash \bot$$
$$A_9 = \begin{bmatrix} bt \vdash bt \leadsto (cr \leadsto w < bs \leadsto d) \\ \mathbf{assume}(bt \leadsto (cr \leadsto w < bs \leadsto d) \not< \circ \mathbf{not}(ca \leadsto (bs \leadsto d < cr \leadsto w)) \\ ca \leadsto (bs \leadsto d < cr \leadsto w)) \end{bmatrix}$$
$$A_{10} = \begin{bmatrix} ca \vdash ca \leadsto (bs \leadsto d < cr \leadsto w) \\ \mathbf{assume}(ca \leadsto (bs \leadsto d < cr \leadsto w) \not< \circ \mathbf{not}(bt \leadsto (cr \leadsto w < bs \leadsto d)) \\ bt \leadsto (cr \leadsto w < bs \leadsto d)) \end{bmatrix}$$
$$A_{11} = [ \vdash \top \leadsto (bt \leadsto (cr \leadsto w < bs \leadsto d) < ca \leadsto (bs \leadsto d < cr \leadsto w)) \vdash \\ bt \leadsto (cr \leadsto w < bs \leadsto d) < ca \leadsto (bs \leadsto d < cr \leadsto w)]$$

Argument $A_4$ attacks arguments $A_2$, $A_3$ and $A_5$, argument $A_5$ attacks arguments $A_1$, $A_3$ and $A_4$, argument $A_6$ attacks argument $A_5$, argument $A_7$ attacks argument $A_4$, argument $A_9$ attacks arguments $A_7$, $A_8$ and $A_{10}$, argument $A_{10}$ attacks arguments $A_6$, $A_8$ and $A_9$, and argument $A_{11}$ attacks argument $A_9$. Given these attack relations both the stable and the preferred semantics give us one argument extension: $\{A_2, A_5, A_7, A_{10}, A_{11}\}$. Hence, *today will be wet in London since CNN forecast rain.*

*The Example of Amgoud and Vesic.* Amgoud and Vesic [1] argue that Modgil's approach [11] can result in extensions of which the arguments support inconsistent conclusions. These inconsistencies are not visible at the level of the argumentation framework because arguments are viewed as atoms. The solution of Amgoud and Vesic is to reverse the attack relation. This solution can be invalid if the attack relation is a result of applying an undercutting defeater.

The approach described in this paper correctly handles the motivating example of Amgoud and Vesic [1]. Since this example is formulated in terms of natural language sentences with which argument and attack relations are associated, we first need to reformulate the example in the language of a logic.

- This violin is expensive since it was made by Stradivari: $s \rightsquigarrow e$.
- additional information: $s$
- The violin was not made by Stradivari: $\neg s$.
- since the first statement is from an expert while the second is from a child, we have the preference relation: $\top \rightsquigarrow \neg s < s$.

Using the formulation of the problem in propositional logic, we can derive the following arguments:

$$A_1 = [s \vdash s]$$
$$A_2 = [s \vdash s \rightsquigarrow e \vdash e]$$
$$A_3 = [\neg s \vdash \neg s]$$
$$A_4 = \left[ \begin{matrix} s \\ \neg s \end{matrix} \middle| \vdash \bot \right]$$
$$A_5 = \left[ \begin{matrix} s \\ \textbf{\textit{assume}}(s \nless \neg s) \end{matrix} \middle| \circ \, \textbf{not}(\neg s) \right]$$
$$A_6 = \left[ \begin{matrix} \neg s \\ \textbf{\textit{assume}}(\neg s \nless s) \end{matrix} \middle| \circ \, \textbf{not}(s) \right]$$
$$A_7 = [\vdash \top \rightsquigarrow \neg s < s \vdash \neg s < s]$$

Argument $A_5$ attacks arguments $A_3$, $A_4$ and $A_6$, argument $A_6$ attacks arguments $A_1$, $A_2$, $A_4$ and $A_5$, and argument $A_7$ attacks argument $A_6$. Given these attack relations both the stable and the preferred semantics give us one argument extension: $\{A_1, A_2, A_5, A_7\}$. Hence, *this violin is expensive since it was made by Stradivari.*

*The Example of Dung, Thang and Son.* Dung et al. [7] use the following example formulated in predicate logic extended with defeasible rules.

Sherlock Holmes is investigating a case involving three persons $P_1$, $P_2$ and $S$ together with the dead body of a big man. Furthermore, $S$ is a small child who cannot kill a big man and $P_1$ is a beneficiary from the dead of the big man.

Dung et al. [7] provide the following information and defeasible rules about the case:

1. The knowledge that one of the persons is the murderer is represented by three strict rules:
   $Inno(P_1) \land Inno(S) \rightarrow \neg Inno(P_2)$
   $Inno(P_2) \land Inno(S) \rightarrow \neg Inno(P_1)$
   $Inno(P_1) \land Inno(P_2) \rightarrow \neg Inno(S)$
2. The legal principle that people are considered innocent until proven otherwise could be represented by three defeasible rules:
   $\top \rightsquigarrow Inno(P_1)$
   $\top \rightsquigarrow Inno(P_2)$
   $\top \rightsquigarrow Inno(S)$
3. A "rule-of-thumb" for the investigation is to find out whether the possible suspects have any motives and to focus the investigation on the one with strong motive to commit the crime. Such "rule-of-thumb" can be represented by two conditional preferences:
   $Has\_Motive(P_1) \land \neg Has\_Motive(P_2) \rightsquigarrow (\top \rightsquigarrow Inno(P_1) < \top \rightsquigarrow Inno(P_2))$
   $Has\_Motive(P_2) \land \neg Has\_Motive(P_1) \rightsquigarrow (\top \rightsquigarrow Inno(P_2) < \top \rightsquigarrow Inno(P_1))$
   The rules state that if $P_i$ has a motive and $P_j$ $(i \neq j)$ does not have a motive then the default that $P_j$ is innocent is more preferred than the default that $P_i$ is innocent.
4. A good reason for having a motive to kill is to be a beneficiary from the dead of the deceased:
   $Beneficiary(P_1) \rightarrow Has\_Motive(P_1)$
   $Beneficiary(P_2) \rightarrow Has\_Motive(P_2)$
5. Peoples are normally assumed not to have motives to kill:
   $\top \rightsquigarrow \neg Has\_Motive(P_1)$
   $\top \rightsquigarrow \neg Has\_Motive(P_2)$
6. The information that $S$ is a small child and $P_1$ is a beneficiary from the dead of the big man is represented by the information:
   $Inno(S), Beneficiary(P_1)$

After deriving all relevant arguments and attack relations for the above example[4], we can identify one extension for both the stable and the preferred semantics, which supports the conclusion that person $P_2$ and child $S$ innocent and person $P_1$ is not innocent.

---

[4] We do not have the space to list all relevant arguments and attack relations implied by the example.

### 4.3   The Postulates of Dung, Thang and Son

Dung et al. [7] introduce postulates that an argumentation system for context dependent preferences must obey. They use their postulates to deciding which arguments for preferences are valid. So, arguments for preferences are evaluated in a different way compared to arguments that do not support preferences.

The postulates proposed by Dung et al. are not relevant here because they specifically address arguments for preferences attacking attack relations. This is not the approach used here.

### 4.4   Related Approaches

Of all approaches for context dependent (specificity) preferences, only the work of Dung and Son [6] and of Prakken and Sartor [14] are related. Other approaches focus on preferences between arguments without looking at the structure of the arguments [1,11] or fucus on arguments for preferences attacking attack relations between arguments [7].

*The relation with the approach of Dung and Son*  As pointed out in the Introduction of this paper, Dung and Son [6] propose that the argument for one rule being more specific than another rule, attacks the application of the more general rule. In the absence of undercutting defeaters, the here proposed approach can be related to the work of Dung and Son [6].

**Proposition 3.** *Consider the more restricted language used by Dung and Son [6] where facts are literals, the antecedents of strict and of defeasible rules are conjunctions of literals, and consequences of strict and of defeasible rules are single literals.*

*In the absence of undercutting defeasible rules[5], the special stable semantics in the approach of Dung and Son [6] gives the same results as the here proposed approach under the standard stable semantics.*

*Proof.* We prove the proposition by showing that a preference attack on a more general defeasible rule in the approach of Dung and Son corresponds one to one with a preference attack on an assumption in the undercutting argument attacking the application of the more specific defeasible rule.

Dung and Son define an argument as a set of defeasible rules $\Delta \subseteq \overline{D}$. They distinguish two types of arguments, namely arguments for propositions and arguments for preferences. For each argument $\Delta$ defined by Dung and Son, there is a corresponding argument $A$ in the argumentation system used in this paper such that $\Delta = \tilde{A}$, and vice versa.

Dung and Son consider pairs of arguments supporting conflicting conclusions, which correspond one to one with arguments for inconsistencies given the restricted language. The only relevant case of conflicting arguments is where

---

[5] Note that we are not referring to undercutting arguments that we use to resolve conflicts/inconsistencies.

both arguments have a last defeasible rule, $\varphi \rightsquigarrow \psi$ and $\eta \rightsquigarrow \neg\psi$ respectively. These two arguments *attack each other by conflict*, and therefore both cannot belong to an extension at the same time.[6] A preference argument concerning $\varphi \rightsquigarrow \psi$ and $\eta \rightsquigarrow \neg\psi$ *attacks by specificity* the most general rule of the two in the approach of Dung and Son. Since an extension in Dung and Son's approach is a maximal conflict-free set of defeasible rules, both types of attacks correspond to undercutting arguments. The attack by conflict correspond to the undercutting arguments that are generated by Definition 6. The attack by specificity does not have a direct corresponding undercutting argument in the here proposed approach. Instead a preference argument attacks the assumption that the other rule has no lower preference. This has the same effect as an undercutting attack on the more general rule. Because the undercutting arguments generated by Definition 6, attack the application of defeasible rules, a maximal conflict-free set of defeasible rules used by Dung and Son [6], corresponds to a stable extension of the stable semantics, and vice versa.[7]

*The Relation with the Approach of Prakken and Sartor.* Prakken and Sartor [14] introduce arguments for context dependent preferences and make use of a property of the grounded semantics, namely that an extension can be computed by iteratively applying the characteristic function, to incorporate the preferences between rules in the grounded extension. In case of the grounded semantics, the here proposed approach gives the same result.

Prakken and Sartor use general logic programming rules that are defeasible or strict. We do not have such rules in a defeasible theory. Instead of using general logic programming rules, we can als use strict and defeasible rules plus undercutting rules that attack the application of defeasible rules. This is the representation that is assumed in the following proposition.

**Proposition 4.** *Consider the more restricted language where facts are literals, the antecedents of strict and of defeasible rules are conjunctions of literals, and consequences of strict and of defeasible rules are either single literals or negations of defeasible rules.*

*The here proposed approach supports under the grounded semantics the same conclusions as the approach proposed by Prakken and Sartor [14].*

*Proof.* We will prove the proposition by induction on the application of the characteristic function: $\mathcal{E} = \bigcup_{i>0} G_i$ with $G_0 = \varnothing$ and $G_i = F(G_{i-1})$.

*Induction Hypothesis*: Let $G_i$ be the justified arguments after $i$ iterations of the adapted characteristic function defined by Prakken and Sartor [14]. Let $G'_i$ be

---

[6] An extension is a maximal conflict-free set of defeasible rule in the approach of Dung and Son.

[7] In the original version of the argumentation system used in this paper [18,19], a stable extension was defined as the fixed point of a function $DR(\mathcal{X}) = \{\varphi \rightsquigarrow \psi \mid A \in \mathcal{A}, \mathcal{X} \cap \tilde{A} = \varnothing, \hat{A} = \mathbf{not}(\varphi \rightsquigarrow \psi)\}$ returning a set of defeated rules if $\mathcal{X}$ is a set of defeated rules. $\mathcal{A} - \mathcal{X}$ is a maximal set of default rules given the definition of an extension used by Dung and Son [6].

the justified arguments after $i$ iterations of the standard characteristic function. $G_i \subseteq G_i'$ and all arguments in $G_i' \backslash G_i$ are generated by Definition 6. Applying the characteristic function, the only interesting case is a pair of conflicting arguments for which we have derived a preference relation for the last rules of the two arguments.

*Induction Step*: Let $A_1$ and $A_2$ be two argument supporting opposite conclusions: one of them supporting $p$ and the other $\neg p$, and let $r_1$ and $r_2$ be the last rule of $A_1$ and $A_2$ respectively. Moreover, let all sub-arguments of $A_1$ and $A_2$ be justified in $G_i$. Finally, let $A_3 \in G_i$ be a justified argument for the preference $r_1 < r_2$. Then according to the adapted characteristic function described by Prakken and Sartor, $A_2$ will be acceptable w.r.t. $G_i$, and therefore will belong to $G_{i+1}$.

The here proposed approach will first derive an argument for an inconsistency. From this argument, Definition 6 will generate two undercutting arguments $A_4$ and $A_5$. Argument $A_4$ will undercut the use of the rule $r_1$ assuming that $r_2 \not< r_1$ and argument $A_5$ will undercut the use of the rule $r_2$ assuming that $r_1 \not< r_2$. The justified preference argument $A_3$ for $r_1 < r_2$ will attack $A_5$. Therefore, $A_4$ will be justified, which attacks undercut the use of the rule $r_1$. Hence, argument $A_1$ and the argument for the inconsistency will not be justified, and arguments $A_2$ and $A_4$ will be justified and therefore belong to $G_{i+1}'$.

## 5  Conclusion

We have investigated a new way of handling context dependent (specificity) preferences. Undercutting arguments in which we explicitly assume the absence of preferences between defeasible rules or between premises, handle the arguments for inconsistencies in the proposed approach. These undercutting arguments can be attacked by arguments for preferences. The approach is intuitively simple and can handle examples that have been used to motivate alternative approaches. We therefore conclude that the propose approach is able to adequately handle context dependent (specificity) preferences. Moreover, because the approach is intuitively more simple than alternative approaches that have been proposed in the literature, the proposed approaches is to be preferred over the alternatives. Finally, we conclude that it is important to consider the defeasible elements that make up an argument instead of viewing the argument as an atom.

## References

1. Amgoud, L., Vesic, S.: Rich preference-based argumentation frameworks. Int. J. Approximate Reasoning **55**(2), 585–606 (2014). https://doi.org/10.1016/j.ijar.2013.10.010
2. Baroni, P., Giacomin, M., Guida, G.: SCC-recursiveness: a general schema for argumentation semantics. Artif. Intell. **168**, 162–210 (2005)

3. Caminada, M.: Semi-stable semantics. In: Proceedings of the 1st Conference on Computational Models of Argument (COMMA 2006). Frontiers in Artificial Intelligence and Applications, vol. 144. IOS Press (2006)
4. Cramer, M., vab der Torre, L.: SCF2 - an argumentation semantics for rational human judgments on argument acceptability. In: Proceedings of the 8th Workshop on Dynamics of Knowledge and Belief (DKB-2019) and the 7th Workshop KI & Kognition (KIK-2019), pp. 24–35 (2019)
5. Dung, P.M.: On the acceptability of arguments and its fundamental role in non-monotonic reasoning, logic programming and n-person games. Artif. Intell. **77**, 321–357 (1995)
6. Dung, P.M., Son, T.C.: An argument-based approach to reasoning with specificity. Artif. Intell. **133**, 35–85 (2001)
7. Dung, P.M., Thang, P.M., Son, T.C.: On structured argumentation with conditional preferences. In: Proceedings of the AAAI Conference on Artificial Intelligence, vol. 33, pp. 2792–2800 (2019). https://doi.org/10.1609/aaai.v33i01.33012792
8. Dung, P., Mancarella, P., Toni, F.: Computing ideal sceptical argumentation. Artif. Intell. **171**, 642–674 (2007)
9. Dvořák, W., Gaggl, S.A.: Stage semantics and the SCC-recursive schema for argumentation semantics. J. Log. Comput. **26**(4), 1149–1202 (2016). https://doi.org/10.1093/logcom/exu006
10. Geffner, H., Pearl, J.: Conditional entailment: bridging two approaches to default reasoning. Artif. Intell. **53**, 209–244 (1992)
11. Modgil, S.: Reasoning about preferences in argumentation frameworks. Artif. Intell. **173**(9), 901–934 (2009). https://doi.org/10.1016/j.artint.2009.02.001
12. Pollock, J.L.: Defeasible reasoning. Cogn. Sci. **11**, 481–518 (1987)
13. Poole, D.: On the comparison of theories: preferring the most specific explanation. In: Proceedings of the Ninth International Joint Conference on Artificial Intelligence, pp. 144–147 (1985)
14. Prakken, H., Sartor, G.: Argument-based extended logic programming with defeasible priorities. J. Appl. Non-Class. Log. **7**(1), 25–75 (1997)
15. Roos, N.: A preference logic for non-monotonic reasoning. Technical report, 88-94, Delft University of Technology, Faculty of Technical Mathematics and Informatics (1988). ISSN 0922-5641
16. Roos, N.: Preference logic: a logic for reasoning with inconsistent knowledge. Technical report, 89-53, Delft University of Technology, Faculty of Technical Mathematics and Informatics (1989). ISSN 0922-5641
17. Roos, N.: A logic for reasoning with inconsistent knowledge. Artif. Intell. **57**, 69–103 (1992)
18. Roos, N.: On resolving conflicts between arguments. Technical report, TR-CTIT-97-37 Centre for Telematics and Information Technology, University of Twente, Enschede (1997)
19. Roos, N.: On resolving conflicts between arguments. Comput. Intell. **16**, 469–497 (2000)
20. Roos, N.: Preferential model and argumentation semantics. In: Proceedings of the 13th International Workshop on Non-Monotonic Reasoning (NMR-2010) (2010)
21. Roos, N.: A semantic tableau method for argument construction. In: Baratchi, M., Cao, L., Kosters, W.A., Lijffijt, J., van Rijn, J.N., Takes, F.W. (eds.) BNAIC/Benelearn 2020. CCIS, vol. 1398, pp. 122–140. Springer, Cham (2021). https://doi.org/10.1007/978-3-030-76640-5_8

22. Simari, G.R., Loui, R.P.: A mathematical treatment of defeasible reasoning and its implementation. Artif. Intell. **53**, 125–157 (1992)
23. Toulmin, S.: The Uses of Argument. Cambridge University Press, Cambridge (1958)
24. Verheij, B.: Two approaches to dialectical argumentation: admissible sets and argumentation stages. In: Proceedings of the Biannual International Conference on Formal and Applied Practical Reasoning (FAPR) Workshop, pp. 357–368 (1996)

# Model-Based Reinforcement Learning with State Abstraction: A Survey

Rolf A. N. Starre[1(✉)], Marco Loog[2], and Frans A. Oliehoek[1]

[1] Delft University of Technology, Delft, The Netherlands
{r.a.n.starre,f.a.oliehoek}@tudelft.nl
[2] Radbout University, Nijmegen, The Netherlands
marco.loog@ru.nl

**Abstract.** Model-based reinforcement learning methods are promising since they can increase sample efficiency while simultaneously improving generalizability. Learning can also be made more efficient through state abstraction, which delivers more compact models. Model-based reinforcement learning methods have been combined with learning abstract models to profit from both effects. We consider a wide range of state abstractions that have been covered in the literature, from straightforward state aggregation to deep learned representations, and sketch challenges that arise when combining model-based reinforcement learning with abstraction. We further show how various methods deal with these challenges and point to open questions and opportunities for further research.

**Keywords:** Model-based RL · State Abstraction · MDPs

## 1 Introduction

With roots in sequential analysis [77], Reinforcement Learning (RL) is a general framework for learning how to act near-optimally in sequential decision-making problems. A key challenge for RL is sample efficiency. Sample efficiency is important because, in many problems, it can be expensive, in time or monetary costs, to collect samples. The combination of Model-based Reinforcement Learning (MBRL) and abstraction is of interest for improving the sample efficiency of learning methods that aim to find solutions for sequential decision-making problems. We define MBRL as an RL method that explicitly learns a model of the environment. MBRL provides a way to find solutions to complex problems efficiently [71] and allows for transfer in shifting or related tasks [1,53]. The state representation, the input to RL methods, plays an essential role in the learning process. A state representation will often contain irrelevant details, e.g., when the input is an image, a large amount can consist of a background that has no direct relevance to the task. Abstracting the state representation to remove irrelevant parts for optimal decision-making allows RL methods to learn much faster. Learning to decide which parts of the state representation are relevant is a key aspect of abstraction learning.

T. Calders et al. (Eds.): BNAIC/Benelearn 2022, CCIS 1805, pp. 133–148, 2023.
https://doi.org/10.1007/978-3-031-39144-6_9

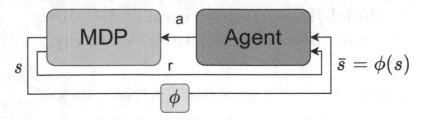

**Fig. 1.** RL with abstraction, the agent observes $\bar{s} = \phi(s)$ instead of $s$. Image from [70].

State abstraction can be carried out in various ways, ranging from state aggregation [2,44] to deep learned representations [63,66]. We provide a high-level view of the promising research in the field, covering a wide range of different types of state abstractions known from the literature.

Recently MBRL, abstraction learning, and related topics have received much attention. There are surveys of decision-making under uncertainty [36], MBRL in general [53], deep MBRL [62], and representation learning in both robotics [42] and MBRL [32]. Our work takes a broad view of abstraction and focuses on the additional challenges that arise when combining MBRL and abstraction [1,57, 69,70]. The contributions of this work are the following: We detail challenges that arise from the combination of MBRL with abstraction using the view of abstraction plus RL as a Partially Observable MDP (POMDP). We show how different approaches for MBRL with state abstraction deal with these challenges, providing a unified view of a wide range of approaches in the process. We identify open questions and opportunities for further research.

## 2    An Overview of State Abstraction for RL

We consider RL in sequential decision-making problems, which can be defined as a Markov decision process (MDP) [64]: $\langle S, A, T, R, \gamma \rangle$, where $S$ is a set of states $s \in S$, $A$ a set of actions $a \in A$, $T$ a transition function $T(s'|s,a) = \Pr(s'|s,a)$, $R$ a reward function $R(s,a)$ which gives the reward received when the agent executes action $a$ in state $s$, and $\gamma$ the discount factor ($0 \leq \gamma < 1$). For realistic problems, the state space of the MDP representation is often too large to tackle directly. One way to reduce the size is to use compact representations such as state abstractions. Section 2.1 characterizes different state abstractions methods and briefly describes some of their properties. Section 2.2 describes how abstraction in an MDP can be viewed as a POMDP and the resulting challenge.

### 2.1    Characterization of Abstractions

State abstraction can be used to reduce the problem size by clustering states into abstract states. This clustering can be defined by using an abstraction function $\phi$, which maps (or aggregates) ground states $s$ to abstract states $\bar{s}$, where the bar notation denotes objects in the abstract space. Here we consider a discrete state space and write this mapping as $\phi(s) = \bar{s}$, such that the abstract state space can be written as $\bar{S} = \{\phi(s) \mid s \in S\}$. The agent then uses the abstract states $\bar{s}$ and the rewards for learning transitions and rewards over the abstract state space. State abstraction can result in an abstract state space that is much smaller than the original state space, $|\bar{S}| \ll |S|$, which can make learning easier.

In the planning setting, where we have access to the model of a problem, many different abstraction functions have been considered [2,44]. Abstractions group states based on specific criteria of the state or state-action pairs. An example is the (stochastic) bisimulation [21], also known as model-irrelevance abstraction [44]. In this abstraction, states are only grouped if their reward and transition functions in the abstract space are the same, i.e., $\phi(s_1) = \phi(s_2)$ iff

$$\forall_{a \in A} \, R(s_1, a) = R(s_2, a), \tag{1}$$

$$\text{and } \forall_{\bar{s}' \in \bar{S}} \, T(\bar{s}'|s_1, a) = T(\bar{s}'|s_2, a). \tag{2}$$

Here $T(\bar{s}'|s, a)$ is the transition to an abstract state $\bar{s}'$ which is defined as

$$T(\bar{s}'|s, a) := \sum_{s' \in \bar{s}'} T(s'|s, a). \tag{3}$$

If we have access to the MDP, we can compute a more compact abstract MDP [13] and find a solution for this smaller problem. An important aspect of these abstractions is whether or not (near) optimal policies for the original policy can be obtained when the policy is learned from the abstract problem. Several results showing that this is possible have been obtained for multiple forms of abstraction [2,44]. These results make abstractions interesting for RL as they show that it is possible to significantly reduce the problem size while still being able to obtain (near) optimal policies for the original problem.

To allow for further reduction in the problem size, approximate versions of abstractions, such as the $\epsilon$-bisimulation, have been considered [2,44]. In the approximate versions, the grouping criteria are relaxed. E.g., in the $\epsilon$-bisimulation, the transition and reward functions for grouped states will be close but not necessarily the same, i.e., $\phi(s_1) = \phi(s_2)$ iff

$$\forall_{a \in A} \, |R(s_1, a) - R(s_2, a)| \leq \epsilon, \tag{4}$$

$$\text{and } \forall_{\bar{s}' \in \bar{S}} \, |T(\bar{s}'|s_1, a) - T(\bar{s}'|s_2, a)| \leq \epsilon, \tag{5}$$

where $T(\bar{s}'|s, a)$ is defined as in (3). Several other examples of exact and approximate state abstraction functions can be found in the literature [2,44]. For a given MDP, it is possible to build an abstract MDP using $\epsilon$-bisimulation criteria [14]. Recent work has introduced transitive state abstractions, which can be computed efficiently [1]. If we have a compact model, the goal is to find a good policy. A potential issue is that if a learned model only approximates the true model, minor errors can compound when planning for long horizons [73,81]. Results for planning have shown that for particular approximate state representations, such as $\epsilon$-bisimulation, the learned policy can still be approximately optimal [2]. There is a similar result for using RL in an abstract MDP [72]. However, these results assume that we have access to the MDP or an abstract MDP, which requires the problem to be known, and this is typically not the case in RL.

## 2.2  Abstraction in an MDP as a POMDP

In the general case of MBRL in an unknown MDP with an abstraction $\phi$, the situation will be as depicted in Fig. 1. Without abstraction, the agent receives a state $s$ as an observation. With abstraction, the agent instead observes an abstract state $\bar{s} = \phi(s)$ through the abstraction function $\phi$. In this case, the agent will no longer know precisely which state it is in, making the environment (a special case of) a POMDP [3,6,32,52,69,70]. Abstraction can be seen as a special case of POMDPs because the observation results from *perceptual aliasing*, i.e., multiple states are perceived as the same. Perceptual aliasing may not be a problem when the resulting problem behaves as an MDP, as for a bisimulation [21,45], but this is often not the case [1,57,70].

To formalize the combination of abstraction and RL in an MDP as a special case of a POMDP, we first give the general definition of an infinite horizon POMDP, [34], which can be described by the tuple $\langle S, A, T, R, \Omega, O, \gamma \rangle$, where $S, A, T, R,$ and $\gamma$ are the same as in the MDP. The $\Omega$ is a finite set of observations $o \in \Omega$ that an agent can receive, and $O$ is an observation function $O(o|a, s') = \Pr(o|a, s')$ that gives the probability of receiving an observation $o$ after taking an action $a$ and ending in state $s'$. Now, when an RL agent acts in an MDP but receives observations through $\phi$, the uncertainty is only due to perceptual aliasing, which means that the observation is a deterministic function of the state: $O(o|a, s') = \Pr(o = \phi(s')|a, s') = \Pr(o = \phi(s')|s')$. For deterministic functions $\phi$, this is 1 iff $o = \phi(s')$. The abstraction function $\phi$ has taken the role of the observation function $O$, with the observation space being $\bar{S}$.

Since we can view the combination of abstraction and RL in an MDP as a special case of a POMDP, RL methods for POMDPs could be used to find a solution. A common approach to finding solutions in POMDPs is through Bayesian RL, for which the Bayes-Adaptive POMDP (BA-POMDP) provides a framework [65]. Extensions of Bayesian RL for POMDPs are covered in the survey of Ghavamzadeh et al. [20]. In Deep RL, using recurrent neural networks is one way in which partial observability has been addressed [30,78]. Specific focus has been on using variational inference methods [29,75] and belief tracking [35, 47,78]. However, these POMDP approaches are often general solutions for any POMDP, and they are not necessarily optimal for the special case of the POMDP induced by abstraction.

Instead of applying POMDP solution methods, it can be tempting to treat the resulting problem as a Markov problem and try to find a solution in this way. For instance, this could be tempting when the abstraction clusters together states with similar transition and reward functions in the abstract space, such as with a $\epsilon$-bisimulation abstraction. However, it has been observed that treating this problem as a Markov process can lead to policies that are far from optimal, and there could be no guarantee of finding an optimal solution [1,57,70]. In general, non-stationarity of the collected data, due to changing behavior of the policy, has been shown to lead to worse performance in Deep RL [28], and non-stationarity due to perceptual aliasing can lead to similar problems when not addressed. Therefore, to find good solutions, methods that combine RL and abstraction should take into account perceptual aliasing.

## 3 Utilizing Given Abstraction Functions

This section presents an overview of the literature that utilizes an abstraction function for MBRL. First, Sect. 3.1 discusses the relation between abstract MDPs and Robust MDPs (RMDPs) and how solution methods for RMDP can allow for obtaining better policies when using an abstract learned model. Section 3.2 considers the RL setting where we do not have such a model, but we are given some abstraction function $\phi$ and see how abstraction can be leveraged to improve performance. Section 3.3 deals with the setting where we are given a set of abstractions and have to learn which one leads to optimal performance. Afterward, Sect. 4 deals with the setting where we do not have an abstraction function $\phi$ and have to learn one online.

### 3.1 Robust Optimization

The RMDP [80], and the related Bounded Parameter MDP (BPMDP) [22], extend the MDP definition by allowing for uncertainty in the transition and reward functions, as quantified by intervals. This uncertainty is generally motivated by not having enough data to be sure about the transition functions but still being able to give some confidence intervals. Another motivation is inherent uncertainty, for instance caused by having a $\epsilon$-bisimulation, where the uncertainty intervals are $\epsilon$ wide. If we learn an $\epsilon$-bisimulation model and can estimate $\epsilon$, we could apply solution methods for RMDP, this makes solution methods for RMDP interesting for RL with abstraction.

To solve problems with inherent uncertainty, the RMDP includes an additional set of outcomes $B$. The transition probabilities and reward function are a function of both $a \in A$ and $b \in B$. From a game-theoretic perspective, $B$ can be seen as the actions of the adversary [61], which can be state-dependent and decide over the distribution of the transition and reward function from within the specified intervals. The solution to an RMDP also includes the policy of the adversary. For general uncertainty sets for $B$, it has been shown that the problem of finding an optimal robust policy is strongly NP-hard [80]. In order to find solutions in polynomial time, two main uncertainty sets for $B$ have been considered: s-rectangular and s, a-rectangular sets [61,80]. In the first case, the adversary can independently choose an outcome for each state $s$. In the second case, the adversary can choose an outcome for each state $s$ and action $a$ independently. Recent work has also given results when the uncertainty sets are less strict [23,51]. Taking into account the uncertainty with robust optimization can lead to better policies for the real environment [46,80].

There has also been some work that combines abstraction with RMDP [46, 61]. The RAAM algorithm [61] receives an abstraction function and an MDP as input. It first constructs an RMDP and uses this to compute an approximately optimal policy for the original MDP. It is shown that this can be beneficial in the limit; bounds on the performance are given that are similar to the bounds for $\epsilon$-bisimulation abstractions in planning [2]. The RAAM approach was later extended by Lim and Autef [46], who use a kernel-based approach, of which state abstraction can be seen as a special case.

The work in this section shows that uncertainty about the transition and reward functions can be dealt with in a principled way, given some uncertainty intervals. While some work connects this work to abstraction, it only focuses on results in the limit.

## 3.2  Leveraging an Abstraction Function

Often in RL, the environment will be unknown, but sometimes we have access abstraction function $\phi$. This $\phi$ could, for instance, come from a domain expert or result from the discretization of a continuous problem. With $\phi$, one could try to learn an abstract model, which is typically done by collecting data and then constructing a maximum likelihood model for the transition and reward functions in the abstract space. If we learn a correct abstract model and find the optimal policy for this problem, this solution can be near-optimal in the true MDP, depending on the abstraction used [2]. Learning in this way could be more sample-efficient than learning a model of the full MDP because the abstract space is smaller than the original state space.

One difficulty in this setting is learning a correct abstract model in the first place. In RL, samples can usually be considered independent, and this is used to show that an accurate model can be learned. In the combination of RL and abstraction, samples can no longer be considered independent due to perceptual aliasing [27,69,70]. In order to give sample efficiency results for RL plus abstraction, some work assumes that the collected samples are independent [17,60]. The work by Paduraru et al. [60] assumes that they receive a data set with independent and identically distributed (i.i.d.) samples and show a trade-off between the quality of the abstraction and the quality of the transition model. The quality of the abstraction is measured in terms of the $\epsilon$ of $\epsilon$-bisimulation. A larger $\epsilon$ means a coarser abstraction and a larger error. The second error relates to the number of samples we can get for a state-action pair, where a coarser abstraction gives more samples per state-action pair and a lower error. Like the work by Paduraru et al. [60], other work has also shown that the error of the agent can be decomposed into multiple components, which are based on the asymptotic bias of the representation and overfitting due to limited data (variance) [17,67]. This bias-variance trade-off indicates that using abstractions can be especially beneficial when the available data is limited while being less beneficial when much data is available, which has been illustrated in experiments [17].

The assumption that the generated data consists of independent samples does not hold in general. Another way to show that we can learn an accurate abstract model is by looking at convergence in the limit. The convergence to an accurate estimation of the abstract model is possible under several conditions, e.g., when the policy is fixed or when the abstraction is a bisimulation [27,69]. Having to use a fixed policy can be seen as a downside because a changing policy that explores helps to learn efficiently [71]. Another downside is that, in the limit, using the full model will be better than using an abstract model since only the error introduced by the bias remains, which is zero for the full model.

The work by Starre et al. [70] has recently shown that an accurate abstract model can still be learned by applying martingale theory [11]. They give the first finite-sample performance analysis for model-based RL plus abstraction by extending the results of an existing algorithm (R-MAX [9]) with the use of an $\epsilon$-bisimulation abstraction.

This section shows that abstractions can lead to better performance with fewer data, trading it off with less accuracy when much data is available. For these methods to work, it is required to already have a good abstraction function, which can be challenging.

### 3.3 Abstraction Selection

While the work in the previous section mainly focused on the case where we have one particular abstraction function, there is also a considerable amount that has focused on state representation selection, where the agent is provided with a set of state representations (or abstraction functions). It is usually assumed that a domain expert provides these representations, and the goal is to select the best representation, often in terms of regret.

Most of this work focuses on finding representations that make the problem Markov instead of focusing on finding good approximate abstractions. In order to deal with perceptual aliasing, most work assumes that the provided set contains a Markov model of the environment [25,48,49,54,59]. In order to find a correct representation in the online setting, these algorithms eliminate non-Markov models by comparing the obtained rewards during execution with a threshold based on a Markov model. The work by Lattimore et al. [41] considers a similar setting where the dynamics of the true environment depend arbitrarily on the history of actions, rewards, and observations. Instead of getting a set of representation functions, they assume access to a given set of models, one of which is a correct model of the true environment. In this way, they can compare the calculated expected reward for the given model with the rewards obtained during the process and eliminate the unlikely models.

Other work does not assume that a Markov representation is available [31,58], these both use an $\epsilon$-bisimulation type abstraction. The work of Ortner et al. [58] builds on the work of Maillard et al. [48] by removing the necessity of having a Markov representation in the set of available representations. However, the analysis is invalid since there is an issue in the proof on which they build [18]. They also do not take into perceptual aliasing since they use a concentration inequality that requires i.i.d. samples. The work by Jiang et al. [31] deals with perceptual aliasing by explicitly assuming in their analysis that a data set consisting of samples that are i.i.d. is available. They give a performance bound for policies based on a learned abstract model and split the error into two components, similar to some of the work mentioned in Sect. 3.2 [17,60]. These two components are used to create an algorithm that decides which representation should be used based on the available data.

The methods in this section show that we can learn to select a correct (Markov) representation, given an initial set of representations. Most of these methods are not very scalable, as they are tabular, and finding a good (Markov) representation/abstraction in larger problems can be challenging.

## 4    Online Abstraction Learning

The previously discussed works have mostly assumed that an abstract representation (or a set thereof) is readily available. However, this is not always possible. In this section, we consider the situation where such an abstraction is unavailable and has to be learned first while simultaneously learning about the environment. Two early studies on this topic provided promising experimental results [40,52]. Section 4.1 covers tabular approaches, which have mostly been more theoretical, and Sect. 4.2 covers deep learned representations focused on scaling up.

### 4.1    Tabular Approaches

The combination of MBRL and abstraction has also been approached theoretically. The work by Bernstein and Shimkin [7] gives results for online abstraction when the transition functions are deterministic. The work by Ortner [57] explores the more general case of stochastic transition functions when trying to learn a $\epsilon$-bisimulation. To learn a $\epsilon$-bisimulation they maintain an interval on the estimation of the transition and reward functions for each state-action pair, which is used to create a BPMDP [22]. Subsequently, the BPMDP is abstracted by clustering the states that overlap in the transition and reward function for all actions, but only if they have a similar amount of samples. They give an example to show that clustered states must have a similar amount of samples for all the actions to obtain good performance. This is an interesting observation since it points out a problem that should be taken into account when learning an abstraction in combination with MBRL. A downside of the method is that it focuses on the computational benefit abstraction can bring; from the perspective of sample efficiency, a method that utilizes abstraction to learn more efficiently is desirable.

In the Bayesian RL setting, the work by Mandel et al. [50] proposes an algorithm that does online clustering and exploration. The clustering is done over state-action pairs rather than only over states. State-action abstractions allow for a broader class of abstractions since state abstractions can be considered a subset of state-action abstractions while potentially still being optimality preserving.

This gives additional power in doing the abstraction since, in some domains, there could be no similar states while similar state-action pairs exist. State-action pairs are grouped when the relative outcomes are likely to be the same. Relative outcomes are similar to observations. Given a relative outcome, the agent knows both the transition and reward. However, it needs to learn the distribution over relative outcomes for each state.

Work in block MDPs, or MDPs with rich observations, is a related approach where the assumption is that each state can generate multiple different observations [5, 15, 24, 39, 82]. Instead of having multiple states that generate the same observation (due to the abstraction function), each type of observation is only generated by one state, but each state can generate multiple observations. This is similar to representation learning, specifically to learning a bisimulation [5, 15, 82]. A common approach in this setting is to use spectral methods [5, 24, 39]. For these to work, it is necessary to be able to uniquely identify states from the observation function. While this is possible for model-irrelevance abstractions, this is generally not possible in the abstraction setting.

The focus of tabular approaches has been on block MDPs, which can lead to a considerable reduction in the state space in suitable problems. However, this does require the problem to have many states with the same behavior in an abstract space, i.e., there needs to be a bisimulation abstraction. This restricts the number of problems to which these methods can be applied.

## 4.2    Deep Learned Representations

There have also been several Deep RL approaches that focus on learning compact state representations, which can be viewed as an instance of state abstraction. For instance, the approaches by Sermanet et al. [68], Thomas et al. [74], Biza and Platt [8], François-Lavet et al. [16], Van der Pol et al. [63], Schrittwieser et al. [66], Allen et al. [3], and Ye et al. [81]. One crucial notion for abstraction in deep RL is a collapse of the latent representation [3, 12, 16, 63]. When considering only the transition function, it would be optimal to cluster all states into exactly one abstract state. It has been shown that losses that require both the transition and reward function of grouped states to be the same can avoid this collapse [19], making it essential to group states based on both transitions and rewards.

Recently, multiple contrastive methods have been used to learn compact representations for predicting the next state [4, 37, 56]. Their representation learning tries to maximize the mutual information between the present and future samples. To train the network, they use positive and negative next-state samples, where the positive samples are transitions that occurred, while the negative samples are transitions that did not occur. These negative samples should help prevent the potential collapse of the state representation. Their methods do not use the model to plan the policy but instead use actor-critic and policy optimization methods on top of the representation. The proposed representation learning method was able to help improve the performance of these methods.

**Table 1.** Characterization of MBRL methods in combination with a type of state abstraction.

| Section | Method | Environment | Model | Abstraction $\phi$ | Abstraction Type | Theory | Scalability | Perceptual Aliasing |
|---|---|---|---|---|---|---|---|---|
| 2.1 | Planning- | MDP | Given | Constructed | Many | V | ~ | Not an issue |
| | Tabular RL | Abstract MDP | Given | Build-in | Bisimulation related | V | X | Not an issue |
| 3.1 | Robust Optimization | MDP | Given (interval) | Build-in | Bisimulation | V | ~ | Assumption on uncertainty |
| | Robust Optimization | MDP + $\phi$ | Given | Given | Bisimulation related | ~ | X | Not an issue |
| 3.2 | Tabular RL | MDP + $\phi$ | Unknown | Given | Bisimulation related | V | X | Assumptions on data gathering |
| 3.3 | Abstraction Selection | MDP + $[\phi_1, \cdots, \phi_n]$ | Unknown | Given | Several | V | X | Markov representation, assumption on data gathering |
| 4.1 | Tabular RL | MDP + $\phi$ | Unknown | Learned | Bisimulation related | V | X | Markov representation, specific check |
| | Bayesian RL | MDP + $\phi$ | Unknown | Learned | $(s,a)$-abstraction | V | X | Markov representation |
| | Spectral Methods | Block-MDP | Unknown | Learned | Bisimulation related | V | ~ | Markov representation |
| 4.2 | Deep RL | MDP + $\phi$ | Unknown | Learned | Bisimulation related | ~ | V | Markov representation, potential problem |
| | Contrastive Loss | MDP + $\phi$ | Unknown | Learned | Bisimulation related | X | V | Markov representation, potential problem |
| | Linear Latent Representations | MDP + $\phi$ | Unknown | Learned | Linear Function | X | V | Markov representation, potential problem |

Other work has focused on learning deep representations for robotics [12, 33, 43]. This has investigated adding several types of robotic priors to bias the representation learning, which are added to the network as an auxiliary loss [30]. These priors encode knowledge about physics, e.g., that changes in the state are often gradual rather than abrupt. The state-representation objectives were instrumental in generalizing, as they significantly improved the results in the test domain. This shows that learning a compact model of the environment can be beneficial even if the model itself is not directly used for planning. Other methods for robotics focus on finding compact linear representations of a problem and finding a policy for this smaller model [76, 79, 83]. This has shown promising results for robotics, where many of the essential state features could be approximately linear.

Most of the work in this section focused on learning exact abstractions. They try to reduce the problem so that the resulting latent representation still makes the problem an MDP. This can be difficult to ensure, especially in Deep RL, so it is likely that the resulting representation is an approximate abstraction. Since most work does not acknowledge this, they do not consider the resulting perceptual aliasing, and algorithms can experience the problem illustrated by [57]: when states with a different number of visitations are grouped, this can lead to suboptimal policies. When this is not taken into account, this can lead an agent to be stuck in a suboptimal loop.

## 5   Discussion and Conclusion

We summarize our overview in Table 1, which compares the approaches on the type of environment, whether or not a model is given, how an abstraction $\phi$ is obtained, what kind of abstraction is used, available theoretical support, scalability, and how they deal with perceptual aliasing.

The methods in Sects. 2 and 3 generally have strong theoretical support (V) in the form of bounded loss (e.g., [2, 80]), finite-sample guarantees (e.g., [60, 70]), or regret bounds (e.g., [49]). Most of these methods are not (X) scalable due to being tabular or only somewhat scalable ($\sim$) due to needing to be given a model, which in many cases is not possible. In most of these works, the problem of perceptual aliasing does not arise, either because of assumptions on data gathering or because an MDP, or MDP representation, is provided. Without assuming that samples are independent, Starre et al. [70] show that finite-sample bounds for MBRL in an MDP with an $\epsilon$-bisimulation can be obtained. *Extending these results to other types of abstractions is still an open question.*

In Sect. 3.2, we saw a bias-variance trade-off with abstractions [17, 31, 60, 67]. Because of this trade-off, *an interesting direction would be to combine learning multiple representations with abstraction selection to decide which representation to use at which time.*

As discussed in Sect. 3.1, results for optimization under uncertainty could make it interesting to maintain confidence intervals for the learned models and use robust optimization to find policies. Since the model will generally not be completely accurate during learning, robust optimization could improve performance [46]. Tabular work discussed in Sects. 3.1 and 4.1 investigated this idea [57,61], *scaling such approaches to larger problems is an interesting future direction.*

Most of the focus has been on abstractions related to bisimulation. As touched upon in Sect. 4.1, abstractions that aggregate state-action pairs can be more potent than state abstractions [50]. An open question is *what are the best types of abstraction to use?* Non-deterministic abstraction [69], temporal abstraction, or combinations of abstractions could be powerful but have not been as well studied [38].

In work by Schrittwieser et al. [66], there is some indication that, in online planning, using a coarser learned model rather than the true model can be beneficial. With limited planning time, planning with a compact learned model outperformed planning with the true model of the environment. *There could be a trade-off for learning between the coarseness of the model and the allotted planning time; a coarser model could perform better with a shorter planning time but worse with a longer planning time.*

The methods in Sect. 4.2 focus on learning abstractions that result in a Markov representation, e.g., bisimulation abstractions. However, *during learning, when the abstraction is likely not a Markov representation, perceptual aliasing occurs. How can the resulting non-stationarity be addressed?* In Sect. 4.1, we saw that the tabular work by Ortner [57] deals with perceptual aliasing, but to do so, it maintains visitation counts for all state-action pairs. Methods that can maintain counts in an approximate way, such as pseudo-counts [72], could enable a scalable version of the approach by Ortner [57]. Another approach to deal with perceptual aliasing in a more sample-efficient way could be using an algorithm such as ITER [28], which tackles the general non-stationarity of the data distribution caused by the RL algorithm. The idea of the algorithm is to frequently transfer the knowledge of the trained network to a new network and then use the new network for training. The knowledge is transferred through samples that are obtained from the collected data set as if they had been generated with the final policy of the trained network.

In multi-agent RL, the challenge is to behave optimally in the presence of other agents whose behavior may be non-stationary [26]. *Approaches for the multi-agent RL problem that address non-stationarity could be insightful for the combination of RL and abstraction.* One approach that could be relevant is trying to capture the non-stationarity that is the result of perceptual aliasing, which could, for instance, be done by using influence-based abstraction [55]. Influence-based abstraction aims to abstract a problem into a smaller local problem with a predictor that quantifies the influence of variables outside the local problem on the local problem. Given an accurate predictor, this results in a Markov problem. Such a predictor could capture the non-stationarity due to perceptual aliasing and improve performance. Influence-based abstraction has been applied together with Deep model-free RL, using a recurrent neural network to capture the influence, which has shown promising results [10].

Other approaches in multi-agent RL do not deal with the non-stationarity but simply ignore it by abstracting away the internal states of the other agents. Since this can be seen as a special case of the non-stationarity in the combination of RL and abstraction, insights from this combination on how to deal with non-stationarity as a result of perceptual aliasing could provide interesting directions for these multi-agent RL approaches.

**Acknowledgement.** This project had received funding from the European Research Council (ERC) under the European Union's Horizon 2020 research and innovation programme (grant agreement No. 758824—INFLUENCE).

# References

1. Abel, D., Arumugam, D., Lehnert, L., Littman, M.: State abstractions for lifelong reinforcement learning. In: ICML (2018)
2. Abel, D., Hershkowitz, D., Littman, M.: Near optimal behavior via approximate state abstraction. In: ICML (2016)
3. Allen, C., Parikh, N., Gottesman, O., Konidaris, G.: Learning markov state abstractions for deep reinforcement learning. In: NeurIPS (2021)
4. Anand, A., Racah, E., Ozair, S., Bengio, Y., Côté, M.A., Hjelm, R.D.: Unsupervised state representation learning in atari. In: NeurIPS (2019)
5. Azizzadenesheli, K., Lazaric, A., Anandkumar, A.: Reinforcement learning in rich-observation mdps using spectral methods. arXiv (2016)
6. Bai, A., Srivastava, S., Russell, S.J.: Markovian state and action abstractions for MDPs via hierarchical MCTS. In: IJCAI (2016)
7. Bernstein, A., Shimkin, N.: Adaptive-resolution reinforcement learning with polynomial exploration in deterministic domains. ML **81**, 359–397 (2010)
8. Biza, O., Platt, R.: Online abstraction with MDP homomorphisms for deep learning. arXiv (2018)
9. Brafman, R.I., Tennenholtz, M.: R-max-a general polynomial time algorithm for near-optimal reinforcement learning. JMLR **3**, 213–231 (2002)
10. Suau de Castro, M., Congeduti, E., Starre, R., Czechowski, A., Oliehoek, F.: Influence-based abstraction in deep reinforcement learning. In: AAMAS Workshop on Adaptive Learning Agents (2019)
11. Chow, Y.S., Teicher, H.: Probability Theory: Independence, Interchangeability, Martingales. Springer, New York (2003)
12. De Bruin, T., Kober, J., Tuyls, K., Babuška, R.: Integrating state representation learning into deep reinforcement learning. RA-L **3**(3), 1394–1401 (2018)
13. Dean, T., Givan, R.: Model minimization in Markov decision processes. In: AAAI/IAAI (1997)
14. Dean, T., Givan, R., Leach, S.: Model reduction techniques for computing approximately optimal solutions for Markov decision processes. In: UAI (1997)
15. Du, S., Krishnamurthy, A., Jiang, N., Agarwal, A., Dudik, M., Langford, J.: Provably efficient RL with rich observations via latent state decoding. In: ICML (2019)

16. François-Lavet, V., Bengio, Y., Precup, D., Pineau, J.: Combined reinforcement learning via abstract representations. In: AAAI (2019)
17. François-Lavet, V., Rabusseau, G., Pineau, J., Ernst, D., Fonteneau, R.: On overfitting and asymptotic bias in batch reinforcement learning with partial observability. JAIR **65**, 1–30 (2019)
18. Fruit, R., Pirotta, M., Lazaric, A.: Near optimal exploration-exploitation in non-communicating Markov decision processes. In: NeurIPS (2018)
19. Gelada, C., Kumar, S., Buckman, J., Nachum, O., Bellemare, M.G.: Deepmdp: learning continuous latent space models for representation learning. In: ICML (2019)
20. Ghavamzadeh, M., Mannor, S., Pineau, J., Tamar, A.: Bayesian reinforcement learning: a survey. Found. Trends Mach. Learn. **8**, 359–483 (2015)
21. Givan, R., Dean, T., Greig, M.: Equivalence notions and model minimization in Markov decision processes. Artif. Intell. **147**(1–2), 163–223 (2003)
22. Givan, R., Leach, S., Dean, T.: Bounded-parameter Markov decision processes. Artif. Intell. **122**(1–2), 71–109 (2000)
23. Goyal, V., Grand-Clement, J.: Robust Markov decision process: beyond rectangularity. arXiv (2018)
24. Guo, Z.D., Doroudi, S., Brunskill, E.: A PAC RL algorithm for episodic POMDPs. In: AISTATS (2016)
25. Hallak, A., Di-Castro, D., Mannor, S.: Model selection in markovian processes. In: SIGKDD (2013)
26. Hernandez-Leal, P., Kaisers, M., Baarslag, T., de Cote, E.M.: A survey of learning in multiagent environments: dealing with non-stationarity. arXiv (2017)
27. Hutter, M.: Extreme state aggregation beyond Markov decision processes. TCS **650**, 73–91 (2016)
28. Igl, M., Farquhar, G., Luketina, J., Boehmer, W., Whiteson, S.: Transient non-stationarity and generalisation in deep reinforcement learning. In: ICLR (2021)
29. Igl, M., Zintgraf, L., Le, T.A., Wood, F., Whiteson, S.: Deep variational reinforcement learning for pomdps. In: ICML (2018)
30. Jaderberg, M., et al.: Reinforcement learning with unsupervised auxiliary tasks. arXiv (2016)
31. Jiang, N., Kulesza, A., Singh, S.: Abstraction selection in model-based reinforcement learning. In: ICML (2015)
32. Jie, N.: Representation learning for model-based reinforcement learning: a survey (2021). https://tinyurl.com/jieRep
33. Jonschkowski, R., Brock, O.: Learning state representations with robotic priors. Auton. Robots **39**, 407–428 (2015)
34. Kaelbling, L.P., Littman, M.L., Cassandra, A.R.: Planning and acting in partially observable stochastic domains. Artif. Intell. **101**(1–2), 99–134 (1998)
35. Karkus, P., Hsu, D., Lee, W.S.: QMDP-Net: deep learning for planning under partial observability. arXiv (2017)
36. Keith, A.J., Ahner, D.K.: A survey of decision making and optimization under uncertainty. Ann. Oper. Res. **300**(2), 319–353 (2021)
37. Kipf, T., van der Pol, E., Welling, M.: Contrastive learning of structured world models. In: ICLR (2019)
38. Konidaris, G.: On the necessity of abstraction. Curr. Opin. Behav. Sci. **29**, 1–7 (2019)
39. Krishnamurthy, A., Agarwal, A., Langford, J.: Pac reinforcement learning with rich observations. arXiv (2016)

40. Kuvayev, L., Sutton, R.S.: Model-based reinforcement learning with an approximate, learned model. In: Yale Workshop on Adaptive and Learning Systems (1996)
41. Lattimore, T., Hutter, M., Sunehag, P.: The sample-complexity of general reinforcement learning. In: ICML (2013)
42. Lesort, T., Díaz-Rodríguez, N., Goudou, J.F., Filliat, D.: State representation learning for control: an overview. Neural Netw. **108**, 379–392 (2018)
43. Lesort, T., Seurin, M., Li, X., Díaz-Rodríguez, N., Filliat, D.: Deep unsupervised state representation learning with robotic priors: a robustness analysis. In: IJCNN (2019)
44. Li, L., Walsh, T.J., Littman, M.L.: Towards a unified theory of state abstraction for MDPs. In: ISAIM (2006)
45. Li, L.: A unifying framework for computational reinforcement learning theory. Ph.D. thesis, Rutgers University-Graduate School-New Brunswick (2009)
46. Lim, S.H., Autef, A.: Kernel-based reinforcement learning in robust Markov decision processes. In: ICML (2019)
47. Ma, X., Karkus, P., Hsu, D., Lee, W.S., Ye, N.: Discriminative particle filter reinforcement learning for complex partial observations. In: ICLR (2019)
48. Maillard, O.A., Nguyen, P., Ortner, R., Ryabko, D.: Optimal regret bounds for selecting the state representation in reinforcement learning. In: ICML (2013)
49. Maillard, O.A., Ryabko, D., Munos, R.: Selecting the state-representation in reinforcement learning. In: NeurIPS (2011)
50. Mandel, T., Liu, Y.E., Brunskill, E., Popovic, Z.: Efficient bayesian clustering for reinforcement learning. In: IJCAI (2016)
51. Mannor, S., Mebel, O., Xu, H.: Robust MDPs with k-rectangular uncertainty. MOOR **41**(4), 1484–1509 (2016)
52. McCallum, A.K.: Reinforcement learning with selective perception and hidden state. University of Rochester (1996)
53. Moerland, T.M., Broekens, J., Jonker, C.M.: Model-based reinforcement learning: a survey. arXiv (2020)
54. Nguyen, P., Maillard, O.A., Ryabko, D., Ortner, R.: Competing with an infinite set of models in reinforcement learning. In: AISTATS (2013)
55. Oliehoek, F.A., Witwicki, S.J., Kaelbling, L.P.: Influence-based abstraction for multiagent systems. In: AAAI (2012)
56. Van den Oord, A., Li, Y., Vinyals, O.: Representation learning with contrastive predictive coding. arXiv (2018)
57. Ortner, R.: Adaptive aggregation for reinforcement learning in average reward Markov decision processes. Ann. Oper. Res. **208**, 321–336 (2013)
58. Ortner, R., Maillard, O.A., Ryabko, D.: Selecting near-optimal approximate state representations in reinforcement learning. In: ALT (2014)
59. Ortner, R., Pirotta, M., Lazaric, A., Fruit, R., Maillard, O.A.: Regret bounds for learning state representations in reinforcement learning. In: NeurIPS (2019)
60. Paduraru, C., Kaplow, R., Precup, D., Pineau, J.: Model-based reinforcement learning with state aggregation. In: European Workshop on RL (2008)
61. Petrik, M., Subramanian, D.: RAAM: the benefits of robustness in approximating aggregated MDPs in reinforcement learning. In: NeurIPS (2014)
62. Plaat, A., Kosters, W., Preuss, M.: High-accuracy model-based reinforcement learning, a survey. arXiv (2021)
63. Van der Pol, E., Kipf, T., Oliehoek, F.A., Welling, M.: Plannable approximations to MDP homomorphisms: equivariance under actions. In: AAMAS (2020)
64. Puterman, M.L.: Markov Decision Processes: Discrete Stochastic Dynamic Programming. Wiley, Hoboken (2014)

65. Ross, S., Pineau, J., Chaib-draa, B., Kreitmann, P.: A Bayesian approach for learning and planning in partially observable Markov decision processes. JMLR **12**, 1729–1770 (2011)
66. Schrittwieser, J., et al.: Mastering atari, go, chess and shogi by planning with a learned model. Nature **588**(7839), 604–609 (2020)
67. Serban, I.V., Sankar, C., Pieper, M., Pineau, J., Bengio, Y.: The bottleneck simulator: a model-based deep reinforcement learning approach. JAIR **69**, 571–612 (2020)
68. Sermanet, P., et al.: Time-contrastive networks: self-supervised learning from video. In: ICRA (2018)
69. Singh, S.P., Jaakkola, T., Jordan, M.I.: Reinforcement learning with soft state aggregation. In: NeurIPS (1995)
70. Starre, R.A.N., Loog, M., Oliehoek, F.A.: An analysis of abstracted model-based reinforcement learning. arXiv (2022)
71. Strehl, A.L., Littman, M.L.: An analysis of model-based interval estimation for Markov decision processes. JCSS **74**(8), 1309–1331 (2008)
72. Taïga, A.A., Courville, A., Bellemare, M.G.: Approximate exploration through state abstraction. arXiv (2018)
73. Talvitie, E.: Model regularization for stable sample rollouts. In: UAI (2014)
74. Thomas, V., et al.: Disentangling the independently controllable factors of variation by interacting with the world. arXiv (2018)
75. Tschiatschek, S., Arulkumaran, K., Stühmer, J., Hofmann, K.: Variational inference for data-efficient model learning in pomdps. arXiv (2018)
76. Van Hoof, H., Chen, N., Karl, M., van der Smagt, P., Peters, J.: Stable reinforcement learning with autoencoders for tactile and visual data. In: IROS (2016)
77. Wald, A.: Statistical Decision Functions. Wiley, Hoboken (1950)
78. Wang, Y., Tan, X.: Deep recurrent belief propagation network for POMDPs. In: AAAI (2021)
79. Watter, M., Springenberg, J.T., Boedecker, J., Riedmiller, M.: Embed to control: a locally linear latent dynamics model for control from raw images. In: NeurIPS (2015)
80. Wiesemann, W., Kuhn, D., Rustem, B.: Robust Markov decision processes. MOOR **38**(1), 153–183 (2013)
81. Ye, W., Liu, S., Kurutach, T., Abbeel, P., Gao, Y.: Mastering atari games with limited data. In: NeurIPS (2021)
82. Zhang, A., et al.: Invariant causal prediction for block MDPs. In: ICML (2020)
83. Zhang, M., Vikram, S., Smith, L., Abbeel, P., Johnson, M., Levine, S.: Solar: deep structured representations for model-based reinforcement learning. In: ICML (2019)

# Symmetry and Dominance Breaking
# for Pseudo-Boolean Optimization

Daimy Van Caudenberg$^{(\boxtimes)}$ and Bart Bogaerts

Vrije Universiteit Brussel, Brussels, Belgium
{daimy.stefanie.van.caudenberg,bart.bogaerts}@vub.be

**Abstract.** It is well-known that highly symmetric problems can often be challenging for combinatorial search and optimization solvers. One technique to avoid this problem is to introduce so-called symmetry breaking constraints, which eliminate some symmetric parts of the search space. In this paper, we focus on *pseudo-Boolean optimization problems*, which are specified by a set of 0–1 integer linear inequalities (also known as *pseudo-Boolean constraints*) and a linear objective. Symmetry breaking has already been studied in this context; however previous work could only deal with symmetries of the entire optimization problem. In this paper, we show how to handle *weak symmetries*: symmetries of the constraints that do not necessarily need to respect the objective. We show that weak symmetries induce a *dominance relation* and that pseudo-Boolean constraints are a natural target formalism to write the dominance breaking constraints in. We implemented these ideas on top of a state-of-the-art symmetry breaking tool for SAT, and in doing so also transfer modern symmetry breaking techniques to pseudo-Boolean optimization. We experimentally validate our approach on the latest pseudo-Boolean competition, as well as on hard combinatorial instances and conclude that the effect of breaking (weak) symmetries depends greatly on the type of solving algorithm used.

**Keywords:** Symmetry breaking · Dominance breaking · Pseudo-Boolean optimization

## 1 Introduction

Hard combinatorial decision and optimization problems often exhibit symmetries. It is well-known that when these symmetries are not properly taken into account, solvers can easily get stuck exploring many symmetric versions of the search space. To overcome this limitation, a variety of techniques has been developed; we here make the distinction between *static* (prior to the search) and *dynamic* (during search) symmetry handling techniques.

This work was partially supported by Fonds Wetenschappelijk Onderzoek – Vlaanderen (FWO) (project G070521N); computational resources and services were provided by the VSC (Flemish Supercomputer Center), funded by FWO and the Flemish Government.

*Static* symmetry handling techniques all perform *symmetry breaking*: that is, they add new constraints that eliminate some, but not all symmetric assignments. One way to achieve this is by adding so-called *lex-leader constraints*, which discard all assignments that are lexicographically larger than their symmetric counterpart. This type of symmetry breaking (with lex-leader or other constraints) is used in various fields [3,11,13,14,16,17,20,22,23,27,30,40].

*Dynamic* symmetry handling techniques come in different flavours. Most methods work on a set of symmetries of the input formula, but some also detect symmetries during the search [5]. Some methods actually *break* the symmetries (and hence potentially also remove satisfying assignments), e.g., by adopting a branching method that takes symmetries into account [36], or by lazily posting the symmetry breaking constraints that static techniques would also add [28,32]. Other methods only eliminate unsatisfiable regions of the search space [7]; the most common such technique is *symmetric learning*, which allows a solver to learn symmetric versions of learned clauses or no-goods when constructing an unsatisfiability proof [6,15,18,26,31,37].

The advantage of static techniques is that they are solver- and algorithm-agnostic: they can be combined with any type of search algorithm and hence are also compatible with future developments. The main drawback of static techniques is that it is difficult to know in advance which symmetry breaking constraints will be effective (will contribute to decreasing the search space), while adding all possible symmetry breaking constraints is too costly.

In this paper, we study static symmetry breaking techniques for *pseudo-Boolean optimization*, where we are given a set $F$ of 0–1 integer linear inequalities and a linear term $f$ (i.e. respectively the pseudo-Boolean constraints and the objective) and are asked to search for a solution to $F$ that minimizes $f$. We are not the first to study symmetries in this setting: already in 2004, Aloul et al. [2] extended SHATTER [3] (a symmetry breaking preprocessor for SAT) to pseudo-Boolean optimization. They detect symmetries $\sigma$ of the entire optimization problem: permutations (of literals) $\sigma$ such that $\sigma(F) = F$ and $\sigma(f) = f$, i.e. $\sigma(F)$ is syntactically equal to $F$ and similarly for $f$. For such symmetries, they add (a clausal encoding of) lex-leader constraints: a set of clauses that expresses that a solution should be lexicographically smaller than its symmetric counterpart. In this paper, we will show that many of the techniques can be generalized to a more general setting. We will define a *weak symmetry* of $(F, f)$ to be a symmetry of $F$, that not necessarily preserves $f$. Some care is needed when adding breaking constraints in this setting. We will show that weak symmetries give rise to a *dominance relation* [10] and will describe constraints that break weak symmetries in a sound way, roughly expressing that we are only interested in assignments that

– are at least as good (in terms of the objective) as their symmetric counterpart, and
– are lexicographically smaller than (or equal to) their symmetric counterpart, in case they have the same objective value.

As it turns out, this can easily be expressed as pseudo-Boolean constraints.

We implemented this idea on top of BREAKID, a symmetry breaking pre-processor for SAT [16]. The resulting tool (which we call BREAKIDPB) differs from SHATTER in the following ways:

- first and foremost, it can handle weak symmetries,
- it integrates all the improvements of BREAKID [16], such as detection of so-called *row-interchangeability*, and
- it can break symmetries with a native pseudo-Boolean encoding (rather than a clausal encoding).

We experimentally validate our techniques on the latest pseudo-Boolean competition, as well as on hard combinatorial instances. Our results are mixed: depending on which type of search algorithm is used to solve the resulting problem (after symmetry breaking), we see that (weak) symmetry breaking can have a very positive or a very negative impact. Moreover, we observed an interesting side-effect where weak symmetry breaking had a positive impact on instances that do not exhibit weak symmetries.

The rest of this paper is structured as follows. In Sect. 2 we present the necessary background for understanding our work. Section 3 describes the framework of dominance relations and how so-called *weak symmetries* fit within this framework. In Sect. 4 we explain how BREAKID was extended into BREAKIDPB and Sect. 5 contains the experimental results.

*Publication History.* This paper is based on the bachelor thesis of the first author [38]. A short version of this paper was presented at the BNAIC/BeneLearn 2022 conference [39]. The current paper extends the short version with more examples, a precise description of the graph that is created, and more extensive experiments.

## 2 Preliminaries

In this section, we recall some standard definitions related to pseudo-Boolean optimization. A *literal* $\ell$ over a Boolean variable $x$ is $x$ itself or its negation $\overline{x} = 1 - x$, where variables take values 0 (false) or 1 (true). A *pseudo-Boolean (PB) constraint* $C$ is a 0–1 linear inequality

$$\sum_i a_i \ell_i \geq A, \tag{1}$$

where $a_i$ and $A$ are integers. Without loss of generality, we will often assume that PB constraints are *normalized*; i.e., that all literals $\ell_i$ are over distinct variables and that the *coefficients* $a_i$ and the *degree (of falsity)* $A$ are non-negative, but most of the time we will not need this. A *pseudo-Boolean formula* $F$ is a conjunction $\bigwedge_j C_j$ of PB constraints, which we can also think of as the set $\bigcup_j \{C_j\}$ of constraints in the formula, choosing whichever viewpoint seems most convenient. An *assignment* $\alpha$ is a function from a set of variables $V$ to $\{0, 1\}$. An assignment is *complete* for $F$ if it assigns a value to all the variables in $F$.

Slightly abusing notation, we extend an assignment to literals in the natural way, by respecting negation where $\alpha$ is defined and being constant where $\alpha$ is not defined. I.e., if $\alpha$ is the assignment of the set of variables $V$ we will write $\alpha(\overline{x})$ to mean $1 - \alpha(x)$ if $x \in V$ and to denote $\overline{x}$ if $x \notin V$. The (normalized) constraint $C$ in (1) is *satisfied* by $\alpha$ (denoted $\alpha \models C$) if $\sum_{\alpha(\ell_i)=1} a_i \geq A$. A PB formula is satisfied if all of its constraints are satisfied. A *pseudo-Boolean optimization problem*[1] is a tuple $(F, f)$ with $F$ a PB formula and $f$ a linear objective $\sum_i w_i \ell_i$. We write $f^\alpha$ for the value of $f$ in $\alpha$, i.e., for $\sum_i w_i \alpha(\ell_i)$. An assignment $\alpha$ is an *(optimal) solution* to $(F, f)$ if $\alpha \models F$ and $f^\alpha \leq f^\beta$ for each $\beta$ that satisfies $F$.

Let $\pi$ be a permutation of the set of literals over variables in $F$ (i.e., a bijection on the set of literals) that respects negation. We extend $\pi$ to various semantic objects in the expected way:

- pseudo-Boolean Constraints $\pi(\sum_i a_i l_i \geq A) = \sum_i a_i \pi(l_i) \geq A$,
- to pseudo-Boolean formulas: $\pi(C_1 \wedge \ldots \wedge C_n) = \pi(C_1) \wedge \ldots \wedge \pi(C_n)$,
- to linear terms: $\pi(f)(\sum_i w_i \ell_i) = \sum_i w_i \pi(\ell_i)$, and
- to assignments: $\pi(\alpha) = \alpha \circ \pi^{-1}$,

where the last, seemingly strange, condition guarantees for instance that $\alpha \models F$ if and only if $\pi(\alpha) \models \pi(F)$. We call $\pi$ a *(syntactic) symmetry*[2] of $F$ if $\pi(F) = F$ and a *strong symmetry* of $(F, f)$ if additionally $\pi(f) = f$. In that case, $\alpha$ is an optimal solution of $(F, f)$ if and only if $\pi(\alpha)$ is.

# 3   Weak Symmetries

So far, in the literature, only symmetries of pseudo-Boolean optimization problems that preserve the formula $F$ and objective function $f$ have been considered. However, we know that in many problems, symmetries of $F$ show up that do not preserve $f$. Take for instance a nurse scheduling problem where large sets of nurses are interchangeable (given that some basic features, e.g. their degrees, are equal), but their preferences are not (the soft constraints, e.g. whether they prefer working during the weekends or night shifts). This gives rise to the following definition.

**Definition 1.** *Every symmetry $\omega$ of $F$ is called a* weak symmetry *of the optimization problem $(F, f)$.*

The strategy for breaking *strong* symmetries, as employed, e.g., by Aloul et al. [1] is to add *lex-leader* constraints. That is, given an order on the variables, for each detected[3] strong symmetry $\sigma$, they add a set $LL_\sigma$ of pseudo-Boolean constraints such that for each total assignment $\alpha$, $\alpha$ can be extended to a model

---

[1] Decision problems are a special case where $F = 0$.

[2] More general definitions of symmetry exist, but all practical use cases of symmetry detection and elimination use syntactic symmetries.

[3] In practice, this is typically a set of generators of the group of strong symmetries.

of $LL_\sigma$ if and only if $\alpha$ is lexicographically smaller than (or equal to) $\sigma(\alpha)$. When working with *weak symmetries*, this strategy is no longer applicable. Indeed, it might be the case that $\sigma(\alpha)$ is lexicographically smaller than $\alpha$, but also has a worse objective than $\alpha$. In that case, we do not want to derive constraints that exclude $\alpha$. In the rest of this section, we will show in detail how to handle weak symmetries. As a theoretic framework, we will use *dominance relations* as studied in the field of constraint programming [10]. In the rest of this section, we describe how to use this framework (in the context of PB formulas) to generate breaking constraints for weak symmetries, how to detect these symmetries, and how BREAKID can be adapted to handle weak symmetries.

### 3.1  Dominance Relations

A dominance relation describes a pair of assignments, where one *dominates* the other when that assignment is better than the other in some "suitable sense". That "suitable sense" can be comparing the objective of the problem, or it can be something more complex. Similar to symmetries, these relations can be used to prune the search tree. Dominance relations can be exploited to add formulas that prevent the search from exploring non-dominant assignments, which we will call *Static Dominance Breaking*.

**Definition 2.** *A dominance relation $\preceq$ (for $(F, f)$) is a pre-order (a reflexive and transitive binary relation) on the set of assignments (that assign values to all variables in $F$ and $f$) such that whenever $\alpha \preceq \beta$ it holds that*

- $f^\alpha \leq f^\beta$
- *if $\beta \models F$, then also $\alpha \models F$.*

I.e., the dominance relation should respect the problem specified by the couple $(F, f)$ in the sense that non-models of $F$ cannot dominate models of $F$ and whenever one assignment dominates another, it should be at least as good as the other assignment in terms of the objective function. As usual, our preorder $\preceq$ induces a partial order $\prec$ (an irreflexive, transitive and asymmetric binary relation) where $\alpha \prec \beta$ if and only if $\alpha \preceq \beta$ and $\beta \not\preceq \alpha$.

*Example 1.* Assume $S$ is a set of strong symmetries of $(F, f)$. In that case, the relation $\preceq_S$ defined as

$$\{(\sigma(\alpha), \alpha) \mid \sigma \in \langle S \rangle \wedge \sigma(\alpha) \leq_{lex} \alpha\}, \tag{2}$$

where $\langle S \rangle$ denotes the group generated by $S$, is a dominance relation for $(F, f)$.

We now define what we mean by a dominance breaking formula. As we will see later in Proposition 1, soundness of a dominance breaking formula means that we can safely add it to $F$, without changing the objective value. One observation regarding this definition is that in the context of SAT and PB solving, contrary to the CP setting where our definition of dominance relation was borrowed from, formulas to break symmetries or dominance relations will typically contain fresh variables (sometimes also called *extension variables*). This is precisely why the definition that follows refers to *extensions* of an assignment $\alpha$, which are assignments $\alpha'$ that agree with $\alpha$ wherever $\alpha$ is defined.

**Definition 3.** *Let $\preceq$ be a dominance relation. A set $D$ of pseudo-Boolean constraints is called a* sound dominance breaking formula *for $\preceq$ if for each assignment $\alpha$ that cannot be extended to a model of $D$, there exists some assignment $\beta$ with $\beta \prec \alpha$.*

*$D$ is called* complete *if additionally whenever $\beta \prec \alpha$, $\alpha$ cannot be extended to a model of $D$.*

Rephrased, a sound dominance breaking formula is a formula that does not eliminate $\preceq$-minimal assignments; it is complete if it eliminates all non-$\preceq$-minimal assignments.

**Proposition 1.** *If $D$ is a sound dominance breaking formula, then at least one optimal solution of $(F, f)$ can be extended to an optimal solution of $(F \cup D, f)$. Hence,*

$$(F, f) \quad and \quad (F \cup D, f)$$

*have the same optimal objective value.*

To see why this proposition holds, note that whenever $\alpha$ cannot be extended to satisfy $D$, this means that there exists another assignment that is *strictly* better. As a result, $D$ only prunes assignments that are strictly dominated, and it is safe to add $D$ to the pseudo-Boolean formula $F$ in the sense that we are guaranteed not to prune all optimal solutions.

*Example 2.* If, as before, $LL_\sigma$ is a set of lex-leader constraints, then

$$\bigcup_{\sigma \in \mathcal{S}} LL_\sigma$$

is a sound dominance breaking formula for the dominance relation $\preceq_\mathcal{S}$ from Example 1.

## 3.2   Weak Symmetries and Dominance Relations

The constraints in the previous example are precisely what SHATTER [1] adds for breaking strong symmetries. We now turn our attention to weak symmetries by showing that they indeed also define a dominance relation and by constructing a sound dominance breaking formula for them.

**Proposition 2.** *Let $\mathcal{W}$ be a set of weak symmetries of $(F, f)$. The relation $\preceq_\mathcal{W}$ defined as*

$$\left\{ (\omega(\alpha), \alpha) \;\middle|\; \begin{array}{l} \omega \in \langle \mathcal{W} \rangle \\ \wedge\, f^{\omega(\alpha)} \leq f^\alpha \\ \wedge\, (f^{\omega(\alpha)} = f^\alpha \Rightarrow \omega(\alpha) \leq_{lex} \alpha) \end{array} \right\}$$

*is a dominance relation for $(F, f)$.*

*Proof.* Reflexivity follows since *id* (the identity function) is in $\langle \mathcal{W} \rangle$ (it is its neutral element). Transitivity holds since composition is internal in $\langle \mathcal{W} \rangle$.     □

Now we construct a dominance breaking formula for this dominance relation. We will again assume that for each weak symmetry $\omega$, we have PB formula $LL_\omega$ such that $\alpha$ can be extended to a model of $LL_\omega$ if and only if $\alpha$ is lexicographically smaller than (or equal to) $\omega(\alpha)$. Slightly abusing notation, we will write

$$(f = \omega(f)) \Rightarrow LL_\omega$$

to denote a PB formula that is satisfied precisely by those assignments $\alpha$ for which $f^\alpha \neq \omega(f)^\alpha$ or for which $\alpha \models LL_\omega$. We will later show how to construct such a formula.

The idea of our dominance breaking formula is to discard candidate solutions whose symmetric variant has a strictly better solution (according to the objective function), as well as candidate solutions whose symmetric variants have an equally good objective function value, but that are lexicographically larger than their symmetric counterpart.

**Proposition 3.** *Let $\mathcal{W}$ be a set of weak symmetries of $(F, f)$. For every $\omega$ in $\mathcal{W}$, the PB formula $BF_\omega$ defined as*

$$\left\{ \begin{array}{c} f \leq \omega(f) \\ (f = \omega(f)) \Rightarrow LL_\omega \end{array} \right\} \tag{3}$$

*forms a sound dominance breaking formula for $\preceq_\mathcal{W}$.*

Intuitively, the first constraint discards candidate solutions whose symmetric variant has a strictly better solution and the second constraint discards candidate solutions whose symmetric variants have an equally good objective function value, but that are lexicographically larger than their symmetric counterpart.

*Proof (Proof of Proposition 3).* We only have to show soundness. Hence, assume $\alpha$ cannot be extended to an assignment that satisfies $BF_\omega$. We claim that in that case $\omega(\alpha) \prec_\mathcal{W} \alpha$. The fact that $\omega(\alpha) \preceq_\mathcal{W} \alpha$ is immediate: since $\alpha$ cannot be extended to satisfy $BF_\omega$, there are two possible situations:

- either $\alpha \not\models f \leq \omega(f)$, but in this case clearly $(\omega(\alpha), \alpha) \in \preceq_\mathcal{W}$,
- or $\alpha \models f = \omega(f)$, and $\alpha$ cannot be extended to satisfy $LL_\omega$, but in this case $\alpha \not\leq_{lex} \omega(\alpha)$ and hence $\omega(\alpha) \leq_{lex} \alpha$ and again $(\omega(\alpha), \alpha) \in \preceq_\mathcal{W}$.

We also need to show that $\alpha \not\preceq_\mathcal{W} \omega(\alpha)$. Assume towards contradiction that $\alpha \preceq_\mathcal{W} \omega(\alpha)$. In that case, by the definition of $\preceq_\mathcal{W}$, there must be some $\omega' \in \mathcal{W}$ such that

- $\omega'(\omega(\alpha)) = \alpha$,
- $f^{\omega'(\omega(\alpha))} \leq f^{\omega(\alpha)}$, and
- $f^{\omega'(\omega(\alpha))} = f^{\omega(\alpha)} \Rightarrow \omega'(\omega(\alpha)) \leq_{lex} \omega(\alpha)$

Hence we find that

$$f^\alpha = f^{\omega'(\omega(\alpha))} \leq f^{\omega(\alpha)} \leq f^\alpha,$$

and $f^\alpha = f^{\omega(\alpha)}$. But using the last item, we then find that $\alpha \leq_{lex} \omega(\alpha)$, which contradicts our earlier assumption that $\alpha$ cannot be extended to satisfy $BF_\omega$.     □

### 3.3   Encoding the Symmetry Breaking Formula

What remains to be explained is how the pseudo-Boolean encoding of (3) is constructed. In order to explain this, we first recall that BREAKID's encoding of $LL_\omega$ consists of the clauses (written here as pseudo-Boolean formulas)

$$y_0 \geq 1, \tag{4a}$$
$$\overline{y}_{j-1} + \overline{x}_{i_j} + \omega(x_{i_j}) \geq 1, \qquad 1 \leq j \leq n \tag{4b}$$
$$\overline{y}_j + y_{j-1} \geq 1, \qquad 1 \leq j < n \tag{4c}$$
$$\overline{y}_j + \overline{\omega(x_{i_j})} + x_{i_j} \geq 1, \qquad 1 \leq j < n \tag{4d}$$
$$y_j + \overline{y}_{j-1} + \overline{x}_{i_j} \geq 1, \text{ and} \qquad 1 \leq j < n \tag{4e}$$
$$y_j + \overline{y}_{j-1} + \omega(x_{i_j}) \geq 1, \qquad 1 \leq j < n \tag{4f}$$

where $\{x_{i_1}, \ldots, x_{i_n}\}$ is the *support* of $\omega$ (i.e., all variables $x$ such that $\omega(x) \neq x$), ordered so that $i_j \leq i_k$ if and only if $j \leq k$. In this formula, each $y_j$ is a fresh variable representing that up to $x_{i_j}$, $\alpha$ and $\omega(\alpha)$ are equal. Equation (4b) does the actual breaking.

What is important to note in this formula is that all the actual breaking is conditional on $y_0$ being true (as specified in (4a)). Indeed, if we would instead replace (4a) by $\overline{y}_0 \geq 1$, then (4c) would imply that all $y$-variables are false, and all constraints in this formula are trivially satisfied. In other words, if $y_0$ is false, adding constraints (4b–4f) has no impact on the models of $F$. Thus, we can encode (3) as

$$f \leq \omega(f), \tag{5a}$$
$$M \cdot \overline{y}_0 + f - \omega(f) \geq 0, \tag{5b}$$
$$M \cdot y_0 + \omega(f) - f \geq 1, \text{ and} \tag{5c}$$
$$\text{Equations (4b–4f)}, \tag{5d}$$

with $M$ a sufficiently large integer. Here, constraints (5b) and (5c) encode that $y_0$ holds if and only if $f \geq \omega(f)$ (in combination with the first constraint, this means that $f$ and $\omega(f)$ are in fact equal). To see this, note for instance that in case $y_0$ is false, (5b) is trivially satisfied. If $y_0$ is true on the other hand, (5b) expresses that $f \geq \omega(f)$. Similarly, (5c) is trivially satisfied when $y_0$ is true and otherwise expresses that $f \not\geq \omega(f)$.

## 4   Extending BreakID

In this section, we discuss some implementation details of our extension of BREAKID (the symmetry breaker for SAT) into BREAKIDPB (the symmetry breaker for pseudo-Boolean optimization problems), with support for breaking both weak and strong symmetries.

In our implementation, we did not use arbitrary precision arithmetic; hence we only support integer coefficients of limited size. Such a restriction is not uncommon in the pseudo-Boolean world: in the competitions, *SMALLINT* tracks (where the sum of all coefficients in a constraint does not surpass $2^{20}$) are common.

First, we discuss how symmetries are detected in BREAKIDPB, next we explain how BREAKIDPB breaks weak and strong symmetries for pseudo-Boolean optimization functions and finally we discuss the compatibility of these extensions with the existing optimizations of BREAKID.

## 4.1  Detecting (Weak) Symmetries

To detect symmetries, BREAKIDPB first transforms the input problem into a graph that represents a simplified version of its syntax tree. This transformation guarantees a one-to-one correspondence between (syntactic) symmetries of the problem at hand and automorphisms (i.e. symmetries) of the graph. Next, an algorithm for searching graph automorphisms is employed [27]. This is a common strategy for symmetry detection [3, 20].

*Remark 1.* The graph automorphism problem is not known to be solvable in polynomial time nor is it NP-complete [9, 29]. The best currently accepted algorithm [4] runs in quasi-polynomial time and was introduced in 2016 (and corrected in 2017). For several specific classes of graphs, polynomial time algorithms are known [24, 25]. In practice, several graph isomorphism solvers (including the one that BREAKID uses) exist that perform very well on inputs without particular combinatorial structure.

BREAKID uses the following technique to generate a graph corresponding to a given pseudo-Boolean problem:

- The nodes are organized as follows:
  - for each literal $\ell_i$ the graph has a node with colour "1". These nodes represent the literals.
  - For each term $w_i\ell_i$ that occurs in constraint $\sum_i w_i\ell_i \geq n$, there is a node with colour "$w_i$". These nodes represent the terms. For the special case where $w_i = 1$, no new node is created since the literal equals the term in this case.
  - For each constraint $\sum_i w_i\ell_i \geq n$, there is a node with colour "$n$" distinct from all term-colours, uniquely determined by the degree of the constraint. These nodes represent the constraints.
- The edges are organized as follows:
  - each literal is connected with its negation (i.e., there is an edge $(x, \overline{x})$).
  - Each term $w_i\ell_i$ is connected to $\ell_i$.
  - Each constraint node $\sum_i w_i\ell_i \geq n$ is connected to all terms $w_i\ell_i$ (which happens to be the node for $\ell_i$ in case $w_i = 1$).

If the graph needs to contain the objective function $f$ as well it is extended as follows:

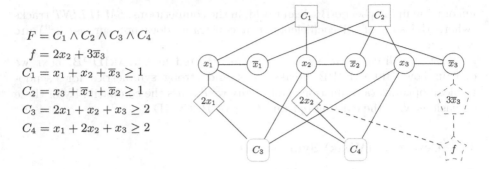

$$F = C_1 \wedge C_2 \wedge C_3 \wedge C_4$$
$$f = 2x_2 + 3\overline{x}_3$$
$$C_1 = x_1 + x_2 + \overline{x}_3 \geq 1$$
$$C_2 = x_3 + \overline{x}_1 + \overline{x}_2 \geq 1$$
$$C_3 = 2x_1 + x_2 + x_3 \geq 2$$
$$C_4 = x_1 + 2x_2 + x_3 \geq 2$$

**Fig. 1.** Example of the graph constructed for a pseudo-Boolean optimization problem $(F, f)$. The different vertex shapes represent different colours. The dashed edges and nodes are only required for detecting strong symmetries; in the case of weak symmetry detection, they are simply omitted.

– A single extra node with a unique colour is added. This node represents the objective. Moreover, for each term $w_i \ell_i$ that occurs in the objective $f = \sum_i w_i \ell_i$, there is a node with colour "$w_i$".
– The objective node is connected to all terms occurring in it. As before, each term $w_i \ell_i$ is connected to $\ell_i$.

In case we wish to detect *weak* symmetries instead of strong symmetries, the only modification needed is to remove the nodes that are only created for representing the objective; in Fig. 1, this means: dropping all dashed nodes and edges. Automorphisms of the resulting graph then correspond directly to weak symmetries.

The graph we construct differs slightly, but in a non-fundamental way from the graph used by SHATTER [1]. The main difference is that we do not need a special treatment for clauses compared to general PB constraints. Next, the terms of (pseudo-Boolean) constraints are added differently.

*Example 3.* Figure 1 contains an example of a pseudo-Boolean optimization problem and its corresponding graph. The optimization problem at hand has no strong symmetries, but exhibits the weak symmetry $(x_1, x_2)(\overline{x}_1, \overline{x}_2)$ (in disjoint cycle notation).

## 4.2   Breaking Weak Symmetries

To break symmetries, BREAKIDPB generates the formulas described in Eqs. (5a–5d). For strong symmetries, the standard symmetry breaking constraints of Eqs. (4a–4f) are used instead.

Next to this, our implementation also supports an alternative encoding of the dominance breaking formula. The difference is that instead of using clauses, we use general pseudo-Boolean constraints. As a consequence, fewer introduced variables and fewer constraints are needed, at the cost of using larger (exponentially growing) exponents. Preliminary experiments showed, however, that for the current solvers, it does not make a big difference which encoding is used.

*Example 4 (Example 3, continued).* The symmetry breaking formulas added for the weak symmetry $(x_1, x_2)(\overline{x_1}, \overline{x_2})$ are the following:

$$2x_1 - 2x_2 \geq 0, \qquad\qquad \text{application of (5a)} \qquad \text{(6a)}$$
$$-2x_1 + 2x_2 - 2y_0 \geq -2, \qquad\qquad \text{application of (5b)} \qquad \text{(6b)}$$
$$2x_1 - 2x_2 + 3y_0 \geq 1, \qquad\qquad \text{application of (5c)} \qquad \text{(6c)}$$
$$1x_1 - 1x_2 - 1y_0 \geq -1. \qquad\qquad \text{application of (4b)–(4f)} \qquad \text{(6d)}$$

Constraints (6b) and (6c) encode that $y_0$ holds if and only if $2x_2 + 3\overline{x_3} \geq 2x_1 + 3\overline{x_3}$ (in short, if $f \geq \omega(f)$). Together with (6a) this means that $f$ and $\omega(f)$ are in fact equal. If $y_0$ is true, (6b) states that $f \geq \omega(f)$ and (6c) is trivially satisfied. Similarly if $y_0$ is false, (6b) is trivially satisfied. In this case (6c) expresses that $f \not\geq \omega(f)$. The last constraint (6d) performs the actual symmetry breaking.

## 4.3   Compatibility with Previous Optimizations

Compared to SHATTER, BREAKID introduced three optimizations for static symmetry breaking for SAT problems. The three introduced optimizations are a compact encoding of the lex-leader constraints, the exploitation of row interchangeability, and the generation of binary symmetry breaking clauses.

The first optimization is a *compact encoding of lex-leader constraints*. A more compact encoding of lex-leader constraints reduces the overhead introduced by adding the constraints to the problem. This more compact encoding is exactly the encoding used for $LL_\omega$ in the dominance breaking formulas generated by BREAKIDPB as described in Equation refce.

The second optimization is the *exploitation of row interchangeability*. This is a type of symmetry present when a subset of variables can be structured as a two-dimensional matrix where each permutation of the rows induces a symmetry. If such a structure of symmetries can be found, the group of symmetries that forms this structure can be broken as a whole. This can also be applied to pseudo-Boolean optimization problems since the implementation detects this kind of symmetries based on symmetries detected in the generated graph. The detected row-symmetries are then broken using the implemented symmetry breaking constraints. For problems where there are weak symmetries present in the structure, dominance breaking formulas are used instead of symmetry breaking constraints to break those symmetries.

Lastly, it is known that posting lex-leader constraints for all detected symmetries in a symmetry group can be infeasible. Hence, often lex-leader constraints are only added for the generators of the symmetry group. BREAKID introduced an alternative; the generation of *binary symmetry breaking clauses*. These are short symmetry breaking clauses, equivalent to posting symmetry breaking constraints in the compact encoding given in Eqs. 4b–4f with $j = 1$. These very

**Table 1.** This table contains for each benchmark family the:
- total number of instances (#Inst.),
- number of instances that exhibit strong (#$\mathcal{S}$) or weak (#$\mathcal{W}$) symmetries,
- number of instances solved without symmetry breaking (#Solved plain),
- number of extra instances solved (+) or no longer solved (−) by enabling certain symmetry breaking techniques:
- "Effect $\mathcal{S}$" breaks strong symmetries (compared to no breaking)
- "Effect $\mathcal{W}$" breaks weak symmetries (compared to "Effect $\mathcal{S}$")
- "Effect Opt. $X$" adds BREAKID's optimizations to configuration $X$

| | #Inst. | #$\mathcal{S}$ | #$\mathcal{W}$ | #Solved | Effect $\mathcal{S}$ | | Effect Opt. $\mathcal{S}$ | | Effect $\mathcal{W}$ | | Effect Opt. $\mathcal{W}$ | |
|---|---|---|---|---|---|---|---|---|---|---|---|---|
| | | | | plain | + | − | + | − | + | − | + | − |
| ROUNDINGSAT (without LP integration) with core-guided optimization | | | | | | | | | | | | |
| Knapsack | 783 | 660 | 361 | 329 | **7** | 6 | 13 | **24** | **10** | 6 | 13 | **14** |
| MiplibOpt | 291 | 156 | 66 | 77 | 2 | **3** | 2 | **4** | 0 | 0 | **3** | 2 |
| PbCompOpt | 1600 | 982 | 574 | 967 | 14 | **15** | 11 | **40** | 10 | **14** | 12 | **23** |
| Crafted | 1514 | 1349 | 216 | 1165 | 30 | **208** | 48 | **174** | 11 | **37** | 47 | **62** |
| ROUNDINGSAT (without LP integration) with linear SAT–UNSAT search | | | | | | | | | | | | |
| Knapsack | 783 | 660 | 361 | 336 | **13** | 3 | 8 | **20** | 5 | **6** | 13 | **15** |
| MiplibOpt | 291 | 171 | 76 | 75 | **2** | **2** | 2 | **4** | **1** | 0 | 3 | **4** |
| PbCompOpt | 1600 | 982 | 574 | 870 | **19** | 16 | 8 | **36** | 5 | **12** | 9 | **27** |
| Crafted | 1514 | 1349 | 216 | 344 | **105** | 59 | **153** | 48 | 12 | **31** | **507** | 44 |
| ROUNDINGSAT (with LP integration) with core-guided optimization | | | | | | | | | | | | |
| Knapsack | 783 | 660 | 361 | 710 | 12 | **33** | 16 | **54** | 7 | **66** | 22 | **31** |
| MiplibOpt | 291 | 168 | 75 | 96 | **5** | 2 | 3 | **8** | 0 | **2** | 4 | **5** |
| PbCompOpt | 1600 | 982 | 570 | 958 | **38** | 15 | 16 | **64** | 9 | **21** | 12 | **45** |
| Crafted | 1514 | 1343 | 216 | 849 | 80 | **332** | **100** | 67 | 20 | **54** | **359** | 36 |

short clauses are then posted for a large set of symmetries in the symmetry group. Since we know that the effect of the first constraints added is higher, this is a cost-effective way to break symmetries. For pseudo-Boolean optimization problems, this option is available as well. The decision was made however to only generate binary breaking clauses for strong symmetries of pseudo-Boolean problems. Since generating binary breaking clauses is done to prevent the overhead of posting many long clauses, adding the longer dominance breaking constraints for each weak symmetry used defeats the purpose.

## 5   Experiments

We implemented our techniques on top of BREAKID bundled with SAUCY [27] for detection of graph automorphisms; our implementation is available online at https://bitbucket.org/krr/breakid/branch/pb_optimization (commit 46cc058 was used for the experiments). As a back-end solver we used ROUNDINGSAT [21] (commit b5de84db). The resources available to solve and break instances were

16GB of memory and 2600 s on an Intel(R) Xeon(R) Gold 6148 CPU running CentOS 7 with Linux kernel 3.10.

We tested our tool with three configurations of ROUNDINGSAT as a back-end:

- two configurations compiled without LP integration:
  - the default configuration, which uses core-guided optimization [19]
  - and a configuration that uses linear SAT–UNSAT search.
- One configuration with LP integration using linear SAT–UNSAT search.

As benchmarks, we used all collections used in the work that introduced this core-guided optimization in ROUNDINGSAT:

- **PbCompOpt**: The linear fixed–precision pseudo-boolean optimization problems of the latest *pseudo-Boolean competition* [35]. (1600 instances)
- **Knapsack**: A set of knapsack instances from the paper *Where Are the Hard Knapsack Problems?* [34] converted to PB. (783 instances)
- **MiplibOpt**: A collection of 0–1 ILP optimization instances from the benchmark sets MIPLIB 2, 3, 2003, 2010 and 2017 to PB. Some instances were rescaled to make them suitable for fixed–precision solvers. [12] (291 instances)
- **Crafted**: A set of crafted combinatorial benchmarks inspired by proof complexity. [33] (1514 instances)

Cactus plots, showing how many instances could be solved up to optimality within a certain time, for all BREAKIDPB configurations and all benchmark sets can be found in Figs. 2, 3 and 4. Table 1 contains for each benchmark set the number of instances, the number of those that exhibit strong and/or weak symmetries, as well as for different configurations how many instances can be solved by modifying one dimension (e.g., including weak symmetries) that could not be solved before (and dually, how many can no longer be solved now).

When analyzing the results using *core-guided search without LP integration* as a back-end (Fig. 2), the results are discouraging. The effect of adding symmetry breaking is only very small, and on the **Crafted** benchmark set, symmetry breaking even deteriorates performance. The same holds for adding weak symmetries and/or the optimizations BREAKID implements compared to SHATTER: the effect on most benchmark sets is small, while on **Crafted** we only observe negative effects.

On the other hand, when using *linear SAT–UNSAT without LP integration* search as a back-end (Fig. 3), we notice the opposite effect: the impact of adding symmetry breaking techniques is generally positive and on the **Crafted** benchmark set, BREAKID's optimizations and *weak* symmetry breaking reinforce one another.

Interestingly, and seemingly contradictory, on this **Crafted** benchmark set, adding weak symmetry breaking also has a positive effect on many instances that do not exhibit weak symmetries. The explanation of why this is possible relates to the *graph* used for detecting the symmetries. When performing weak symmetry breaking, this graph contains no node for the objective function and is

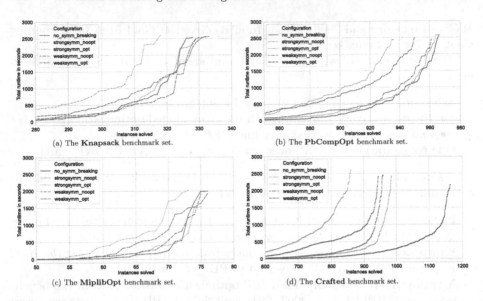

(a) The **Knapsack** benchmark set.

(b) The **PbCompOpt** benchmark set.

(c) The **MiplibOpt** benchmark set.

(d) The **Crafted** benchmark set.

**Fig. 2.** Runtime ($Y$-axis) needed to solve a number ($X$-axis) of optimization problems to optimality for the different BREAKIDPB configurations with the core-guided optimization configuration of ROUNDINGSAT.

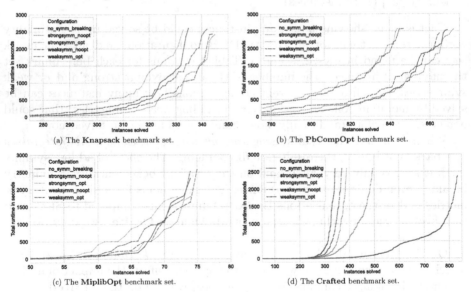

(a) The **Knapsack** benchmark set.

(b) The **PbCompOpt** benchmark set.

(c) The **MiplibOpt** benchmark set.

(d) The **Crafted** benchmark set.

**Fig. 3.** Runtime ($Y$-axis) needed to solve a number ($X$-axis) of optimization problems to optimality for the different BREAKIDPB configurations with the linear SAT–UNSAT search configuration of ROUNDINGSAT.

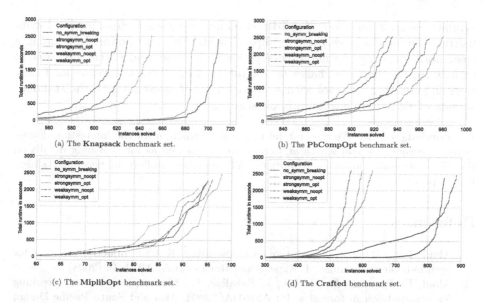

(a) The **Knapsack** benchmark set.

(b) The **PbCompOpt** benchmark set.

(c) The **MiplibOpt** benchmark set.

(d) The **Crafted** benchmark set.

**Fig. 4.** Runtime ($Y$-axis) needed to solve a number ($X$-axis) of optimization problems to optimality for the different BREAKIDPB configurations with the linear SAT–UNSAT search configuration of ROUNDINGSAT with linear solver integration.

generally simpler and smaller (see Fig. 1 for an example). Upon manual inspection of several instances, we noticed that with this simpler graph, it is easier for BREAKIDPB to find the underlying *structure* of the symmetry group (in particular, detecting row-interchangeability), and hence it makes it easier to break the symmetry group completely.

The same effect can be observed when using *linear SAT–UNSAT search with LP integration* as a back-end (Fig. 4). Symmetry breaking has some inpact on the number of solved instances and for the **Crafted** benchmarkt set we notice once again that the optimizations reinforce *weak* symmetry breaking.

## 6    Conclusion

In this paper, we have studied static symmetry breaking for pseudo-Boolean optimization problems. We defined the novel notion of *weak symmetries*, which do not necessarily respect the objective function. We developed the theory showing how to statically break weak symmetries and implemented a tool that performs static symmetry breaking for both strong and weak symmetries. Our experimental validation shows that the effect of breaking (weak) symmetries depends greatly on the type of solving algorithm used, where we generally observed negative effects with core-guided optimization and positive effects with linear SAT–UNSAT search when not using LP integration. As a surprising side-effect of this investigation, we discovered that even for optimization problems where all symmetries are strong, doing the detection as if we are searching for weak symmetries can have a large positive impact on the breaking power. Developing a clear understanding of when precisely this is the case, and potentially, how to exploit this further, are challenges for future work. Another avenue for future work is extending our tool with support for *proof logging*, which the standard version of BREAKID has recently obtained [8].

**Acknowledgement.** We are grateful to Jakob Nordström for the interesting discussions on pseudo-Boolean search and optimization, as well as for providing details on the different configurations of ROUNDINGSAT and where to find the benchmarks used in this paper.

# References

1. Aloul, F.A., Ramani, A., Markov, I.L., Sakallah, K.A.: Symmetry breaking for pseudo-boolean formulas. J. Expe. Algorithmics (JEA) **12**, 1–14 (2008)
2. Aloul, F., Ramani, A., Markov, I., Sakallah, K.: Shatterpb: symmetry-breaking for pseudo-boolean formulas. In: ASP-DAC 2004: Asia and South Pacific Design Automation Conference 2004 (IEEE Cat. No. 04EX753), pp. 884–887 (2004). https://doi.org/10.1109/ASPDAC.2004.1337720
3. Aloul, F.A., Sakallah, K.A., Markov, I.L.: Efficient symmetry breaking for Boolean satisfiability. IEEE Trans. Comput. **55**(5), 549–558 (2006). https://doi.org/10.1109/TC.2006.75
4. Babai, L.: Graph isomorphism in quasipolynomial time. In: Proceedings of the Forty-Eighth Annual ACM Symposium on Theory of Computing, pp. 684–697 (2016)
5. Benhamou, B., Nabhani, T., Ostrowski, R., Saïdi, M.R.: Dynamic symmetry breaking in the satisfiability problem. In: Proceedings of the 16th International Conference on Logic for Programming, Artificial intelligence, and Reasoning. LPAR-16, Dakar, Senegal (2010)
6. Benhamou, B., Nabhani, T., Ostrowski, R., Saïdi, M.R.: Enhancing clause learning by symmetry in SAT solvers. In: Proceedings of the 2010 22Nd IEEE International Conference on Tools with Artificial Intelligence, ICTAI 2010, vol. 1, pp. 329–335. IEEE Computer Society, Washington, DC (2010). https://doi.org/10.1109/ICTAI.2010.55
7. Benhamou, B., Saïs, L.: Tractability through symmetries in propositional calculus. J. Autom. Reason. **12**(1), 89–102 (1994)
8. Bogaerts, B., Gocht, S., McCreesh, C., Nordström, J.: Certified symmetry and dominance breaking for combinatorial optimisation. In: Thirty-Sixth AAAI Conference on Artificial Intelligence, AAAI 2022, Thirty-Fourth Conference on Innovative Applications of Artificial Intelligence, IAAI 2022, The Twelveth Symposium on Educational Advances in Artificial Intelligence, EAAI 2022 Virtual Event, 22 February–1 March 2022, pp. 3698–3707. AAAI Press (2022). https://ojs.aaai.org/index.php/AAAI/article/view/20283
9. Booth, K.S., Colbourn, C.J.: Problems polynomially equivalent to graph isomorphism. Technical report CS-77-04, Department of Computer Science, University of Waterloo (1979)

10. Chu, G., Stuckey, P.J.: A generic method for identifying and exploiting dominance relations. In: Milano, M. (ed.) CP 2012. LNCS, pp. 6–22. Springer, Heidelberg (2012). https://doi.org/10.1007/978-3-642-33558-7_4
11. Crawford, J.M., Ginsberg, M.L., Luks, E.M., Roy, A.: Symmetry-breaking predicates for search problems. In: Principles of Knowledge Representation and Reasoning, pp. 148–159. Morgan Kaufmann (1996)
12. Devriendt, J.: MIPLIB 0–1 instances in OPB format (2020). https://doi.org/10.5281/zenodo.3870965
13. Devriendt, J., Bogaerts, B.: BreakID: static symmetry breaking for ASP (system description). In: Bogaerts, B., Harrison, A. (eds.) Ninth workshop on Answer Set Programmin and Other Computing Paradigms: Proceedings, 2016, New York City, New York, USA, 16 October 2016, pp. 25–39 (2016). http://docs.google.com/viewer?a=v&pid=sites&srcid=ZGVmYXVsdGRvbWFpbnxhc3BvY3AyMDE2fGd4OjU4NTA0YTc3N2VkYWWYyMWM
14. Devriendt, J., Bogaerts, B., Bruynooghe, M.: BreakIDGlucose: on the importance of row symmetry in SAT. In: Proceedings of the Fourth International Workshop on the Cross-Fertilization Between CSP and SAT (CSPSAT) (2014). https://lirias.kuleuven.be/handle/123456789/456639
15. Devriendt, J., Bogaerts, B., Bruynooghe, M.: Symmetric explanation learning: effective dynamic symmetry handling for SAT. In: Gaspers, S., Walsh, T. (eds.) SAT 2017. LNCS, vol. 10491, pp. 83–100. Springer, Cham (2017). https://doi.org/10.1007/978-3-319-66263-3_6
16. Devriendt, J., Bogaerts, B., Bruynooghe, M., Denecker, M.: Improved static symmetry breaking for SAT. In: Creignou, N., Le Berre, D. (eds.) SAT 2016. LNCS, vol. 9710, pp. 104–122. Springer, Cham (2016). https://doi.org/10.1007/978-3-319-40970-2_8
17. Devriendt, J., Bogaerts, B., Bruynooghe, M., Denecker, M.: On local domain symmetry for model expansion. Theory Pract. Logic Program. 16(5–6), 636–652 (2016). https://doi.org/10.1017/S1471068416000508. https://www.cambridge.org/core/article/on-local-domain-symmetry-for-model-expansion/96E8AB07EB4C02D502B68687B23AC21C
18. Devriendt, J., Bogaerts, B., De Cat, B., Denecker, M., Mears, C.: Symmetry propagation: improved dynamic symmetry breaking in SAT. In: IEEE 24th International Conference on Tools with Artificial Intelligence, ICTAI 2012, Athens, Greece, 7–9 November 2012, pp. 49–56. IEEE Computer Society (2012). https://doi.org/10.1109/ICTAI.2012.16
19. Devriendt, J., Gocht, S., Demirović, E., Nordström, J., Stuckey, P.J.: Cutting to the core of pseudo-boolean optimization: combining core-guided search with cutting planes reasoning. In: Proceedings of the AAAI Conference on Artificial Intelligence, vol. 35, pp. 3750–3758 (2021)
20. Drescher, C., Tifrea, O., Walsh, T.: Symmetry-breaking answer set solving. AI Commun. 24(2), 177–194 (2011)
21. Elffers, J., Nordström, J.: Divide and conquer: towards faster pseudo-Boolean solving. In: Lang, J. (ed.) Proceedings of the Twenty-Seventh International Joint Conference on Artificial Intelligence, IJCAI 2018, 13–19 July 2018, Stockholm, Sweden, pp. 1291–1299. ijcai.org (2018). https://doi.org/10.24963/ijcai.2018/180
22. Flener, P., et al.: Breaking row and column symmetries in matrix models. In: Van Hentenryck, P. (ed.) CP 2002. LNCS, vol. 2470, pp. 462–477. Springer, Heidelberg (2002). https://doi.org/10.1007/3-540-46135-3_31
23. Gent, I.P., Smith, B.M.: Symmetry breaking in constraint programming. In: Proceedings of ECAI-2000, pp. 599–603. IOS Press (2000)

24. Grohe, M.: Fixed-point definability and polynomial time on graphs with excluded minors. In: 2010 25th Annual IEEE Symposium on Logic in Computer Science, pp. 179–188 (2010). https://doi.org/10.1109/LICS.2010.22
25. Grohe, M.: Logical and structural approaches to the graph isomorphism problem. In: Chatterjee, K., Sgall, J. (eds.) MFCS 2013. LNCS, vol. 8087, p. 42. Springer, Heidelberg (2013). https://doi.org/10.1007/978-3-642-40313-2_4
26. Heule, M., Keur, A., Maaren, H.V., Stevens, C., Voortman, M.: CNF symmetry breaking options in conflict driven SAT solving (2005)
27. Katebi, H., Sakallah, K.A., Markov, I.L.: Symmetry and satisfiability: an update. In: Strichman, O., Szeider, S. (eds.) SAT 2010. LNCS, vol. 6175, pp. 113–127. Springer, Heidelberg (2010). https://doi.org/10.1007/978-3-642-14186-7_11
28. Kirchweger, M., Szeider, S.: SAT modulo symmetries for graph generation. In: Michel, L.D. (ed.) 27th International Conference on Principles and Practice of Constraint Programming, CP 2021, Montpellier, France (Virtual Conference), 25–29 October 2021. LIPIcs, vol. 210, pp. 34:1–34:16. Schloss Dagstuhl - Leibniz-Zentrum für Informatik (2021). https://doi.org/10.4230/LIPIcs.CP.2021.34
29. Lubiw, A.: Some NP-complete problems similar to graph isomorphism. SIAM J. Comput. **10**(1), 11–21 (1981). https://doi.org/10.1137/0210002
30. Lynce, I., Marques-Silva, J.: Breaking symmetries in SAT matrix models. In: Marques-Silva, J., Sakallah, K.A. (eds.) SAT 2007. LNCS, vol. 4501, pp. 22–27. Springer, Heidelberg (2007). https://doi.org/10.1007/978-3-540-72788-0_6
31. Mears, C., García de la Banda, M., Demoen, B., Wallace, M.: Lightweight dynamic symmetry breaking. Constraints 1–48 (2013). https://doi.org/10.1007/s10601-013-9154-2
32. Metin, H., Baarir, S., Colange, M., Kordon, F.: CDCLSym: introducing effective symmetry breaking in SAT solving. In: Beyer, D., Huisman, M. (eds.) TACAS 2018. LNCS, vol. 10805, pp. 99–114. Springer, Cham (2018). https://doi.org/10.1007/978-3-319-89960-2_6
33. Nordström, J.: Supplementary material for cutting to the core of pseudo-boolean optimization: combining core-guided search with cutting planes reasoning (2022). https://www.csc.kth.se/~jakobn/publications/CoreGuidedPB/
34. Pisinger, D.: Where are the hard knapsack problems? Comput. Oper. Res. **32**(9), 2271–2284 (2005)
35. Roussel, O.: Pseudo-boolean competition 2016 (2016). https://www.cril.univ-artois.fr/PB16/
36. Sabharwal, A.: SymChaff: exploiting symmetry in a structure-aware satisfiability solver. Constraints **14**(4), 478–505 (2009)
37. Schaafsma, B., Heule, M.J.H., van Maaren, H.: Dynamic symmetry breaking by simulating Zykov contraction. In: Kullmann, O. (ed.) SAT 2009. LNCS, vol. 5584, pp. 223–236. Springer, Heidelberg (2009). https://doi.org/10.1007/978-3-642-02777-2_22
38. Van Caudenberg, D.: Static symmetry and dominance handling for pseudo-Boolean optimization (2022). Bachelor thesis; Bogaerts, Bart (supervisor). https://www.bartbogaerts.eu/MScBScStudents/2022-Daimy/BScThesisDaimy.pdf
39. Van Caudenberg, D., Bogaerts, B.: Static symmetry and dominance breaking for pseudo-Boolean optimization. In: BNAIC/BeNeLearn 2022 (2022)
40. Walsh, T.: Symmetry breaking constraints: recent results. CoRR abs/1204.3348 (2012)

# Examining Speaker and Keyword Uniqueness: Partitioning Keyword Spotting Datasets for Federated Learning with the Largest Differencing Method

Paul C. Wallbott[1], Sascha Grollmisch[2] (ID), and Thomas Köllmer[2]([envelope]) (ID)

[1] Fraunhofer Institute for Intelligent Analysis and Information Systems IAIS, Sankt Augustin, Germany
paul.wallbott@iais.fraunhofer.de
[2] Fraunhofer Institute for Digital Media Technology IDMT, Ilmenau, Germany
{sascha.grollmisch,thomas.koellmer}@idmt.fraunhofer.de

**Abstract.** Federated learning is a powerful training strategy for neural networks where several independent clients train a model without the need of sharing potentially sensitive data. However, real world client-local data is usually biased: A single client might have access to only a few lighting conditions in computer visions, patient groups in a hospital or speakers and keywords in a smart device performing keyword spotting. We help researchers to better understand and estimate the expected performance impacts by introducing a new method to partition a given dataset into an arbitrary amount of clients, each with unique properties, to simulate such conditions.

We apply the method to partition the Google Speech Command dataset into clients with non-overlapping speakers and additionally unique keywords and share the script to create the novel *GSC-FL* dataset. The results, using convolutional neural networks, show that the performance of the final model is stable up to at least 16 clients and models trained only on local data are clearly outperformed by federated learning. However, unique speakers for each client have a negative performance impact and it increases even more with unique keywords. Our script can be applied with only minor adjustments to partition any other dataset for federated learning investigations as well.

**Keywords:** speech recognition · keyword spotting · federated learning · deep learning · multiway number partitioning

## 1 Introduction

Keyword spotting (KWS) deals with recognizing keywords such as "yes" or "stop" in a speech audio stream. A special case is the recognition of a selected word to wake-up voice assistant systems like Amazon Alexa or Microsoft Cortana (wakeword detection) before a computationally expensive automatic speech

© The Author(s), under exclusive license to Springer Nature Switzerland AG 2023
T. Calders et al. (Eds.): BNAIC/Benelearn 2022, CCIS 1805, pp. 167–177, 2023.
https://doi.org/10.1007/978-3-031-39144-6_11

recognition is triggered to analyze the semantic meanings of longer phrases. Such wake word or hot word detection systems can be extended by looking for several keywords which allow the hands-free control of industrial machines or the indexing of large audio archives. KWS has seen strong performance improvements with the inclusion of deep learning techniques [1–4], see [5] for a recent review.

These deep learning approaches require large databases to learn robust models which are not overfitting to certain speakers or recording conditions. A simple but expensive way to improve their robustness is to collect and annotate more and more data from a vast user basis which covers different speakers and all keywords. These models can then be adapted to new keywords with few examples using transfer learning [4]. However, the centralized data collection raises several privacy, security, and logistical issues: By sharing speech data (best case with realistic background noise) also other confidential information may be shared, the centralized host needs to be fully trusted, and raw audio data (or at least a compressed input representation) needs to be transmitted. An alternative solution for obtaining robust models is Federated Learning (FL) [6]. Instead of training the model on a centralized data collection, models are trained directly on many edge devices using locally stored data. Each of these devices, so-called clients, share the parameter changes with a coordination server, which aggregates these changes to update the global model. This newer model is then transferred back to the clients and used for the next training iteration. This process is repeated until convergence or when new data is acquired [7].

The performance of federated learning systems degrades, if the data is not ideally distributed over all clients and unbalanced in terms of locally available classes. The problem of sound event detection makes no exception [8], the same goes for the KWS use case: Not all clients have the same speakers which might lead to a local speaker overfitting. Conversely, not all clients have examples for all keywords since users likely only record keywords of their interest. To the best of our knowledge, the application of FL to KWS has focused on wake-up word detection on small [9] and big [10] datasets but not considered larger keyword vocabulary nor the mentioned distribution problems.

With this paper, we propose the novel *GSC-FL* dataset which covers different realistic data distributions and publish the scripts to create it.[1] It contains pre-defined splits of the Google-Speech Commands (GSC) dataset [11] for fully random, unique speakers, and also unique keywords distributions for each client. These splits were created with the largest differencing method (LDM), see Sect. 2; an approach that can also be applied to other FL distribution scenarios that are unrelated to KWS, such as medical image analysis with unique patients or other sociodemographic characteristics that might bias the local model. With the *GSC-FL* dataset we answer the following research questions and provide deeper insights on FL for KWS: How is the performance of models trained with FL affected when more clients participate that have less data per client? How do unique speakers for each client affect the performance? And lastly: How do unique keywords for each client affect the performance?

---

[1] The scripts can be found here: https://github.com/paul-cw/gsc-fl.git.

## 2    Realistic Data Distribution

To investigate the research questions we need an appropriate FL dataset where each sample from the original dataset is assigned to a specific client. The simplest approach for GSC is to randomly select utterances of each keyword from the whole set. However, for a realistic scenario, it is very unlikely that each speaker records keywords at basically every client which are normally geographically dispersed. A random distribution implicitly assumes this and following experiments might output too optimistic results. We require a more realistic data distribution that reflects particular constraints: Non-overlapping speakers between the resulting clients and the same number of recordings per client. While the former restricts the local variability in terms of speakers, we choose the latter to eliminate effects due to different number of total utterances per client. This problems arises since each speaker contributes a varying amount of keywords to the whole dataset, starting from a single word.

We can formulate the distribution problem as follows: Suppose we have $N$ speakers in the original dataset and write down a set of integers $S = \{i_1, ..., i_N\}$ where $i_n$ is the number of recordings that speaker $n$ contributed to the GSC dataset. We want to split the dataset into $K$ clients, which is then equivalent to finding $K$ subsets of $S$, where the sum of elements in each subset is approximately equal. This problem is known as multiway number partitioning. While in the case of a small number of speakers one could evaluate all possible combinations directly and choose the best one, the vast amount of possible combinations makes this approach unfeasible. We use the largest differencing method (LDM) [12] to search for an optimal solution by minimizing the difference between the subset with the largest and the one with the smallest sum. LDM consecutively replaces the two biggest numbers in $S$ with their difference to achieve this. The resulting partitions are shown in Table 1 and discussed in the next section. To the best of our knowledge, LDM has not been considered for distributing FL datasets.

## 3    The GSC-FL Dataset

We start from the well known Google Speech Commands dataset, which contains 105,829 utterances of 35 keywords from 2,618 different speakers [11]. To prepare it for federated learning, we apply the following processing pipeline:

**First, we Select Keywords:** To get a balanced dataset, we select the 10 commands *yes, no, on, down, stop, right, up, go, left, off* and put the remaining keywords into the *unknown* category. For each speaker, we draw random unknown recordings until the total number of unknown keywords is equal to the speakers average number of recordings of the 10 keywords above. We create silence utterances, mix in background noise and add the same amount of unknown utterances to each speaker. The resulting dataset has 12 classes: 10 keywords, unknown, and silence.

**Second, we Create Clients for Federated Learning:** We assign each utterance in the training dataset[2] a client id for the splits into K = [2 ... 512] clients. This is done in two ways: For the **iid split**, we randomly split the utterances into K equal sized clients with a locally balanced amount of keywords. For the **speaker split**, we create K clients with the condition that all utterances of a given speaker go to one client only, while optimizing for identical number of recordings on each client using LDM, see Sect. 2. While the first split provides an optimal baseline with overlapping speakers on the different clients, the second split ensures that all utterances of a given speaker are mapped to only one client. The results in Table 1 show the roughly balanced splits with respect to the number of utterances and speakers over the resulting clients.

**Third, we Create Unique Keywords:** We drop the utterances of the keywords *up, go, left, off* from all but one client (or two in the case of K = 8). This corresponds to the most difficult scenario where each client has unique speakers and also partially unique keywords. The dropped utterance are also removed from the centralized dataset for a fair comparison.

The resulting datasets are shown for K = 8 in Fig. 1. One can see that the split is slightly more imbalanced intra-class wise for the speaker splitting but still shows a balanced data distributions. The slight increase in class imbalance is due to the non trivial task of creating K clients from the dataset. We measure the class imbalance on a client $c$ as the deviation from the mean number of utterances per keyword:

$$\alpha_c = 100 * \frac{\sum_{k=1}^{K} |N_{ck} - N_c|}{2N_c(K-1)} \tag{1}$$

$$N_c = \frac{\sum_{k=1}^{K} N_{ck}}{K} \tag{2}$$

Where $K$ is the number of classes on the client, $N_{ck}$ the number of utterances of class $k$ on client $c$ and $N_c$ is the average number of utterances per keyword on client $c$. We have normalized the measure to $\alpha_c \in [0, 100]$, where equally distributed keywords result in $\alpha_c = 0$ and unequally distributed keywords in $\alpha_c = 100$. The non iid-ness is then defined as:

$$\alpha = \frac{1}{K} \sum_{c=1}^{K} \alpha_c \tag{3}$$

where $K$ is the number of clients and $\alpha_c$ defined above.

## 4   Experimental Setup

This section describes the input representation obtained from the raw audio data as well as the neural network architecture that is used in the following experiments.

---

[2] We use the predefined train, validation, test split that comes with the dataset.

**Table 1.** Average dataset properties and the corresponding standard deviation after splitting into several clients in the unique speakers setup. Average speakers/utterances (utt.) are obtained by averaging the number of speakers/utterances over all clients. The non-iidness ($\alpha$) is defined in equation (3). The value for the iid split is $\alpha = 1.1$ for all splits.

| #clients (K) | speakers | utt./kw | $\alpha_{speaker}$ | $\alpha_{iid}$ |
|---|---|---|---|---|
| 2 | $1004.0 \pm 4.2$ | $1535.5 \pm 0.1$ | $1.1 \pm 0.6$ | $1.1 \pm 0.0$ |
| 4 | $502.0 \pm 1.4$ | $767.7 \pm 0.0$ | $1.4 \pm 0.3$ | $1.1 \pm 0.0$ |
| 8 | $251.0 \pm 1.2$ | $383.9 \pm 0.0$ | $1.7 \pm 0.3$ | $1.1 \pm 0.0$ |
| 16 | $125.5 \pm 1.1$ | $191.9 \pm 0.0$ | $2.2 \pm 0.4$ | $1.1 \pm 0.0$ |
| 32 | $62.8 \pm 0.8$ | $96.0 \pm 0.0$ | $2.9 \pm 0.7$ | $1.1 \pm 0.0$ |
| 64 | $31.4 \pm 0.7$ | $48.0 \pm 0.0$ | $3.8 \pm 1.0$ | $1.1 \pm 0.1$ |
| 128 | $15.7 \pm 0.5$ | $24.0 \pm 0.0$ | $5.8 \pm 1.5$ | $1.2 \pm 0.3$ |
| 256 | $7.8 \pm 1.4$ | $12.0 \pm 0.0$ | $7.5 \pm 2.1$ | $1.4 \pm 0.6$ |
| 512 | $3.9 \pm 1.5$ | $6.0 \pm 0.5$ | $9.9 \pm 4.0$ | $1.5 \pm 1.6$ |

## 4.1 Input Representation

The dataset contains one second long raw audio recordings with a sampling rate of 16 kHz. We extract 40 MFCC with a sliding window of $l = 40$ ms and a stride of $s = 20$ ms as in [2], resulting in a $49 \times 40$ dimensional input matrix for each input file. To create realistic silence utterances, we add the Google Speech Command specific background noise with a fixed amplitude to the silent utterances.

## 4.2 Model

For fast algorithmic iterations and the feasible execution, all experiments focus on small footprint models with less than 100k parameters. It must be noted, that the general accuracy might be increased with larger models with millions of parameters as in [4], but this is not the focus of this paper. Furthermore, these small models are more suitable for FL scenarios, where each client needs to train models locally and has likely only restricted hardware resources.

There are a variety of different small footprint models that have been tested on the Google Speech Command dataset, mostly recurrent neural networks (RNN) and convolutional neural networks (CNN) based architectures, see [2,3] for comparative studies of different architectures. For our purposes we use the small footprint model with temporal convolutions introduced in [13], which has only 65k parameters while achieving near state-of-the-art performance. We choose the authors' TC-ResNet8 architecture. The residual blocks contain batch normalization layers in the original formulation, which we replace with group normalization layers [14]. These were shown to be more suitable for FL [8].

## 4.3   Objective and Training Procedure

Since it is a multi-class single-label problem, we use the Categorical Cross Entropy loss to optimize the model. For the final evaluation, we pick the best

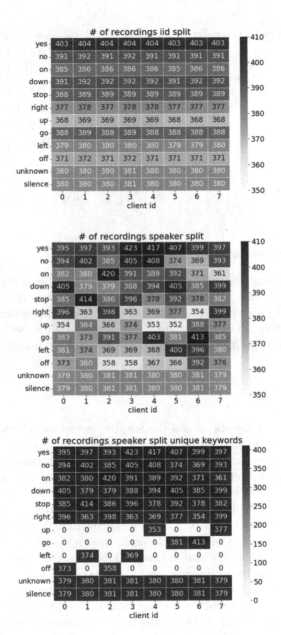

**Fig. 1.** Utterance distribution by keyword and client id. Color encodes the number of recordings for each combination with the different splitting methods described.

training weights in terms of F-score (f1) on the fixed validation dataset. All results are reported for the pre-defined test set which is independent of the FL training data distribution. For a meaningful comparison, we hold as many parameters fixed as possible. That includes a batch size of 32 as well as the (client side) Adam optimizer [15]. We compare different learning rates and find the common 0.001 works best on average. We fix the dropout rate by running experiments with $K = 2$ and $K = 32$ clients. The former benefits from bigger dropout rates, while the latter achieves best results with no dropout. Dropout is therefore set to a rate of 0.1 as a compromise. The results could be further improved with data augmentation, hyper parameter optimization, and learning rate schedulers.

**Non-FL Training.** To understand the benefit each client can obtain from participating in the FL process, we calculate individual models on all clients in a non-federated manner. We quote the $F$-score on the test set of the best model from all clients in the split as the result from non-federated learning. We train for 250 epochs and use early stopping with a patience of 10 epochs. The larger the number of clients, the less data is available for individual models and we expect more gain by participating in the FL process.

**FL Training.** For federated learning we use the standard federated averaging algorithm [6] with a learning rate of 1. We run the code three times to account for randomness during training. Throughout the experiments, we train for 250 epochs (600 for the unique keyword settings due to slower convergence) and quote the $F$-score on the test set. We run one epoch per client for each federated averaging round. In such a round, all clients participate in the training process.

## 5   Results

The following section presents the results for federated compared to non-federated training and details the outcomes for the unique speakers and keyword scenarios.

### 5.1   FL vs. Non-FL Training

The final results for FL on the iid split are shown in Table 2. We see that FL has a positive impact compared to the local training on each client and that the difference to the non-federated F-score is positive in every case. This is expected, since the federated setup makes use of the full dataset, not only the $K$th fraction as the baseline runs do. The performance of the final model is stable up to 16 clients and decreases by 4% points with 64 clients. This can be attributed to the smaller amount of local data.

## 5.2 Unique Speakers

Comparing iid and speaker splits in Table 2, one can see that the federated performance in the speaker split is roughly equal to the iid baseline for up to 16 clients and only moderately diverges up to 128 clients with 16 speakers each. With less than 10 speakers per client as in 256 and 512, the gap is increasing. One reason might be the models overfitting to local speakers since the amount of speakers is reduced with an increased number of clients. Another reason could be due to the increasing class imbalance on each client, which is shown in Table 1. This is due to the constraint of equal number of recordings and unique speakers on each client, which is harder to fulfill the more clients are used. In general, speaker overfitting might be a challenge for real world applications where one client equals one household with less than five speakers.

**Table 2.** Mean $F$-scores and standard deviation on the test set for iid ($F_{iid}$) and speaker ($F_{speaker}$) splits, as well as the best result for models trained locally ($F_{local}$) on each client without federated learning on the iid split. The best result for a fixed number of clients is bold.

| #clients (K) | $F_{iid}$ [%] | $F_{speaker}$ [%] | $F_{local}$ [%] |
|---|---|---|---|
| 1 | 94.6 | 94.5 | 94.6 |
| 2 | 94.6 ± 0.3 | **94.7 ± 0.2** | 91.9 |
| 4 | 94.6 ± 0.3 | **94.8 ± 0.6** | 90.1 |
| 8 | 94.5 ± 0.2 | **94.6 ± 0.3** | 87.4 |
| 16 | **94.5 ± 0.1** | 94.1 ± 0.2 | 83.6 |
| 32 | **92.9 ± 0.3** | 92.5 ± 0.1 | 79.2 |
| 64 | **91.0 ± 0.3** | 90.1 ± 0.3 | 75.2 |
| 128 | **87,7 ± 0.2** | 87.0 ± 0.8 | 65.3 |
| 256 | **84,1 ± 0.2** | 80.9 ± 1.0 | 55.7 |
| 512 | **77,7 ± 1.6** | 74.8 ± 1.9 | 42.9 |

**Table 3.** The F-scores (F) with federated learning (FL) for the splits into 4 and 8 clients with unique keywords (kws) are shown in comparison to the centralized F-scores (centr.) that are obtained using the full dataset with adjusted keyword utterances.

| speaker split | centr. 4 | FL 4 | centr. 8 | FL 8 |
|---|---|---|---|---|
| $F$ all kws [%] | 93.1 | 84.5 | 92.6 | 86.8 |
| $F$ shared kws [%] | 93.6 | 88.6 | 93.4 | 90.2 |
| $F$ unique kws [%] | 92.1 | 76.2 | 91.2 | 80.0 |

## 5.3    Unique Keywords

The results for the unique vocabulary setting are shown in Table 3. The centralized F-scores are higher than the results achieved in the federated setup. The total amount of utterances for each keyword can be ruled out as a reason since the total utterances were also adjusted in the centralized training. This explains also the lower performance compared to Table 2. The results indicate that the misbalanced client data has a negative impact on the performance of the FL model. For 8 clients the accuracy improves since two clients have examples of each unique keyword leading to a higher training impact of the unique keywords in the averaging step of FL. As expected, the F-score is lower for the unique keywords than the shared ones that are present at each client. They also converge slower, as can be inferred from the learning curves in Fig. 2. The shared vocabulary is converging after 50 epochs, while the unique keywords are reaching an F-score of 0.5. Even after the 600 epochs, federated models don't show full convergence for the unique keywords. The FL averaging process might need to be adjusted when classes are unique for some clients to address this, in future work.

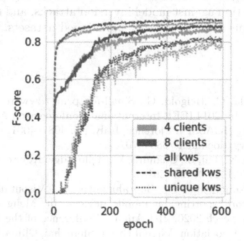

**Fig. 2.** The *F*-score on the validation set is shown for the unique keyword setting for the speaker split.

## 6    Conclusion

Federated Learning is a promising approach in keyword spotting use cases, where a central collection of training data is not feasible or has undesired consequences, such as possible privacy violations in case of a data breach. To facilitate research on this topic, we publish the *GSC-FL* dataset, a partitioned version of the Google

Speech Command dataset into unique speakers and unique keyword splits. We interpret the creation of such a dataset as a multiway number partitioning problem and create our dataset with the help of the largest differencing method. We suggest that this approach can be used for similar federated learning studies, where a centrally collected dataset, that contains multiple instances from the same source or any other property of interest, needs to be distributed efficiently without overlapping instances to a variable number of FL clients.

In our experiments on *GSC-FL*, we showed that the model benefits from the federated learning compared to local training, as expected. In the iid split, where speakers are present on several clients, the performance decreases with more than 16 clients and drops considerably with 512. This is caused by fewer training examples per client. Unique speakers do not influence the results negatively when more than 10 speakers contribute to each client. With only a handful of speakers, the performance degrades due to speaker overfitting and an increased class imbalance caused by the unique speaker setting. Additionally, unique keywords and therefore unique classes for each client affect the performance negatively which leaves room for improvements.

The proposed dataset and our results highlight directions for future research on federated learning in the context of KWS, such as testing different aggregation schemes, the protection against model inversion attacks, and methods to address local bias, that occur with realistically partitioned datasets.

# References

1. Chen, G., Parada, C., Heigold, G.: Small-footprint keyword spotting using deep neural networks. In: 2014 IEEE International Conference on Acoustics, Speech and Signal Processing (ICASSP), Florence, Italy, pp. 4087–4091. IEEE (2014). http://ieeexplore.ieee.org/document/6854370/
2. Zhang, Y., Suda, N., Lai, L., Chandra, V.: Hello Edge: Keyword Spotting on Microcontrollers. arXiv:1711.07128 (2018)
3. Rybakov, O., Kononenko, N., Subrahmanya, N., Visontai, M., Laurenzo, S.: Streaming keyword spotting on mobile devices. In: Meng, H., Xu, B., Zheng, T.F. (eds.) Interspeech 2020, 21st Annual Conference of the International Speech Communication Association, Virtual Event, Shanghai, China, 25–29 October 2020, ISCA, pp. 2277–2281 (2020). https://doi.org/10.21437/Interspeech.2020-1003
4. Mazumder, M., Banbury, C., Meyer, J., Warden, P., Reddi, V.J.: Few-shot keyword spotting in any language. In: Hermansky, H., Cernocký, H., Burget, L., Lamel, L., Scharenborg, O., Motlícek, P. (eds.) Interspeech 2021, 22nd Annual Conference of the International Speech Communication Association, Brno, Czechia, 30 August–3 September 2021, ISCA, pp. 4214–4218 (2021). https://doi.org/10.21437/Interspeech.2021-1966
5. López-Espejo, I., Tan, Z., Hansen, J.H.L., Jensen, J.: Deep spoken keyword spotting: an overview. IEEE Access **10**, 4169–4199 (2022). https://doi.org/10.1109/ACCESS.2021.3139508
6. McMahan, B., Moore, E., Ramage, D., Hampson, S., Arcas, B.A.: Communication-efficient learning of deep networks from decentralized data. In: Proceedings of the 20th International Conference on Artificial Intelligence and Statistics (2017)

7. Kairouz, P., McMahan, H.B., et al.: Advances and open problems in federated learning. Found. Trends® Mach. Learn. **14**(1–2), 1–210 (2021). https://doi.org/10.1561/2200000083

8. Johnson, D.S., et al.: DESED-FL and URBAN-FL: federated learning datasets for sound event detection. In: 29th European Signal Processing Conference, EUSIPCO 2021, Dublin, Ireland, 23–27 August 2021, pp. 556–560. IEEE (2021). https://doi.org/10.23919/EUSIPCO54536.2021.9616102

9. Leroy, D., Coucke, A., Lavril, T., Gisselbrecht, T., Dureau, J.: Federated learning for keyword spotting. In: IEEE International Conference on Acoustics, Speech and Signal Processing, ICASSP 2019, Brighton, United Kingdom, 12–17 May 2019, pp. 6341–6345. IEEE (2019). https://doi.org/10.1109/ICASSP.2019.8683546

10. Hard, A., et al.: Training keyword spotting models on non-IID data with federated learning. In: Meng, H., Xu, B., Zheng, T.F. (eds.) Interspeech 2020, 21st Annual Conference of the International Speech Communication Association, Virtual Event, Shanghai, China, 25–29 October 2020, ISCA, pp. 4343–4347 (2020). https://doi.org/10.21437/Interspeech.2020-3023

11. Warden, P.: Speech Commands: A Dataset for Limited-Vocabulary Speech Recognition, arXiv:1804.03209 (2018)

12. Karmarkar, N., Karp, R.M.: The differencing method of set partitioning. Computer Science Division (EECS), University of California Berkeley (1982)

13. Choi, S., et al.: Temporal convolution for real-time keyword spotting on mobile devices. In: Kubin, G., Kacic, Z. (eds.) Interspeech 2019, 20th Annual Conference of the International Speech Communication Association, Graz, Austria, 15–19 September 2019, ISCA, pp. 3372–3376 (2019). https://doi.org/10.21437/Interspeech.2019-1363

14. Wu, Y., He, K.: Group normalization. In: Ferrari, V., Hebert, M., Sminchisescu, C., Weiss, Y. (eds.) ECCV 2018. LNCS, vol. 11217, pp. 3–19. Springer, Cham (2018). https://doi.org/10.1007/978-3-030-01261-8_1

15. Kingma, D.P., Ba, J.: Adam: a method for stochastic optimization. In: Bengio, Y., LeCun, Y. (eds.) 3rd International Conference on Learning Representations, ICLR 2015, San Diego, CA, USA, 7–9 May 2015, Conference Track Proceedings (2015). http://arxiv.org/abs/1412.6980

# Author Index

T. Calders et al. (Eds.): BNAIC/Benelearn 2022, CCIS 1805, p. 179, 2023.
https://doi.org/10.1007/978-3-031-39144-6

Printed in the United States
by Baker & Taylor Publisher Services